Illinois Central College
Learning Resource Center

GRANGERS

THE
METAPHYSICAL
POETS

Oxford University Press, Ely House, London W. 1

GLASGOW   NEW YORK   TORONTO   MELBOURNE   WELLINGTON
CAPE TOWN   SALISBURY   IBADAN   NAIROBI   LUSAKA   ADDIS ABABA
BOMBAY   CALCUTTA   MADRAS   KARACHI   LAHORE   DACCA
KUALA LUMPUR   HONG KONG   TOKYO

THE
METAPHYSICAL
POETS

Selected and Edited by

HELEN GARDNER

SECOND EDITION

OXFORD UNIVERSITY PRESS

This selection was first published by
Penguin Books Ltd. in 1957

© *Helen Gardner,* 1967

SECOND EDITION 1967
REPRINTED 1967

PRINTED IN GREAT BRITAIN

TO

ELSIE DUNCAN-JONES

PREFACE TO THE SECOND EDITION

WHEN I made this selection in 1957 my work in preparation for my edition of Donne's Love Poems was in its early stages. As it proceeded I came to the conclusion that the text needed a more radical revision than I had thought. The text therefore of Donne's Love Poems in the first edition of this anthology and reprintings of it should be described as Grierson's text with minor modifications. For a second edition, I have substituted the text of my edition of *John Donne: Elegies and Songs and Sonnets*, 1965, and have also made some corrections in the notes. I have to thank Mr. C. B. Ricks for calling my attention to some superior readings in a broadside edition of Rochester's 'Upon Nothing', which I have adopted into the text of 1691.

H. G.

August 1966

CONTENTS

CONTENTS

CONTENTS

CONTENTS

CONTENTS

CONTENTS

CONTENTS

CONTENTS

INTRODUCTION

THE term 'metaphysical poets' came into being long after the poets to whom we apply it were dead. Samuel Johnson, who coined it, did so with the consciousness that it was a piece of literary slang, that he was giving a kind of nickname. When he wrote in his *Life of Cowley* that 'about the beginning of the seventeenth century appeared a race of writers that may be termed the metaphysical poets', his 'may be termed' indicates that he did not consider that these poets had the right to be called 'metaphysical' in the true sense. He was adapting a witty sally from Dryden who, writing in 1693, said of Donne:

He affects the metaphysics, not only in his satires, but in his amorous verses, where nature only should reign; and perplexes the minds of the fair sex with nice speculations of philosophy, when he should engage their hearts, and entertain them with the softnesses of love. In this . . . Mr Cowley has copied him to a fault.

Between Dryden and Johnson comes Pope, who is reported by Spence to have remarked that 'Cowley, as well as Davenant, borrowed his metaphysical style from Donne'. But the only writer I know of before Dryden who spoke as if there were a 'metaphysical school' is Drummond of Hawthornden (1585–1649) who, in an unfortunately undated letter, speaks of poets who make use of 'Metaphysical *Ideas* and *Scholastical Quiddities*'.

What we call metaphysical poetry was referred to by contemporaries as 'strong lines', a term which calls attention to other elements in metaphysical poetry than its fondness for indulging in 'nice speculations of philosophy' in unusual contexts. The term is used in connexion with prose as well as with verse—indeed the earliest use I know of is by a prose writer—and so invites us to look at metaphysical poetry in a wider context. Like the later term 'metaphysical', the term 'strong-lined' is a term of disapprobation. It too is a kind of slang, a phrase which would seem to have been coined by those who disliked this way of writing. Thus Burton, in the preface to

The Anatomy of Melancholy (1621), contrasts his own 'loose free style' with 'neat composition, strong lines, hyperboles, allegories', and later speaks disparagingly of the 'affectation of big words, fustian phrases, jingling termes, strong lines, that like *Acastes* arrows caught fire as they flew'; and Quarles, in the preface to *Argalus and Parthenia* (1629), declares:

I have not affected to set thy understanding on the Rack, by the tyranny of *strong lines*, which (as they fabulously report of *China* dishes) are made for the third *Generation* to make use of, and are the meere itch of wit; under the colour of which, many have ventured (trusting to the *Oedipean* conceit of their ingenious Reader) to write *non-sense*, and felloniously father the created expositions of other men; not unlike some painters, who first make the picture, then, from the opinions of better judgements, conclude whom it resembles.

These are complaints against an established manner in prose and verse. It is a manner which developed in the last decade of the sixteenth century with the cry everywhere for 'More matter and less words'. In prose, Cicero, the model for the sixteenth century, was dethroned in favour of the Silver Latin writers, Seneca and Tacitus. Recommending Sir Henry Savile's translation of Tacitus in 1591, Antony Bacon commends Tacitus because he 'hath written the most matter with the best conceit in the fewest words of any Historiographer', and adds 'But he is hard. *Difficilia quae pulchra*; the second reading will please thee more than the first, and the third than the second.' The same conception that difficulty is a merit is applied to poetry in Chapman's preface to *Ovid's Banquet of the Sense* (1595), where he declares that poetry, unlike oratory, should not aim at clarity: 'That Poetry should be as pervial as oratory and plainness her special ornament, were the plain way to barbarism.' Poetry, like prose, should be close-packed and dense with meaning, something to be 'chewed and digested', which will not give up its secrets on a first reading. In the 1590's also formal satire first appeared in English, and the satirists took as their model Persius, the most obscure of Roman satirists, and declared that satire should be 'hard of conceit and harsh of style'. The same period sees the vogue of the epigram and the great popularity of Martial.

What came to be called by its denigrators the 'strong-lined' style had its origins in this general desire at the close of Elizabeth's reign for concise expression, achieved by an elliptical syntax, and accompanied by a staccato rhythm in prose and a certain deliberate roughness in versification in poetry. Along with this went admiration for difficulty in the thought. Difficulty is indeed the main demerit in this way of writing for those who dislike it, and the constant complaint of its critics is that it confuses the pleasures of poetry with the pleasures of puzzles. It is one of its merits for those who approve it. Jasper Mayne, in his elegy on Donne, put his finger on one of the delights of reading 'strong-lined' verse when he said

> Wee are thought wits, when 'tis understood.

It makes demands upon the reader and challenges him to make it out. It does not attempt to attract the lazy, and its lovers have always a certain sense of being a privileged class, able to enjoy what is beyond the reach of vulgar wits. The great majority of the poets included in this book did not write to be read by all and sundry. Few of them published their poems. They were 'Chamber poets', as Drayton, with the jealousy of the professional for the amateur, complains. Their poems passed from hand to hand in manuscript. This is a source of both weakness and strength. At times the writing has the smell of a coterie, the writer performing with a self-conscious eye on his clever readers. But at its best it has the ease and artistic sincerity which comes from being able to take for granted the understanding of the audience for whom one writes.

The first characteristic that I shall isolate in trying to discuss the admittedly vague and, it is often thought, unsatisfactory term 'metaphysical poetry' is its concentration. The reader is held to an idea or a line of argument. He is not invited to pause upon a passage, 'wander with it, and muse upon it, and reflect upon it, and bring home to it, and prophesy upon it, and dream upon it' as a 'starting-post towards all the "two-and-thirty Palaces" '. Keats's advice can be followed profitably with much poetry, particularly with Elizabethan and Romantic poetry; but metaphysical poetry demands that we pay attention and read on. For this reason I have resisted the temptation to print excerpts from longer poems. It is, of course, possible and pleasurable to linger over passages of striking beauty and originality, but, on the whole, I think that to do so is to miss the special pleasure that metaphysical poetry has to give. It does not aim at providing, to quote Keats again, 'a little Region to wander in', where lovers of poetry 'may pick and choose, and in which images are so numerous that many are forgotten and found new in a second Reading'. A metaphysical poem tends to be brief, and is always closely woven. Marvell, under the metaphor of a garland, characterizes his own art finely in 'The Coronet' when he speaks of a 'curious frame' in which the flowers are 'set with Skill and chosen out with Care'. And Donne in a sermon, speaking of the Psalms as especially dear to him in that they were poems, stresses the same elements of deliberate art (curiosity), and economy of language, when he defines psalms as

Such a form as is both curious, and requires diligence in the making, and then when it is made, can have nothing, no syllable taken from it, nor added to it.

Concentration and a sinewy strength of style is the mark of Ben Jonson as well as of Donne, and such adjectives as 'strenuous' and 'masculine' applied to him by his admirers point to a sense in which he too was in some degree a 'strong-lined' man, and explain why so many younger writers were able to regard both him and Donne as equally their masters. Behind both, as behind much of the poetry of their followers, lies the classical epigram, and there is some truth in saying that a metaphysical poem is an expanded epigram. Almost all the poets in this collection exercised their skill in the writing of epigrams. Their efforts make on the whole very dreary reading; but the vogue of the epigram helped to form the taste for witty poetry. The desire for concentration and concision marks also the verse forms characteristic of seventeenth-century lyric. It appears in the fondness for a line of eight syllables rather than a line of ten, and in the use of stanzas employing lines of varying length into which the sense seems packed, or of stanzas built on very short lines. A stanza of Donne or Herbert is not, like rhyme royal or a Spenserian stanza, an ideal mould, as it were, into which the words have flowed. It is more like a limiting frame in which words and thoughts are compressed, a 'box where sweets compacted lie'. The metaphysical poets favoured either very simple verse forms, octosyllabic couplets or quatrains, or else stanzas created for the particular poem, in which length of line and rhyme scheme artfully enforced the sense. In a poem not included here, 'The Triple Foole', Donne suggests, in passing, this conception of the function of rhyme and metre:

> I thought, if I could draw my paines,
> Through Rimes vexation, I should them allay,
> Griefe brought to numbers cannot be so fierce,
> For, he tames it, that fetters it in verse.

The second characteristic of metaphysical poetry, its most immediately striking feature, is its fondness for conceits, and here, of course, Jonson and Donne part company. A conceit is a comparison whose ingenuity is more striking than its justness, or, at least, is more immediately striking. All comparisons discover likeness in things unlike: a comparison becomes a conceit when we are made to concede likeness while being strongly conscious of unlikeness. A brief comparison can be a conceit if two things patently unlike, or which we should never think of together, are shown to be alike in a single point in such a way, or in such a context, that we feel their incongruity. Here a conceit is like a spark made by striking two stones together. After the flash the stones are just two stones. Metaphysical poetry abounds in such flashes, as when Cartwright in his New Year's poem (p. 160), promising to be a new man, declares that he will not be new as the year is new when it begins again its former cycle, and then thinks of two images of motion without progression, the circulation of the blood and a mill:

> Motion as in a Mill
> Is busie standing still.

The wit of this depends on our being willing to suppress our memory of other features of mills, and particularly on our not allowing ourselves to think that mills are very usefully employed grinding corn while 'standing still'. Normally metaphor and simile allow and invite the mind to stray beyond the immediate point of resemblance, and in extended or epic simile, which is the diametrical opposite of the conceit, the poet himself expatiates freely, making the point of comparison a point of departure. In an extended conceit, on the other hand, the poet forces fresh points of likeness upon us. Here the conceit is a kind of 'hammering out' by which a difficult join is made. I borrow the phrase from Shakespeare's poet-king Richard II, who occupies himself in prison composing a conceited poem:

> I have been studying how I may compare
> This prison where I live unto the world:
> And for because the world is populous,
> And here is not a creature but myself,
> I cannot do it; yet I'll hammer it out.
> My brain I'll prove the female to my soul. . . .

Longer conceits set themselves to 'prove' likeness. They may, as here, start from a comparison which the speaker owns is far from obvious and then proceeds to establish. Or they may start from one that is immediately acceptable generally and then make us accept further resemblances in detail after detail. Thus nobody, I imagine, would think Lady Macbeth is being particularly ingenious when she compares the troubled face of her husband to a book in which men may 'read strange matters'. She leaves our imaginations to give further content to this comparison of finding meaning in a book and meaning in a face and to the deliberately imprecise words 'strange matters'. But when Lady Capulet takes up the same comparison to urge Juliet to wed Count Paris she expands the comparison for us in detail after detail so that it becomes a conceit, and most people would add a very tasteless and ineffective one.

> Read o'er the volume of young Paris' face
> And find delight writ there with beauty's pen;
> Examine every married lineament,
> And see how one another lends content;
> And what obscur'd in this fair volume lies
> Find written in the margent of his eyes.
> This precious book of love, this unbound lover,
> To beautify him, only lacks a cover. . . .
> That book in many eyes doth share the glory
> That in gold clasp locks in the golden story:
> So shall you share all that he doth possess,
> By having him making yourself no less.

Elizabethan poetry, dramatic and lyric, abounds in conceits. They are used both as ornaments and as the basis of songs and sonnets. What differentiates the conceits of the metaphysicals is not the fact that they very frequently employ curious learning in their comparisons. Many of the poets whom we call metaphysical, Herbert for instance, do not. It is the use which they make of the conceit and the rigorous nature of their conceits, springing from the use to which they are put, which is more important than their frequently learned content. A metaphysical conceit, unlike Richard II's comparison of his prison to the world, is not indulged in for its own sake. It is used, as Lady Capulet uses hers, to persuade, or it is used to define, or to prove a point. Ralegh's beautiful comparison of man's life to a play (p. 3) is a good example of a poem which seems to me to hover on the verge of becoming a metaphysical poem. Its concision and completeness and the ironic, colloquially made point at the end—'Onely we dye in earnest, that's no Jest'—bring it very near, but it remains in the region of the conceited epigram and does not cross the border. On the other hand, Lady Capulet's conceit fails to be metaphysical in another way. She does not force us to concede the justness of her initial comparison by developing it, she merely argues from various arbitrarily chosen points of comparison between a book and a bachelor. In a metaphysical poem the conceits are instruments of definition in an argument or instruments to persuade. The poem has something to say which the conceit explicates or something to urge which the conceit helps to forward. It can only do this if it is used with an appearance of logical rigour, the analogy being shown to hold by a process not unlike Euclid's superimposition of triangles. I have said that the first impression a conceit makes is of ingenuity rather than of justice: the metaphysical conceit aims at making us concede justness while admiring ingenuity. Thus, in one of the most famous of all metaphysical conceits, the comparison of the union in absence of two lovers with the relation between the two legs of a compass, Donne sustains the comparison through the whole process of drawing a circle, because he is attempting to give a 'proof by analogy' of their union, by which he can finally persuade his mistress not to mourn. In another of his unfortunately rare asides on the art of poetry, Donne, again speaking of the Psalms, said:

> In all Metricall compositions . . . the force of the whole piece is for the most part left to the shutting up; the whole frame of the Poem is a beating out of a piece of gold, but the last clause is as the impression of the stamp, and that is it that makes it currant.

We might expand this by saying that the brilliant abrupt openings for which metaphysical poetry is famous, are like the lump of gold flung down on the table to be worked; the conceits are part of the beating out by which the metal is shaped to receive its final stamp, which is the point towards which the whole has moved.

Argument and persuasion, and the use of the conceit as their instrument, are the elements or body of a metaphysical poem. Its quintessence or soul is the vivid imagining of a moment of experience or of a situation out of which the need to argue, or persuade, or define arises. Metaphysical poetry is famous for its abrupt, personal openings in which a man speaks to his mistress, or addresses his God, or sets a scene, or calls us to mark this or see that. A great many of the poems in this collection are inspired by actual occasions either of personal, or, less often, public interest. The great majority postulate an occasion. We may not accept that Donne's 'Good Friday' was, actually 'made as I was riding westward that day', as a heading in some manuscripts tells us, but we must accept as we read the poem that he is riding westward and thinking as he rides. Marvell calls us to look at little T. C. in her garden. The child of one of Marvell's friends, Theophila Cornewall, bore the same beautiful name as her elder sister who had died two days after her baptism, a name which has a foreboding ring since the proverb says that the 'Darlings of the Gods' die young. This lovely poem would seem to have arisen from thoughts suggested by the name and family history of a friend's child. Whether Marvell actually caught sight of her in a garden we have no means of knowing. But he does not convey to us his sense of the transience of spring and the dangerous fragility of childhood through general reflections on human life. He calls us to watch with him a child 'in a Prospect of Flowers'. Equally, when his subject belongs to the ideal world of pastoral, not the world of daily life, his nymph is set before us complaining for her fawn while the little beast's life-blood is ebbing away. She tells of her betrayal in love as the tears are running down her cheeks in mourning for the creature who consoled her for that betrayal. Even poems of generalized reflection are given the flavour of spontaneous thought, as when Herbert opens his poem 'Man' (p. 101) with 'My God, I heard this day . . .', and thus gives the poem the air of having sprung from the casual overhearing of a chance remark.

The manner of metaphysical poetry originates in developments in prose and verse in the 1590's. The greatest glory of that decade is that it saw the flowering of the drama. Metaphysical poetry is the poetry of the great age of our drama. Its master John Donne was, we are told, 'a great frequenter of plays' in his youth. As an ambitious young man of social standing he would not have considered writing for the players, and his work is too personal, wilful, and idiosyncratic for us to imagine him doing so with any success. But his strong dramatic imagination of particular situations transforms the lyric and makes a metaphysical poem more than an epigram expanded by conceits. I have begun this volume a little before Donne with poems which in some ways anticipate the metaphysical manner: Ralegh's fine passionate conceit of a pilgrimage, written when he was under sentence of death, some specimens of Fulke Greville's 'close, mysterious and sentencious way of writing', Southwell's meditations, Shakespeare's strange celebration of married chastity in the most 'strong-lined' of all poems, if 'strong lines' are riddles, Alabaster's attempts at the concise expression of theological paradox, Wotton's laconic comment on the greatest scandal of the age. But the minute the reader reaches Donne, he will have the same sense of having arrived as when, in a collection of pre-Shakespearian plays, we hear the voice of Marlowe. Ralegh is too discursive, Greville too heavy and general, Southwell too dogged in his conceits and in his verse, one line padding at the same pace after another, Shakespeare too remote, and too symbolic, creating a static world where Love and Constancy are deified. The vehement, colloquial tone of the Satire 'Of Religion' creates the sense of an actual historical situation in which urgent choices present themselves. In the three splendid Elegies a man is speaking to a woman at a moment when all the faculties are heightened, as in drama, by the thought of what impends. He is about to go to the wars—what will she say to him when he returns, perhaps mutilated? He has to travel and she wants to come with him as his page—he is horrified at the thought of such romantic folly and implores her to be his true mistress and 'home of love'. With the tide of passion rising in him, impatient for the moment when she will be his, he watches her undressing for bed. The sense of the moment gives Donne's wit its brilliance and verve, the aptness and incongruity of the comparisons being created by their contexts. Without this, as in some of his complimentary pieces, he labours to be witty and never becomes 'air-borne'. The fading of this desire to make poems out of particular moments, made imaginatively present rather than remembered, and played over by wit rather than reflected upon, is apparent towards the end of this volume. The metaphysical style peters out, to be replaced by the descriptive and reflective poetry of the eighteenth century, a century which sees the rise of the novel and has virtually no drama.

The strong sense of actual and often very ordinary situations which the metaphysical poets convey makes me agree with Grierson in thinking that words such as 'conceited' or 'fantastic' do not sum up their quality at all. A reader may at times exclaim 'Who would ever think such a thought in such a situation?' He will not exclaim 'Who can imagine himself in such a situation?' Dryden praised Donne for expressing deep thoughts in common language. He is equally remarkable for having extraordinary thoughts in ordinary situations. The situations which recur in seventeenth-century lyric are the reverse of fantastic, and often the reverse of ideal or romantic situations. Thus, a very favourite topic is the pleasure of hearing a beautiful woman sing or play. This domestic subject is, of course, a favourite on the Continent, and not merely with the poets, but with the painters. Such poems usually go beyond compliment to create a sense of the occasion; as Waller, in praising Lady Isabella Rich, whom Dorothy Osborne described as 'Lady Isabella that speaks and looks and plays and sings and all so prettily', expresses exactly the delight which we receive during an actual performance from artistry:

> Such moving sounds from such a careless touch,
> So unconcern'd her selfe, and we so much!

Again there are a great many poems which arise out of the common but unromantic situation of love between persons of very different ages. A mature man may rather ruefully complain to 'a very young Lady'

> That time should mee so far remove
> From that which I was borne to love.

This Horatian theme of the charm of young girls to older men is given various twists. The situation is reversed when Cartwright persuades his Chloe not to mind being older than he is; and at the end of the period Rochester gives us a fresh variation on the theme that age and youth are not so incompatible as the romantics claim by writing a song for 'A Young Lady to her Ancient Lover'.

The most serious and impassioned love poetry of the century argues, or assumes as a base for argument, that love is a relation between two persons loving—'It cannot *be* love till I love her that loves me'. The poems which Donne wrote on the experience of loving where love is returned, poems in which 'Thou' and 'I' are merged into 'We', are his most original and profound contributions to the poetry of human love. It is not possible to find models for such poems as 'The Good-Morrow', 'The Anniversarie', 'The Canonization', and, less perfect but still wonderful, 'The Extasie'. These poems have the right to the title metaphysical in its true sense, since they raise, even when they do not explicitly discuss, the great metaphysical question of the relation of the spirit and the senses. They raise it not as an abstract problem, but in the effort to make the experience of the union of human powers in love, and the union of two human beings in love, apprehensible. We never lose our sense of a 'little roome' which love has made 'an every where'. In the lighter verses of Donne's followers this theme that love is the union of two human beings, not the service of a votarist to a goddess, is handled with a mixture of gallantry, sensibility and good sense that has a peculiar charm:

> 'Tis not how witty, nor how free,
> Nor yet how beautifull she be,
> But how much kinde and true to me.

This is a very characteristic note. There are plenty of high and chivalrous fancies, and the Platonic ideal of love as the union of souls casts its spell; but the tone of the bargain scene in *The Way of the World* is anticipated in many lyrics in which the speaker sets forward the terms on which he is willing to make the 'world without end bargain' of love. The question 'What shall I do if she does not love me?' is often handled and usually with a glance at the old chivalric answer. Suckling's impudent 'The devil take her' is flat blasphemy against the religion of love. King's exquisite 'Tell me no more how fair she is' is chivalrous enough, as is Waller's 'It is not that I love you less'; but earlier servants of love would not, I think, have shown so stoical an acceptance of the fact that their love was hopeless, nor been so sensible in resolving not to keep their wounds green by hearing the lady's praises or by haunting her company. In one of his beautifully tempered songs of love unreturned, Godolphin seriously considers what creates the obligation to constancy. Parting for the wars, or parting to go abroad, or the final parting of death, actual or anticipated, are also favourite subjects. They too inspire poems which are metaphysical in both senses, as lovers ponder such questions as 'Can love subsist without the things that elemented it?' and 'Shall we meet in another world, and, if so, shall we know each other?'

The seventeenth century was, as Cowley said, 'a warlike, various and tragical age'. A glance at the biographical notes will show how many of the poets included in this book at one time or another 'trailed a pike', or 'raised a troop of horse', or went on missions abroad, or played a part in public affairs. They were for the most part men of the world who knew its ways. Their wit, high-flown and extravagant though it is, goes with a strong sense of the realities of daily life, the common concerns of men and women. And in spite of Johnson's accusation of pedantry, it has the flavour of the wit of conversation between friends who urge each other on to further flights. Donne perhaps meant what he said when, in the stanza of 'The Will' in which he restores gifts to those from whom he had received them, he leaves

> To Nature, all that I in Ryme have writ;
> And to my company my wit.

'I know the world and believe in God' wrote Fulke Greville,

a Calvinist who was well acquainted with the winding stair of politics. Donne might have said the same, and Herbert has no need to tell us that he knows the ways of Learning, Honour, and Pleasure; it is apparent in all his poetry that he was not unworldly because of lack of knowledge of the world. The strength of the religious poetry of the metaphysical poets is that they bring to their praise and prayer and meditation so much experience that is not in itself religious. Here too the poems create for us particular situations out of which prayer or meditation arises: Donne riding westward, or stretched out upon his deathbed; Herbert praying all day long 'but no hearing', or noting his own whitening hair, or finding, after a night of heaviness, joy in the morning; Vaughan walking to spend his hour, or sitting solitary at midnight thinking of departed friends. Even with Crashaw, where this sense of the poet's own situation is unimportant, how vividly he dramatizes, rather than narrates, the story of St Teresa, and invokes the weeping Magdalen; and how vigorously he urges the hesitant Countess of Denbigh against delay.

Much stress has been laid recently upon the strongly traditional element in the conceits of metaphysical religious poetry. A good deal that seems to us remote, and idiosyncratic, the paradoxes and the twistings of Scripture to yield symbolic meanings, reaches back through the liturgy and through commentaries on Scripture to the Fathers and can be paralleled in medieval poetry. It is also true that the metaphysical manner of setting a subject, 'hammering it out', and then 'shutting it up' is closely allied to the method of religious meditation and that many metaphysical poems are poetical meditations. And yet, as strongly—or even more strongly—as in reading the secular poetry, the more we suggest common qualities and the more we set the poets in a tradition, the more strongly we are aware of their intensely individual treatment of common themes. How individually, for instance, Herbert treats the old theme of the stages of human life and the traditional lesson of the *Ars Moriendi* in 'Mortification' (p. 103). Who else but Herbert would, with compassionate irony in place of the usual gloom of the moralist, show man as unconsciously amassing at each stage what he needs for his burial? And how tenderly and sympathetically he epitomizes each stage of our strange eventful pilgrimage, catching its very essence: the dreamless sleep of boyhood, the retraction of energies and interests in middle age, and the pathos of old age, unable to speak for rheum. The comparison of sleep to death, and of a bed to a grave, is stock enough. It is transformed by the further haunting image

> Successive nights, like rolling waves,
> Convey them quickly, who are bound for death.

The poem concludes with an old moral for its 'shutting up'; but the moral is made new by the time we reach it, because Herbert has so expanded our understanding of our dying life. The metaphysical style heightens and liberates personality. It is essentially a style in which individuality is expressed. The best pupils in the school of Donne learned from their master how to speak their own minds in their own voices.

For this reason I have contented myself with describing some of the characteristics of metaphysical poetry and have not attempted to construct a definition of 'a metaphysical poem'. Such definitions do not seem to me very profitable, since none of these poets ever thought of himself as writing such a thing, and they usually lead their creators to finding fault with this or that poet for not conforming to the critic's definition. I am aware that I have included in this collection some poems whose presence under its title may be challenged. If I had the space I could defend them all on one ground or another, though my defence would of course have to take the form of 'All these poems are metaphysical, but some are more metaphysical than others'. I am more concerned that readers should find them beautiful and interesting than that they should approve or disapprove of them as conforming or not conforming to the idea of a metaphysical poem. All of them have a certain pungency in their thought, or in their turns of phrase, which makes them, whether profound or flippant, deserve the praise of being 'fine and wittie'.

HELEN GARDNER

St Hilda's College, Oxford

ACKNOWLEDGEMENTS

I should like to thank Mrs Duncan-Jones, Mr John Hayward, and Professor Louis Martz for valuable advice, and Miss Anne Elliott and Miss Jane Lang for help in preparing this book for press.

NOTE ON THE TEXT

As a general rule, the text is that of the first edition, or, with poems which their authors revised, of the first edition of the author's final version. The original spelling has been preserved, with occasional modifications where the retention of older forms might mislead, or where eccentric forms might seem grotesque. Thus I have throughout followed modern usage in distinguishing *than* and *then*, and *whether* and *whither*, and, for example, have printed *Sentry* for *Centry* and added an *e* in forms such as *Judge*. In printing from manuscripts I have allowed myself rather more licence, particularly in reducing scribal reduplication of consonants. The punctuation of the original editions has been altered as little as possible, and I hope in accordance with seventeenth-century practice.

At the end of a poem, or of a group of poems, the source of the text is given. This will usually give the date of a poem's first appearance in print; but in some cases poems had been printed in a miscellany before the author's works were collected. It should also be remembered that many of these poems had been circulating in manuscript for some years before they were printed.

It might be held that an anthologist presenting texts without a critical apparatus should print with the absolute minimum of alteration from his copy-text. But my aim has been to present the best text I can of these poems and to present them in the most appropriate dress. During the seventeenth century great changes took place in the presentation of poems and a poem printed after the Restoration looks very different from the same poem printed twenty years earlier. The later text may correct errors in the earlier or incorporate its author's second thoughts, but to print from it gives a subtly different flavour to the poem. Because of this I have preferred not to take all Cowley and Davenant's poems from the collected editions of 1668 and 1673, but to print from the earlier editions, correcting the text by the final one. Similarly with Waller, whose poems did not appear under his own auspices until 1664, I have preferred to print from the unauthorized edition of 1645, correcting its text by the later one. Cowley, Davenant, and Waller are not Restoration poets, and the heavy punctuation and excessive capitalization of the later editions obscure their quality.

A much more difficult problem is presented by two much greater poets, Donne and Crashaw. Donne's poems were published posthumously, and some of them, by accidents of publication, from inferior manuscript versions. I have printed the Divine Poems from my own edition, and the text of the Love Poems is that of my forthcoming edition. For other poems I have in the main accepted Sir Herbert Grierson's readings. Crashaw's poems were extensively revised by their author. It is usual to print the revised versions from the posthumous *Carmen Deo Nostro*, printed in Paris in 1652. I have preferred to print from the edition of 1648 which, although published after Crashaw had left England and needing correction by the text of 1652, is greatly superior in its presentation of the poems. I have often wondered whether some judgements on Crashaw are not influenced by the exotic printing of *Carmen Deo Nostro*, whose heavy punctuation, weird spellings, and absurd over-capitalization impede recognition of his melodic power. With Crashaw I have also, in one instance, broken my rule of printing the author's final version. I have taken his poem on 'Hope' from the first edition of 1646, in order to preserve the form in which it there appeared, answering Cowley stanza by stanza. The alterations in the later version, which was printed as a separate poem following Cowley's, do not seem to me of such importance as to outweigh the interest of the first version as an 'Answer Poem'.　　　　　　　　　　　　　　H. G.

SIR WALTER RALEGH

(1552?–1618)

The Passionate Mans Pilgrimage, supposed to be written by one at the point of death[1]

Give me my Scallop shell of quiet,
My staffe of Faith to walke upon,
My Scrip of Joy, Immortall diet,
My bottle of salvation:
My Gowne of Glory, hopes true gage,
And thus Ile take my pilgrimage.

Blood must be my bodies balmer,
No other balme will there be given
Whilst my soule like a white Palmer
Travels to the land of heaven,
Over the silver mountaines,
Where spring the Nectar fountaines:
And there Ile kisse
The Bowle of blisse,
And drinke my eternall fill
On every milken hill.
My soule will be a drie before,
But after, it will nere thirst more.

And by the happie blisfull way
More peacefull Pilgrims I shall see,
That have shooke off their gownes of clay,
And goe appareld fresh like mee.
Ile bring them first
To slake their thirst
And then to taste those Nectar suckets[2]

[1] Ralegh was under sentence of death from 17 Nov. to 6 Dec. 1603.
[2] Sweetmeats: usually fruit candied in syrup.

1

At the cleare wells
Where sweetnes dwells,
Drawne up by Saints in Christall buckets.

And when our bottles and all we,
Are fild with immortalitie:
Then the holy paths wee'le travell
Strewde with Rubies thicke as gravell,
Ceelings of Diamonds, Saphire floores,
High walles of Corall and Pearl Bowres.

From thence to heavens Bribeles hall
Where no corrupted voyces brall,
No Conscience molten into gold,
Nor forg'd accusers bought and sold,
No cause deferd, nor vaine spent Journey,
For there Christ is the Kings Atturney:
Who pleades for all without degrees,
And he hath Angells, but no fees.

When the grand twelve million Jury
Of our sinnes with sinfull fury,
Gainst our soules blacke verdicts give,
Christ pleades his death, and then we live,
Be thou my speaker taintles pleader,
Unblotted Lawyer, true proceeder,
Thou movest salvation even for almes:
Not with a bribed Lawyers palmes.

And this is my eternall plea,
To him that made Heaven, Earth and Sea,
Seeing my flesh must die so soone,
And want a head to dine next noone,
Just at the stroke when my vaines start and spred
Set on my soule an everlasting head.
Then am I readie like a palmer fit,
To tread those blest paths which before I writ.

(A. Scoloker, *Daiphantus*, 1604)

What is our Life?

What is our life? a play of passion,
Our mirth the musicke of division,
Our mothers wombes the tyring houses be,
Where we are drest for this short Comedy,
Heaven the Judicious sharpe spectator is,
That sits and markes still who doth act amisse,
Our graves that hide us from the searching Sun,
Are like drawne curtaynes when the play is done,
Thus march we playing to our latest rest,
Onely we dye in earnest, that's no Jest.

(Orlando Gibbons, *Madrigals and Mottets*, 1612)

FULKE GREVILLE, LORD BROOKE
(1554–1628)

Sonnets from Caelica

SONNET 87

When as Mans life, the light of human lust,
In socket of his earthly lanthorne burnes,
That all this glory unto ashes must,
And generation to corruption turnes;
  Then fond desires that onely feare their end,
  Doe vainely wish for life, but to amend.

But when this life is from the body fled,
To see it selfe in that *eternall Glasse,*
Where time doth end, and thoughts accuse the dead,
Where all to come, is one with all that was;
  Then living men aske how he left his breath,
  That while he lived never thought of death.

3

SONNET 88

Man, dreame no more of curious mysteries,
As what was here before the world was made,
The first Mans life, the state of Paradise,
Where heaven is, or hells eternall shade,
  For Gods works are like him, all infinite;
  And curious search, but craftie sinnes delight.

The Flood that did, and dreadfull Fire that shall,
Drowne, and burne up the malice of the earth,
The divers tongues, and *Babylons* downe-fall,
Are nothing to the mans renewed birth;
  First, let the Law plough up thy wicked heart,
  That Christ *may come, and all these types depart.*

When thou hast swept the house that all is cleare,
When thou the dust hast shaken from thy feete,
When Gods All-might doth in thy flesh appeare,
Then Seas with streames above the skye doe meet;[1]
  For Goodnesse onely doth God comprehend,
  Knowes what was first, and what shall be the end.

Chorus Sacerdotum[2]

Oh wearisome Condition of Humanity!
Borne under one Law, to another bound:
Vainely begot, and yet forbidden vanity,
Created sicke, commanded to be sound:
What meaneth Nature by these diverse Lawes?
Passion and Reason, selfe-division cause:
Is it the marke, or Majesty of Power

[1] 'The waters under the firmament will no longer be divided from those
above it.' What 'the waters above the firmament' were is one of the 'curious
mysteries' of creation.
[2] Chorus added at the close of Greville's neo-Senecan drama *Mustapha*.

4

To make offences that it may forgive?
Nature herselfe, doth her own selfe defloure,
To hate those errors she her selfe doth give.
For how should man thinke that[1] he may not doe,
If Nature did not faile, and punish too?
Tyrant to others, to her selfe unjust,
Onely commands things difficult and hard.
Forbids us all things, which it knowes is lust,[2]
Makes easie paines, unpossible reward.
If Nature did not take delight in blood,
She would have made more easie wayes to good.
We that are bound by vowes, and by Promotion,
With pompe of holy Sacrifice and rites,
To teach beleefe in good and still devotion,
To preach of Heavens wonders, and delights:
Yet when each of us, in his owne heart lookes,
He findes the God there, farre unlike his Bookes.

(Certaine Learned and Elegant Workes, 1633)

ROBERT SOUTHWELL

(1561–1595)

Marie Magdalens *Complaint at Christs death*

Sith my life from life is parted:
    Death come take thy portion,
Who survives, when life is murdred,
    Lives by meere extortion.[3]
All that live, and not in God,
Couch theyr life in deaths abode.

Seely starres must needes leave shining,
    When the sunne is shaddowed.
Borrowed streames refraine theyr running,

[1] *that*: that which.   [2] *lust*: pleasure.
[3] 'Lives by absolute torturing of the word's sense.'

When head springs are hindered.
One that lives by others breath,
Dyeth also by his death.

O true life, since thou hast left me,
   Mortall life is tedious,
Death it is to live without thee,
   Death of all most odious.
Turne againe, or take me to thee,
Let me dye or live thou in mee.

Where the truth once was and is not,
   Shaddowes are but vanity:
Shewing want, that helpe they cannot,
   Signes, not salves of misery.
Painted meate no hunger feedes,
Dying life each death exceeds.

With my love, my life was nestled
   In the somme of happinesse;
From my love, my life is wrested
   To a world of heavinesse.
O, let love my life remove,
Sith I live not where I love.

O my soule what did unloose thee
   From thy sweet captivity?
God, not I, did still possesse thee:
   His, not mine thy liberty.
O, too happy thrall thou wert,
When thy prison was his hart.

Spightfull speare, that break'st this prison,
   Seate of all felicity,
Working this, with double treason,
   Loves and lifes delivery:
Though my life thou drav'st away,
Maugre thee my love shall stay.[1]

---

[1] Printed in the first edition of Southwell's poems in 1595.

The Burning Babe

As I in hoarie Winters night stoode shivering in the snow,
Surpris'd I was with sodaine heate, which made my hart to
    glow;
And lifting up a fearefull eye, to view what fire was neare,
A pretty Babe all burning bright did in the ayre appeare;
Who scorched with excessive heate, such floods of teares did
    shed,
As though his floods should quench his flames, which with his
    teares were bred:
Alas (quoth he) but newly borne, in fierie heates I frie,
Yet none approach to warme their harts or feele my fire, but I;
My faultlesse breast the furnace is, the fuell wounding thornes:
Love is the fire, and sighs the smoake, the ashes, shames and
    scornes;
The fewell Justice layeth on, and Mercie blowes the coales,
The mettall in this furnace wrought, are mens defiled soules:
For which, as now on fire I am to worke them to their good,
So will I melt into a bath, to wash them in my blood.
With this he vanisht out of sight, and swiftly shrunk away,
And straight I called unto minde, that it was Christmasse day.

New Heaven, New Warre[1]

Come to your heaven you heavenly quires,
Earth hath the heaven of your desires;
Remove your dwelling to your God,
A stall is now his best abode;
Sith men their homage doe denie,
Come Angels all their fault supplie.

[1] Although printed as a single poem, this is two parallel poems on the
Nativity, or possibly on the Nativity and the Circumcision.

His chilling cold doth heate require,
Come Seraphins in liew of fire;
This little Arke no cover hath,
Let Cherubs wings his body swath:[1]
Come Raphaell, this Babe must eate,
Provide our little Tobie meate.[2]

Let Gabriell be now his groome,
That first tooke up his earhly roome;
Let Michaell stand in his defence,
Whom love hath linck'd to feeble sence,
Let Graces rock when he doth crie,
Let Angels sing his lullabie.

The same you saw in heavenly seate,
Is he that now sucks Maries teate;
Agnize your King a mortall wight,
His borrowed weede lets not your sight:
Come kisse the maunger where he lies,
That is your blisse above the skies.

This little Babe so few dayes olde,
Is come to ryfle Sathans folde;
All hell doth at his presence quake,
Though he himselfe for cold doe shake:
For in this weake unarmed wise,
The gates of hell he will surprise.

With teares he fights and winnes the field,
His naked breast stands for a shield;
His battering shot are babish cryes,
His Arrowes lookes of weeping eyes,
His Martiall ensignes cold and neede,
And feeble flesh his warriers steede.

[1] Two carved Cherubs with outspread wings covered the Mercy-seat above the Ark of the Covenant, the sign of God's tabernacling with men (Exodus xxv).

[2] Raphael the 'sociable Archangel' accompanied Tobias and supplied his needs.

His Campe is pitched in a stall,
His bulwarke but a broken wall:
The Crib his trench, hay stalks his stakes,
Of Sheepheards he his Muster makes;
And thus as sure his foe to wound,
The Angells trumps alarum sound.

My soule with Christ joyne thou in fight,
Stick to the tents that he hath dight;
Within his Crib is surest ward,
This little Babe will be thy guard:
If thou wilt foyle thy foes with joy,
Then flit not from the heavenly boy.

(*St Peters Complaint*, 1602)

WILLIAM SHAKESPEARE

(1564–1616)

The Phoenix and the Turtle[1]

Let the bird of lowdest lay,
On the sole *Arabian* tree,
Herauld sad and trumpet be:
To whose sound chaste wings obay.

---

[1] In the myth the Phoenix, a bird of dazzling beauty and sole of its kind, dwells on a lofty tree in an Eastern Paradise. Every thousand years it flies to a palm-tree in Arabia and there builds itself a nest of spices. Here it is consumed by its own fires and reborn. When full-grown it flies with its own ashes to lay them on the altar of the Temple of the Sun at Heliopolis. Men rejoice at the return of the marvellous bird and other birds assemble. In chorus they accompany the singing Phoenix as it soars to heaven, before flying back alone to its Paradise. Unlike his fellow poets who celebrated the Phoenix (Beauty) and the Turtle Dove (Constancy), Shakespeare, omitting the central element of the bird's death and resurrection, has created out of the myth a myth of his own.

But thou shriking harbinger,
Foule precurrer of the fiend,
Augour of the fevers end,[1]
To this troupe come thou not neere.

From this Session interdict
Every foule of tyrant wing,
Save the Eagle feath'red King,
Keepe the obsequie so strict.

Let the Priest in Surples white,
That defunctive Musicke can,[2]
Be the death-devining Swan,
Lest the *Requiem* lacke his right.

And thou treble-dated Crow,
That thy sable gender mak'st,
With the breath thou giv'st and tak'st,
Mongst our mourners shalt thou go.[3]

Here the Antheme doth commence,
Love and Constancie is dead,
Phoenix and the *Turtle* fled,
In a mutuall flame from hence.

So they loved as love in twaine,
Had the essence but in one,
Two distincts, Division none,
Number there in love was slaine.[4]

---

[1] The screech-owl is a bird of ill-omen.

[2] *can*: is skilled in. The swan was popularly supposed to sing before its own death.

[3] Although crows were said by Pliny to live nine times the time of a man, probably the even longer-lived raven is intended. They were held to conceive their offspring (*gender*) by an exchange of breath.

[4] The logical impossibilities of a completely mutual love are set out in scholastic terms. In two persons was the one substance (*essence*). Though distinguished, they could not be divided: the terms are from logic. Though they were two, they were one and 'one is no number'. Mathematics, or numbering, was made impossible.

Hearts remote, yet not asunder;
Distance and no space was seene,
Twixt this *Turtle* and his Queene;
But[1] in them it were a wonder.

So betweene them Love did shine,
That the *Turtle* saw his right,
Flaming in the *Phoenix* sight;[2]
Either was the others mine.[3]

Propertie[4] was thus appalled,
That the selfe was not the same:[5]
Single Natures double name,
Neither two nor one was called.

Reason in it selfe confounded,
Saw Division grow together:
To themselves yet either neither,
Simple were so well compounded,

That it cried, how true a twaine,
Seemeth this concordant one,
Love hath Reason, Reason none,
If what parts, can so remaine.

Whereupon it made this *Threne*,
To the *Phoenix* and the *Dove*,
Co-supremes and starres of Love,
As *Chorus* to their Tragique Scene.

[1] *But*: except.
[2] 'He saw what was his in her eyes.'
[3] Each was the other's treasure, and equally there was no distinction of 'mine' and 'thine' between them.
[4] *Propertie*: what belongs to an individual (*proprium*); identifying characteristics.
[5] *the selfe*: the self-same. Language here fails as mathematics has before it. Reason recognizing its own defeat celebrates its overthrow in the rest of the poem.

THRENOS

Beautie, Truth, and Raritie,
Grace in all simplicitie,
Here enclosde, in cinders lie.

Death is now the *Phoenix* nest,
And the *Turtles* loyall brest,
To eternitie doth rest.

Leaving no posteritie,
Twas not their infirmitie,
It was married Chastitie.

Truth may seeme, but cannot be,
Beautie bragge, but tis not she,
Truth and Beautie buried be.

To this urne let those repaire,
.That are either true or faire,
For these dead Birds, sigh a prayer.

(Robert Chester, *Loves Martyr*, 1601)

WILLIAM ALABASTER
(1567–1640)

Upon the Ensignes of Christes Crucifyinge[1]

O sweete and bitter monuments of paine,
Bitter to Christ who all the paine endur'd,
But sweete to mee, whose Death my life procur'd,
How shall I full express, such loss, such gaine.
My tongue shall bee my Penne, mine eyes shall raine
Teares for my Inke, the Cross where I was cur'd
Shall be my Booke, where having all abjur'd
And calling heavens to record in that plaine

[1] The first of a set of sonnets on the symbols of the Passion.

Thus plainely will I write: *no sinne like mine.*
When I have done, doe thou Jesu divine
Take up the tarte Spunge of thy Passion
And blot it forth: then bee thy spirit the Quill,
Thy bloode the Inke, and with compassion
Write thus upon my soule: *thy Jesu still.*

Incarnatio est maximum donum Dei

Like as the fountaine of all light created
Doth powre out streams of brightness undefined
Through all the conduits of transparent kinde
That heaven and ayre are both illuminated,
And yet his light is not thereby abated;
So Gods eternall bounty ever shin'd
The beames of beeing, moving, life, sence, minde,
And to all things him selfe communicated.
But see the violent diffusive pleasure
Of goodnes, that left not, till God had spente
Himself by giving us himself his treasure
In making man a God omnipotent.
How might this goodness draw our soules above
Which drew downe God with such attractive Love.
(Bodleian Library, MS. Eng. Poet. e 57)

SIR HENRY WOTTON
(1568–1639)

A Hymn to my God in a night of my late Sicknesse

> *Oh thou great Power,* in whom I move,
> For whom I *live,* to whom I *die,*
> Behold me through thy beams of *love,*
> Whilest on this *Couch* of *tears* I lye;
>   And Cleanse my sordid *soul* within,
>   By thy *Christs Bloud,* the *bath* of sin.

No hallowed oyls, no grains I need,
No rags of Saints, no purging fire,
One rosie drop from *Davids* Seed
Was worlds of seas, to quench thine Ire.
    O pretious Ransome! which once paid,
    That *Consummatum Est* was said:

And said by *him*, that said no more,
But *seal'd* it with his sacred *breath*.
Thou then, that hast dispung'd my score,
And dying, wast the death of *death*;
    Be to me now, on thee I call,
    My Life, my Strength, my Joy, my All.

On his Mistris, the Queen *of* Bohemia[1]

You meaner *Beauties* of the *Night*,
That poorly satisfie our *Eies*
More by your *number*, than your *light*,
You *Common people* of the *Skies*;
    What are you when the *Moon* shall rise?

You curious Chanters of the Wood,
That warble forth *Dame Natures* layes,
Thinking your *Passions* understood
By your weake *accents*; whats your praise
    When *Philomell* her voyce shal raise?

You *Violets*, that first appeare,
By your *pure purpel mantels* knowne,
Like the proud *Virgins* of the *yeare*,
As if the *Spring* were all your own;
    What are you when the *Rose is blowne?*

[1] Elizabeth, daughter of James I, married Frederick, Elector Palatine, in 1613. His acceptance of the Crown of Bohemia in 1619 was the spark which touched off the Thirty Years War. He was driven from his kingdom in 1620, and dubbed 'The Winter King', as his wife was called 'The Queen of Hearts'.

So, when my *Mistris* shal be *seene*
In *form* and *Beauty* of her *mind*,
By *Vertue* first, then *Choyce* a *Queen*,
Tell me, if *she* were not design'd
    Th' *Eclypse* and *Glory* of her kind.[1]

Upon the Sudden Restraint of the Earle of Somerset,[2] *then falling from favor*

Dazel'd thus, with height of place,
Whilst our hopes our wits beguile,
No man markes the narrow space
'Twixt a prison, and a smile.

Then, since fortunes favours fade,
You, that in her armes doe sleep,
Learne to swim, and not to wade;
For, the Hearts of Kings are deepe.

But, if Greatness be so blind,
As to trust in towers of Aire,
Let it be with Goodness lin'd,
That at least, the Fall be faire.

Then though darkned, you shall say,
When Friends faile, and Princes frowne,
Vertue is the roughest way,
But proves at night a *Bed of Downe*.

              (*Reliquiae Wottonianae*, 1651)

---

[1] For a discussion of varying versions of this famous poem, see J. B. Leishman, *The Library*, 1945. The text I print is eclectic.

[2] Robert Carr, Earl of Somerset, favourite of James I. He was placed under arrest at the close of 1615, as was his wife, Frances Howard, divorced wife of the Earl of Essex. In May 1616 they stood their trial for the murder of Sir Thomas Overbury in the Tower.

JOHN DONNE

(1572–1631)

Satyre: Of Religion[1]

Kinde pitty chokes my spleene; brave scorn forbids
Those teares to issue which swell my eye-lids;
I must not laugh, nor weepe sinnes, and be wise,
Can railing then cure these worne maladies?
Is not our Mistresse faire Religion,
As worthy of all our Soules devotion,
As vertue was to the first blinded[2] age?
Are not heavens joyes as valiant to asswage
Lusts, as earths honour was to them? Alas,
As wee do them in meanes, shall they surpasse
Us in the end, and shall thy fathers spirit
Meet blinde[2] Philosophers in heaven, whose merit
Of strict life may be imputed faith, and heare
Thee, whom hee taught so easie wayes and neare
To follow, damn'd? O if thou dar'st, feare this;
This feare great courage, and high valour is.
Dar'st thou ayd mutinous Dutch, and dar'st thou lay
Thee in ships woodden Sepulchers, a prey
To leaders rage, to stormes, to shot, to dearth?
Dar'st thou dive seas, and dungeons of the earth?
Hast thou couragious fire to thaw the ice
Of frozen North discoveries? and thrise
Colder than Salamanders, like divine
Children in th'oven,[3] fires of Spaine, and the line,

[1] Written not later than 1597, perhaps as early as 1593. It belongs to a time when, in Walton's words, Donne 'betrothed himself to no Religion that might give him any other denomination than a Christian'.

[2] *blinded . . . blinde*: without the light of revelation.

[3] Shadrach, Meshach, and Abednego, 'the Three Children', who were unharmed in the midst of the burning fiery furnace (Daniel iii).

Whose countries limbecks[1] to our bodies bee,
Canst thou for gaine beare? and must every hee
Which cryes not, Goddesse, to thy Mistresse, draw,
Or eate thy poysonous words? courage of straw!
O desperate coward, wilt thou seeme bold, and
To thy foes and his (who made thee to stand
Sentinell in his worlds garrison) thus yeeld,
And for forbidden warres, leave th'appointed field?
Know thy foes: The foule Devill (whom thou
Strivest to please,) for hate, not love, would allow
Thee faine, his whole Realme to be quit;[2] and as
The worlds all parts wither away and passe,
So the worlds selfe, thy other lov'd foe, is
In her decrepit wayne, and thou, loving this,
Dost love a withered and worne strumpet; last
Flesh (it selfes death) and joyes which flesh can taste,
Thou lovest; and thy faire goodly soule, which doth
Give this flesh power to taste joy, thou dost loath.
Seeke true religion. O where? Mirreus
Thinking her unhous'd here, and fled from us,
Seekes her at Rome; there, because hee doth know
That shee was there a thousand yeares agoe,
He loves her ragges so, as wee here obey
The statecloth where the Prince sate yesterday.
Crantz to such brave Loves will not be inthrall'd,
But loves her onely, who at Geneva is call'd
Religion, plaine, simple, sullen, yong,
Contemptuous, yet unhansome; As among
Lecherous humors, there is one that judges
No wenches wholsome, but coarse country drudges.
Graius stayes still at home here, and because
Some Preachers, vile ambitious bauds, and lawes
Still new like fashions, bid him thinke that shee
Which dwels with us, is onely perfect, hee
Imbraceth her, whom his Godfathers will

[1] *limbecks*: alembics or stills.
[2] *to be quit*: to be rid of you; i.e. there is no need to court the devil.

Tender to him, being tender, as Wards still
Take such wives as their Guardians offer, or
Pay valewes.[1] Carelesse Phrygius doth abhorre
All, because all cannot be good, as one
Knowing some women whores, dares marry none.
Graccus loves all as one, and thinkes that so
As women do in divers countries goe
In divers habits, yet are still one kinde,
So doth, so is Religion; and this blind-
nesse too much light breeds; but unmoved thou
Of force must one, and forc'd but one allow;
And the right; aske thy father which is shee,
Let him aske his; though truth and falshood bee
Neare twins, yet truth a little elder is;
Be busie to seeke her, beleeve mee this,
Hee's not of none, nor worst, that seekes the best.
To adore, or scorne an image, or protest,
May all be bad; doubt wisely; in strange way
To stand inquiring right, is not to stray;
To sleepe, or runne wrong, is. On a huge hill,
Cragged, and steep, Truth stands, and hee that will
Reach her, about must, and about must goe;
And what the hills suddennes resists, winne so;
Yet strive so, that before age, deaths twilight,
Thy Soule rest, for none can worke in that night.
To will, implyes delay, therefore now doe:
Hard deeds, the bodies paines; hard knowledge too
The mindes indeavours reach, and mysteries
Are like the Sunne, dazling, yet plaine to all eyes.
Keepe the truth which thou hast found; men do not stand
In so ill case here, that God hath with his hand
Sign'd Kings blanck-charters to kill whom they hate,
Nor are they Vicars, but hangmen to Fate.
Foole and wretch, wilt thou let thy Soule be tyed

---

[1] Wards who refused marriages arranged for them by their guardians
had to pay them a sum called 'the value of the marriage'. The recusant,
similarly, had to pay for not attending his parish church.

To mans lawes, by which she shall not be tryed
At the last day? Oh, will it then boot thee
To say a Philip, or a Gregory,
A Harry, or a Martin taught thee this?
Is not this excuse for mere[1] contraries,
Equally strong? cannot both sides say so?
That thou mayest rightly obey power, her bounds know;
Those past, her nature, and name is chang'd; to be
Then humble to her is idolatrie.
As streames are, Power is; those blest flowers that dwell
At the rough streames calme head, thrive and do well,
But having left their roots, and themselves given
To the streames tyrranous rage, alas, are driven
Through mills, and rockes, and woods, and at last, almost
Consum'd in going, in the sea are lost:
So perish Soules, which more chuse mens unjust
Power from God claym'd, than God himselfe to trust.

Elegie: His Picture[2]

Here take my Picture; though I bid farewell,
Thine, in my heart, where my soule dwels, shall dwell.
'Tis like me now, but I dead, 'twill be more
When wee are shadowes both, than 'twas before.
When weather-beaten I come backe; my hand,
Perhaps with rude oares torne, or Sun beams tann'd,
My face and brest of haircloth, and my head
With cares rash sodaine hoarinesse o'rspread,
My body'a sack of bones, broken within,
And powders blew staines scatter'd on my skinne;
If rivall fooles taxe thee to'have lov'd a man,
So foule, and coarse, as, Oh, I may seeme then,

---

[1] *mere*: absolute.
[2] This and the following two poems are from a set of Love Elegies written probably between 1593 and 1596.

This shall say what I was: and thou shalt say,
Doe his hurts reach mee? doth my worth decay?
Or doe they reach his judging minde, that hee
Should like'and love lesse, what he did love to see?
That which in him was faire and delicate,
Was but the milke, which in loves childish state
Did nurse it: who now is growne strong enough
To feed on that, which to'disus'd tasts seemes tough.

(*Poems*, 1633)

Elegie: On his Mistris

By our first strange and fatall interview,
By all desires which thereof did ensue,
By our long sterving hopes, by that remorse[1]
Which my words masculine perswasive force
Begot in thee, and by the memory
Of hurts which spies and rivalls threatned mee,
I calmely beg; but by thy parents wrath,
By all paines which want and divorcement hath,
I conjure thee; and all those oathes which I
And thou have sworne, to seal joint constancie,
Here I unsweare, and over-sweare them thus:
Thou shalt not love by meanes so dangerous.
Temper, oh faire Love, loves impetuous rage,
Be my true mistris still, not my feign'd page.
I'll goe, and, by thy kind leave, leave behinde
Thee, onely worthy to nurse in my minde
Thirst to come back; oh, if thou dye before,
From other lands my soule towards thee shall soare.
Thy (else Almighty) Beauty cannot move
Rage from the seas, nor thy love teach them love,
Nor tame wilde Boreas harshness; Thou hast read
How roughly hee in peices shivered

---

[1] *remorse*: pity.

Faire Orithea, whome he swore hee lov'd.[1]
Fall ill or good, 'tis madness to have prov'd
Dangers unurg'd; Feede on this flatterye,
That absent lovers one in th'other bee.
Dissemble nothing, not a boy, nor change
Thy bodies habit, nor mindes; bee not strange
To thy selfe onely; All will spye in thy face
A blushing womanly discovering grace.
Richly cloth'd Apes are call'd Apes, and as soone
Ecclips'd as bright, wee call the moone, the moone.
Men of France, changeable Camelions,
Spittles of diseases, shops of fashions,
Loves fuellers, and the rightest companie
Of Players which uppon the worlds stage bee,
Will quickly knowe thee,'and knowe thee; and alas
Th'indifferent Italian, as wee passe
His warme land, well content to thinke thee page,
Will haunt thee, with such lust and hideous rage
As Lots faire guests were vext: But none of these,
Nor spungie hydroptique Dutch, shall thee displease,
If thou stay here. Oh stay here, for, for thee
England is only'a worthy gallerie,
To walk in expectation, till from thence
Our greate King call thee into his presence.
When I am gone, dreame mee some happinesse,
Nor let thy lookes our long hid love confesse,
Nor praise, nor dispraise mee, blesse, nor curse
Openly loves force; nor in bed fright thy nurse
With midnights startings, crying out, oh, oh,
Nurse, oh my love is slaine; I saw him goe
Ore the white Alpes, alone; I saw him, I,
Assayld, fight, taken, stabb'd, bleede, fall, and dye.
Augure mee better chance, except dreade Jove
Think it enough for mee, to'have had thy love.

(Poems, 1635)

.[1] In all known versions of the myth, Boreas, the North wind, carried the maiden undamaged to the mountains, where she bore him many children.

Elegie: To his Mistris Going to Bed

Come, Madame, come, all rest my powers defie,
Until I labour, I in labour lye.
The foe oft-times, having the foe in sight,
Is tir'd with standing, though they never fight.
Off with that girdle, like heavens zone glistering
But a farre fairer world encompassing.
Unpin that spangled brest-plate, which you weare
That th'eyes of busy fooles may be stopt there:
Unlace your selfe, for that harmonious chime
Tells me from you that now 'tis your bed time.
Off with that happy buske, whom I envye
That still can be, and still can stand so nigh.
Your gownes going off such beauteous state reveales
As when from flowery meades th'hills shadow steales.
Off with your wyrie coronet and showe
The hairy dyadem which on you doth growe.
Off with those shoes: and then safely tread
In this loves hallow'd temple, this soft bed.
In such white robes heavens Angels us'd to bee
Receiv'd by men; Thou Angel bring'st with thee
A heaven like Mahomets Paradise; and though
Ill spirits walk in white, we easily know
By this these Angels from an evill sprite:
They set our haires, but these the flesh upright.
   Licence my roving hands, and let them goe
Behind, before, above, between, below.
Oh my America, my new found lande,
My kingdome, safeliest when with one man man'd,
My myne of precious stones, my Empiree,
How blest am I in this discovering thee.
To enter in these bonds is to be free,
Then where my hand is set my seal shall be.
   Full nakedness, all joyes are due to thee.
As soules unbodied, bodies uncloth'd must bee

To taste whole joyes. Gems which you women use
Are as Atlanta's balls, cast in mens viewes,
That when a fooles eye lighteth on a gem
His earthly soule may covet theirs not them.[1]
Like pictures, or like bookes gay coverings made
For laymen, are all women thus arraid;
Themselves are mystique bookes, which only wee
Whom their imputed grace will dignify
Must see reveal'd. Then since I may knowe,
As liberally as to a midwife showe
Thy selfe; cast all, yea this white linnen hence.
Here is no pennance, much lesse innocence.
    To teach thee, I am naked first: Why then
What need'st thou have more covering than a man.

                         (*Poems*, 1669)[2]

The Calme[3]

Our storme is past, and that storms tyrranous rage,
A stupid calme, but nothing it, doth swage.
The fable is inverted, and farre more
A blocke afflicts now, than a storke before.[4]
Stormes chafe, and soone weare out themselves, or us;

---

[1] Donne speaks as if it were Atalanta who threw the golden balls to distract Hippomenes, whereas it was *his* ruse to make *her* turn aside in their race.

[2] These last two poems were among the five Elegies 'excepted' in the entry of Donne's *Poems* in the Stationers' Register in 1632, and consequently not printed in the first edition of 1633.

[3] This is the second of two poems written on the Islands Voyage of 1597. The object of the expedition (which was a failure, owing to dissensions between its leaders, Ralegh and Essex) was to intercept the Spanish treasure fleet off the Azores. With its companion piece 'The Storme', 'The Calme' was one of the most popular of Donne's poems.

[4] In Aesop's Fables the frogs asked Zeus for a king and he gave them a Log. Distressed by its immobility they complained and King Log was replaced by a snake which tormented them. During the Middle Ages the snake was transformed into King Stork.

23

In calmes, Heaven laughs to see us languish thus.
As steady'as I can wish, that my thoughts were,
Smooth as thy mistresse glasse, or what shines there,
The sea is now. And, as the Iles which wee
Seeke, when wee can move, our ships rooted bee.
As water did in stormes, now pitch runs out:
As lead, when a fir'd Church becomes one spout.
And all our beauty, and our trimme, decayes,
Like courts removing, or like ended playes.
The fighting place now seamens ragges supply;
And all the tackling is a frippery.[1]
No use of lanthornes;[2] and in one place lay
Feathers and dust, to day and yesterday.
Earths hollownesses, which the worlds lungs are,
Have no more winde than the upper valt of aire.
We can nor lost friends, nor sought foes recover,[3]
But meteorlike, save that wee move not, hover.
Only the Calenture[4] together drawes
Deare friends, which meet dead in great fishes jawes:
And on the hatches as on Altars lyes
Each one, his owne Priest, and owne Sacrifice.
Who live, that miracle do multiply
Where walkers in hot Ovens, doe not dye.
If in despite of these, wee swimme, that hath
No more refreshing, than our brimstone Bath,
But from the sea, into the ship we turne,
Like parboyl'd wretches, on the coales to burne.
Like *Bajazet* encag'd, the shepheards scoffe,[5]
Or like slacke sinew'd *Sampson*, his haire off,
Languish our ships. Now as a Miriade

[1] *a frippery*: a second-hand-clothes shop.
[2] The Admiral, or flag-ship, carried a lantern by which the following ships steered.
[3] Ralegh and his squadron lost touch with the main fleet off Spain and contact was not made until both reached the Azores.
[4] *Calenture*: a disease of sailors in the tropics, in which the delirious patient takes the sea for green fields and attempts to leap into it.
[5] Tamburlaine, the Scythian shepherd, scoffs at the emperor Bajazeth in his cage in Marlowe's *Tamburlaine*, part 1.

Of Ants durst th'Emperours lov'd snake invade,[1]
The crawling Gallies, Sea-gaols, finny chips,
Might brave our Pinnaces, now bed-ridde ships.
Whether a rotten state, and hope of gaine,
Or to disuse mee from the queasie paine
Of being belov'd, and loving, or the thirst
Of honour, or faire death, out pusht mee first,
I lose my end: for here as well as I
A desperate may live, and a coward die.
Stagge, dogge, and all which from, or towards flies,
Is paid with life, or prey, or doing dyes.
Fate grudges us all, and doth subtly lay
A scourge, 'gainst which wee all forget to pray.
He that at sea prayes for more winde, as well
Under the poles may begge cold, heat in hell.
What are wee then? How little more alas
Is man now, than before he was? He was
Nothing; for us, wee are for nothing fit;
Chance, or our selves still disproportion it.
Wee have no power, no will, no sense; I lye,
I should not then thus feele this miserie.

The Flea[2]

Marke but this flea,[3] and marke in this,
How little that which thou deny'st me is;
Mee it suck'd first, and now sucks thee,
And in this flea, our two bloods mingled bee;

---

[1] Suetonius reports that the pet snake of Tiberius was eaten by ants. The Emperor took this as a warning against the power of the multitude.

[2] Donne's love lyrics, scattered in the first edition, were collected together in the second under the heading 'Songs and Sonets'. In my edition I have arranged them in two groups in accordance with my theories as to their probable dates. Here I follow the haphazard order in the edition of 1635.

[3] Fleas were a popular subject for jocose and amatory poetry in all countries at the Renaissance.

Confesse it, this cannot be said
A sinne, or shame, or losse of maidenhead,
    Yet this enjoyes before it wooe,
      And pamper'd swells with one blood made of two,
      And this, alas, is more than wee would doe.

Oh stay, three lives in one flea spare,
Where wee almost, nay more than maryed are:
This flea is you and I, and this
Our mariage bed, and mariage temple is;
Though parents grudge, and you, w'are met,
And cloysterd in these living walls of Jet.
    Though use make thee apt to kill mee,
    Let not to this, selfe murder added bee,
    And sacrilege, three sinnes in killing three.

Cruell and sodaine, hast thou since
Purpled thy naile, in blood of innocence?
 In what could this flea guilty bee,
Except in that drop which it suckt from thee?
Yet thou triumph'st, and saist that thou
Find'st not thy selfe, nor mee the weaker now;
    'Tis true, then learne how false, feares bee;
    Just so much honor, when thou yeeld'st to mee,
    Will wast, as this flea's death tooke life from thee.

The Good-Morrow

I wonder by my troth, what thou, and I
Did, till we lov'd? were we not wean'd till then?
But suck'd on countrey pleasures, childishly?
Or snorted we i'the seaven sleepers den?[1]

[1] Legend tells of seven young men of Ephesus who took refuge in a cave during the persecution of Diocletian and were entombed there. They were found alive over two centuries later.

'Twas so; But this, all pleasures fancies bee.
If ever any beauty I did see,
Which I desir'd, and got, 'twas but a dreame of thee.

And now good morrow to our waking soules,
Which watch not one another out of feare;
For love, all love of other sights controules,
And makes one little roome, an every where.
Let sea-discoverers to new worlds have gone,
Let Maps to others, worlds on worlds have showne,
Let us possesse our world, each hath one, and is one.

My face in thine eye, thine in mine appeares,
And true plaine hearts doe in the faces rest,
Where can we finde two better hemispheares
Without sharpe North, without declining West?
What ever dyes, was not mixt equally;
If our two loves be one, or, thou and I
Love so alike, that none doe slacken, none can die.[1]

Song

Goe, and catche a falling starre,
    Get with child a mandrake roote,
Tell me, where all past yeares are,
    Or who cleft the Divels foot,
Teach me to heare Mermaides singing,
    Or to keep off envies stinging,
            And finde
            What winde
Serves to'advance an honest minde.

[1] Only the simple, or uncompounded, and things compounded of elements between which is no contrariety are free from corruption and immortal.

If thou beest borne to strange sights,
   Things invisible to see,
Ride ten thousand daies and nights,
   Till age snow white haires on thee,
Thou, when thou retorn'st, wilt tell mee
All strange wonders that befell thee,
     And sweare
     No where
Lives a woman true, and faire.

If thou findst one, let mee know,
   Such a Pilgrimage were sweet,
Yet doe not, I would not goe,
   Though at next doore wee might meet,
Though shee were true, when you met her,
And last, till you write your letter,
     Yet shee
     Will bee
False, ere I come, to two, or three.

The Undertaking

I have done one braver thing
   Than all the *Worthies* did,
Yet a braver thence doth spring,
   Which is, to keepe that hid.

It were but madnes now t'impart
   The skill of specular stone,[1]
When he which can have learn'd the art
   To cut it, can finde none.

[1] Donne refers more than once to 'specular stone' as a stone unknown in his own day which the ancients had employed for building temples with transparent walls. He found his information in a book published in 1599.

So, if I now should utter this,
    Others (because no more
Such stuffe to worke upon, there is,)
    Would love but as before.

But he who lovelinesse within
    Hath found, all outward loathes,
For he who colour loves, and skinne,
    Loves but their oldest clothes.

If, as I have, you also doe
    Vertue'attir'd in woman see,
And dare love that, and say so too,
    And forget the Hee and Shee;

And if this love, though placed so,
    From prophane men you hide,
Which will no faith on this bestow,
    Or, if they doe, deride:

Then you'have done a braver thing
Than all the *Worthies* did,
And a braver thence will spring,
    Which is, to keepe that hid.

The Sunne Rising

Busie old foole, unruly Sunne,
    Why dost thou thus,
Through windowes, and through curtaines call on us?
Must to thy motions lovers seasons run?
    Sawcy pedantique wretch, goe chide
    Late schoole boyes, and sowre prentices,
Goe tell Court-huntsmen, that the King will ride,[1]
    Call countrey ants to harvest offices;
Love, all alike, no season knowes, nor clyme,
Nor houres, dayes, months, which are the rags of time.

[1] James I was as passionately addicted to hunting as to theology. The allusion dates the composition of the poem after 1603.

Thy beames, so reverend, and strong
   Why shouldst thou thinke?
I could eclipse and cloud them with a winke,
But that I would not lose her sight so long:
   If her eyes have not blinded thine,
   Looke, and to morrow late, tell mee,
  Whether both the'India's of spice and Myne
  Be where thou leftst them, or lie here with mee.
Aske for those Kings whom thou saw'st yesterday,
And thou shalt heare, All here in one bed lay.

   She'is all States, and all Princes, I,
   Nothing else is.
Princes doe but play us; compar'd to this,
All honor's mimique; All wealth alchimie.
   Thou sunne art halfe as happy'as wee,
   In that the world's contracted thus;
  Thine age askes ease, and since thy duties bee
  To warme the world, that's done in warming us.
Shine here to us, and thou art every where;
This bed thy center is, these walls, thy spheare.

The Canonization

For Godsake hold your tongue, and let me love,
   Or chide my palsie, or my gout,
My five gray haires, or ruin'd fortune flout,
   With wealth your state, your minde with Arts improve,
    Take you a course, get you a place,
    Observe his honour, or his grace,
  Or the Kings reall, or his stamped face[1]
   Contemplate; what you will, approve,
   So you will let me love.

[1] The reference to the King's face seen at Court, or on the coinage, dates this poem, like the last, as after 1603.

Alas, alas, who's injur'd by my love?
  What merchants ships have my sighs drown'd?
Who saies my teares have overflow'd his ground?
  When did my colds a forward spring remove?
    When did the heats which my veines fill
    Adde one man to the plaguie Bill?
Soldiers finde warres, and Lawyers finde out still
  Litigious men, which quarrels move,
  Though she and I do love.

Call us what you will, wee'are made such by love;
  Call her one, mee another flye,
We'are Tapers too, and at our owne cost die,
  And wee in us finde the'Eagle and the Dove;
    The Phoenix ridle hath more wit
    By us, we two being one, are it,
So, to one neutrall thing both sexes fit.
  Wee dye and rise the same, and prove
  Mysterious by this love.

Wee can dye by it, if not live by love,
  And if unfit for tombes or hearse
Our legend bee, it will be fit for verse;
  And if no peece of Chronicle wee prove,
    We'll build in sonnets pretty roomes;
    As well a well wrought urne becomes
The greatest ashes, as halfe-acre tombes,
  And by these hymnes, all shall approve
  Us *Canoniz'd* for Love.

And thus invoke us; You whom reverend love
  Made one anothers hermitage;
You, to whom love was peace, that now is rage;
  Who did the whole worlds soule extract, and drove
    Into the glasses of your eyes,
    So made such mirrors, and such spies,
That they did all to you epitomize,
  Countries, Townes, Courts: Beg from above
  A patterne of your love!

Song

Sweetest love, I do not goe,
   For wearinesse of thee,
Nor in hope the world can show
   A fitter Love for mee;
     But since that I
Must dye at last, 'tis best,
To use my selfe in jest
   Thus by fain'd deaths to dye.

Yesternight the Sunne went hence,
   And yet is here to day,
He hath no desire nor sense,
   Nor halfe so short a way:
     Then feare not mee,
But beleeve that I shall make
Speedier journeyes, since I take
   More wings and spurres than hee.

O how feeble is mans power,
   That if good fortune fall,
Cannot adde another houre,
   Nor a lost houre recall!
     But come bad chance,
And wee joyne to it our strength,
And wee teach it art and length,
   It selfe o'r us to'advance.

When thou sigh'st, thou sigh'st not winde,
   But sigh'st my soule away,
When thou weep'st, unkindly kinde,
   My lifes blood doth decay.
     It cannot bee
That thou lov'st mee, as thou say'st,
If in thine my life thou waste,
   Thou art the best of mee.

Let not thy divining heart
   Forethinke me any ill,
Destiny may take thy part,
   And may thy feares fulfill;
     But thinke that wee
Are but turn'd aside to sleepe;
They who one another keepe
   Alive, ne'r parted bee.

Aire and Angels[1]

Twice or thrice had I lov'd thee,
Before I knew thy face or name;
So in a voice, so in a shapelesse flame,
Angells affect us oft, and worship'd bee;
   Still when, to where thou wert, I came,
Some lovely glorious nothing I did see.
   But since my soule, whose child love is,
Takes limmes of flesh, and else could nothing doe,
   More subtile than the parent is,
Love must not be, but take a body too,
   And therefore what thou wert, and who,
     I bid Love aske, and now
That it assume thy body, I allow,
And fixe it selfe in thy lip, eye, and brow.

Whilst thus to ballast love, I thought,
And so more steddily to have gone,
With wares which would sinke admiration,
I saw, I had loves pinnace overfraught,
   Ev'ry thy haire for love to worke upon
Is much too much, some fitter must be sought;
   For, nor in nothing, nor in things
Extreme, and scatt'ring bright, can love inhere;

[1] The appearance of angels (who are pure spirit) in visible form was explained in scholastic theology by the theory that they made themselves 'bodies' of air condensed to clouds.

33

Then as an Angell, face, and wings
Of aire, not pure as it, yet pure doth weare,
   So thy love may be my loves spheare;
      Just such disparitie
As is twixt Aire and Angells puritie,
'Twixt womens love, and mens will ever bee.

The Anniversarie

All Kings, and all their favorites,
   All glory'of honors, beauties, wits,
The Sun it selfe, which makes times, as they passe,
Is elder by a yeare, now, than it was
When thou and I first one another saw:
All other things, to their destruction draw,
   Only our love hath no decay;
This, no to morrow hath, nor yesterday,
Running it never runs from us away,
But truly keepes his first, last, everlasting day.

Two graves must hide thine and my corse,
   If one might, death were no divorce.
Alas, as well as other Princes, wee,
(Who Prince enough in one another bee,)
Must leave at last in death, these eyes, and eares,
Oft fed with true oathes, and with sweet salt·teares;
   But soules where nothing dwells but love
(All other thoughts being inmates)[1] then shall prove[2]
This, or a love increased there above,
When bodies to their graves, soules from their graves remove.

And then wee shall be throughly blest,
   But wee no more, than all the rest.
Here upon earth, we'are Kings, and none but wee
Can be such Kings, nor of such subjects bee;

---

[1] *inmates*: lodgers, opposed to those who 'dwell'.
[2] *prove*: experience to the full (this love).

Who is so safe as wee? where none can doe
Treason to us, except one of us two.
   True and false feares let us refraine,
Let us love nobly, and live, and adde againe
Yeares and yeares unto yeares, till we attaine
To write threescore: this is the second of our raigne.

Twicknam Garden[1]

Blasted with sighs, and surrounded with teares,
   Hither I come to seeke the spring,
   And at mine eyes, and at mine eares,
Receive such balmes, as else cure every thing;
   But O, selfe traytor, I do bring
The spider love, which transubstantiates all,
   And can convert Manna[2] to gall,
And that this place may thoroughly be thought
   True Paradise, I have the serpent[3] brought.

'Twere wholsomer for mee, that winter did
   Benight the glory of this place,
   And that a grave frost did forbid
These trees to laugh, and mocke mee to my face;
   But that I may not this disgrace
Indure, nor leave this garden, Love let mee
   Some senslesse peece of this place bee;
Make me a mandrake, so I may grow here,
   Or a stone fountaine weeping out my yeare.[4]

[1] Lucy, Countess of Bedford, patroness of Donne, as of many other poets, lived at Twickenham from 1608 to 1617.

[2] *Manna*: the heavenly food of the Israelites in the desert, a type of the Eucharistic wafer. Love performs the Eucharistic miracle in reverse.

[3] Among the Seven Deadly Sins, Envy is represented by a serpent.

[4] Plants and stones can 'detest and love', but are without a 'soul of sense'. The first, or vegetable, soul, is 'of growth', the second, or animal, is 'of sense', the third, or rational soul, is proper to men.

Hither with christall vyals, lovers come,
　　And take my teares, which are loves wine,
　　And try your mistresse Teares at home,
For all are false, that tast not just like mine;
　　Alas, hearts do not in eyes shine,
Nor can you more judge womans thoughts by teares,
　　Than by her shadow, what she weares.
O perverse sexe, where none is true but shee,
　　Who's therefore true, because her truth kills mee.[1]

Loves Growth

I scarce beleeve my love to be so pure
　　As I had thought it was,
　　Because it doth endure
Vicissitude, and season, as the grasse;
Me thinkes I lyed all winter, when I swore,
My love was infinite, if spring make'it more.
But if this medicine, love, which cures all sorrow
With more, not onely bee no quintessence,[2]
But mixt of all stuffes, paining soule, or sense,
And of the Sunne his working vigour borrow,
Love's not so pure, and abstract, as they use
To say, which have no Mistresse but their Muse,
But as all else, being elemented too,
Love sometimes would contemplate, sometimes do.

And yet not greater, but more eminent,
　　Love by the spring is growne;
　　As, in the firmament,
Starres by the Sunne are not inlarg'd, but showne.

[1] No woman is what she seems. His mistress's 'truth' does not manifest real truth but cruelty.

[2] The contrast is between the old medical doctrine 'similia similibus curantur' and the Paracelsian doctrine of cure by the *quintessence*, a pure essence extracted from things and separated from their 'elements', which cured by its 'purity'.

Gentle love deeds, as blossomes on a bough,
From loves awaken'd root do bud out now.
If, as in water stir'd more circles bee
Produc'd by one, love such additions take,
Those like to many spheares, but one heaven make,
For, they are all concentrique unto thee;
And though each spring doe adde to love new heate,
As princes doe in times of action get
New taxes, and remit them not in peace,
No winter shall abate the springs encrease.

The Dreame

Deare love, for nothing lesse than thee
Would I have broke this happy dreame,
    It was a theame
For reason, much too strong for phantasie,
Therefore thou wakd'st me wisely; yet
My Dreame thou brok'st not, but continued'st it,
Thou art so true, that thoughts of thee suffice,
To make dreames truth; and fables histories;
Enter these armes, for since thou thoughtst it best,
Not to dreame all my dreame, let's do the rest.

As lightning, or a Tapers light,
Thine eyes, and not thy noise wak'd mee;
    Yet I thought thee
(For thou lov'st truth) an Angell, at first sight,
But when I saw thou saw'st my heart,
And knew'st my thoughts, beyond an Angels art,
When thou knew'st what I dreamt, when thou knew'st when
Excesse of joy would wake me, and cam'st then,
I doe confesse, it could not chuse but bee
Prophane, to thinke thee any thing but thee.[1]

[1] Only God can know the thoughts of the heart, and only of God can it be said that 'He is Himself only and divinely like Himself'.

Comming and staying show'd thee, thee,
But rising makes me doubt, that now,
    Thou art not thou.
That love is weake, where feare's as strong as hee;
'Tis not all spirit, pure, and brave,
If mixture it of *Feare*, *Shame*, *Honor*, have.
Perchance as torches which must ready bee,
Men light and put out, so thou deal'st with mee,
Thou cam'st to kindle, goest to come; Then I
Will dreame that hope againe, but else would die.

A Valediction: of Weeping[1]

    Let me powre forth
My teares before thy face, whil'st I stay here,
For thy face coines them, and thy stampe they beare,
And by this Mintage they are something worth,
    For thus they bee
    Pregnant of thee;
Fruits of much griefe they are, emblemes of more,
When a teare falls, that thou falls which it bore,
So thou and I are nothing then, when on a divers shore.

    On a round ball
A workeman that hath copies by, can lay
An Europe, Afrique, and an Asia,
And quickly make that, which was nothing, *All*,
    So doth each teare,
    Which thee doth weare,
A globe, yea world by that impression grow,
Till thy teares mixt with mine doe overflow
This world, by waters sent from thee, my heaven dissolved so.

---

[1] The basic conceit is that the tears of each bear the image, or 'stamp', of the other, a variant of the popular notion of lovers 'looking babies' in each others' eyes.

O more than Moone,
Draw not up seas to drowne me in thy spheare,
Weepe me not dead, in thine armes, but forbeare
To teach the sea, what it may doe too soone;
    Let not the winde
    Example finde,
To doe me more harme, than it purposeth;
Since thou and I sigh one anothers breath,
Who e'r sighes most, is cruellest, and hasts the others death.

Loves Alchymie

Some that have deeper digg'd loves Myne than I
Say, where his centrique happinesse doth lie:
    I have lov'd, and got, and told,
But should I love, get, tell, till I were old,
I should not finde that hidden mysterie;
    Oh, 'tis imposture all:
And as no chymique yet th'Elixar[1] got,
    But glorifies his pregnant pot,
    If by the way to him befall
Some odoriferous thing, or med'cinall,
  So, lovers dreame a rich and long delight,
  But get a winter-seeming summers night.

Our ease, our thrift, our honor, and our day,
Shall we, for this vaine Bubles shadow pay?
    Ends love in this, that my man,
Can be as happy'as I can; If he can
Endure the short scorne of a Bridegroomes play?
    That loving wretch that sweares,

[1] The *Elixir Vitae*, which would cure all diseases and indefinitely pro-long life, was sometimes identified with the 'philosophers' stone' of the alchemists, which would purge base metals of their impurities and turn them to gold.

'Tis not the bodies marry,[1] but the mindes,
    Which he in her Angelique findes,
    Would sweare as justly, that he heares,
In that dayes rude hoarse minstralsey, the spheares.
    Hope not for minde in women; at their best
    Sweetnesse and wit, they'are but *Mummy*, possest.[2]

A Nocturnall upon S. Lucies day,[3]
Being the shortest day

'Tis the yeares midnight, and it is the dayes,
Lucies, who scarce seaven houres herself unmaskes,
    The Sunne is spent, and now his flasks[4]
    Send forth light squibs, no constant rayes;
        The worlds whole sap is sunke:
The general balme th'hydroptique earth hath drunk,
Whither, as to the beds-feet, life is shrunke,[5]
Dead and enterr'd; yet all these seeme to laugh,
Compar'd with mee, who am their Epitaph.

Study me then, you who shall lovers bee
At the next world, that is, at the next Spring:
    For I am every dead thing,
    In whom love wrought new Alchimie.

[1] Manuscript spellings suggest that Donne may not have intended the verb 'marry' here, but the noun 'mary' or 'marrow', which gives better sense with the next line: 'it is not the sweetness of her body, but that of her mind which he, like an angel, finds in her', or 'which he finds angelic in her'.

[2] *Mummy*: a medicinal preparation made from mummies, regarded as a universal panacea; also dead flesh, a corpse. Both senses are probably intended.

[3] St. Lucy's day, 13 Dec., was traditionally regarded as the shortest day, the Winter Solstice, when the Sun entered the sign of the Goat (Capricorn). In fact, the true solstice by the old (Julian) Calendar was 12 Dec.

[4] *flasks*: the stars, which were thought to store up light from the sun.

[5] Life *in extremis* shrinks down into the earth, as a dying man huddles at the foot of the bed. One of Hippocrates' signs of imminent death is when the sick man 'makes the beds feet where the head should be'.

For his art did expresse[1]
A quintessence even from nothingnesse,
From dull privations, and leane emptinesse:
He ruin'd mee, and I am re-begot
Of absence, darknesse, death; things which are not.

All others, from all things, draw all that's good,
Life, soule, forme, spirit, whence they beeing have;
  I, by loves limbecke, am the grave
  Of all, that's nothing. Oft a flood
    Have wee two wept, and so
Drownd the whole world, us two; oft did we grow
To be two Chaosses, when we did show
Care to ought else; and often absences
Withdrew our soules, and made us carcasses.

But I am by her death, (which word wrongs her)
Of the first nothing, the Elixer grown;
  Were I a man, that I were one,
  I needs must know; I should preferre,
    If I were any beast,
Some ends, some means; Yea plants, yea stones detest
And love; All, all some properties invest;
If I am ordinary nothing were,
As shadow,'a light and body must be here.[2]

But I am None; nor will my Sunne renew.
You lovers, for whose sake, the lesser Sunne
  At this time to the Goat is runne
  To fetch new lust, and give it you,
    Enjoy your summer all;
Since shee enjoyes her long nights festivall,
Let mee prepare towards her, and let mee call
This houre her Vigill, and her Eve, since this
Both the yeares, and the dayes deep midnight is.

[1] *expresse*: squeeze out.
[2] The distinction is between an 'ordinary nothing', which is the absence of something, and can therefore be said to come from something, and the 'quintessential nothing', which comes from nothing, that is the absolute nothing which was before creation.

JOHN DONNE

The Apparition

When by thy scorne, O murdresse, I am dead,
 And that thou thinkst thee free
From all solicitation from mee,
Then shall my ghost come to thy bed,
And thee, fain'd vestall, in worse armes shall see;
Then thy sicke taper will begin to winke,
And he, whose thou art then, being tyr'd before,
Will, if thou stirre, or pinch to wake him, thinke
 Thou call'st for more,
And in false sleepe will from thee shrinke,
And then poore Aspen wretch, neglected thou
Bath'd in a cold quicksilver sweat wilt lye
 A veryer ghost than I;
What I will say, I will not tell thee now,
Lest that preserve thee;'and since my love is spent,
I'had rather thou shouldst painfully repent,
Than by my threatenings rest still innocent.

A Valediction: forbidding mourning[1]

As virtuous men passe mildly'away,
 And whisper to their soules, to goe,
Whilst some of their sad friends doe say,
 The breath goes now, and some say, no:

So let us melt, and make no noise,
 No teare-floods, nor sigh-tempests move,
'Twere prophanation of our joyes
 To tell the layetie our love.

[1] Walton says that Donne gave these verses to his wife when he left her
to go with Sir Robert Drury to France in Noy. 1611.

42

Moving of th'earth brings harmes and feares,
    Men reckon what it did and meant,
But trepidation of the spheares,
    Though greater farre, is innocent.[1]

Dull sublunary lovers love
    (Whose soule is sense) cannot admit
Absence, because it doth remove
    Those things which elemented it.

But we by'a love, so much refin'd,
    That our selves know not what it is,
Inter-assured of the mind,
    Care lesse, eyes, lips, and hands to misse.

Our two soules therefore, which are one,
    Though I must goe, endure not yet
A breach, but an expansion,
    Like gold to ayery thinnesse beate.

If they be two, they are two so
    As stiffe twin compasses are two,
Thy soule the fixt foot, makes no show
    To move, but doth, if the'other doe.

And though it in the center sit,
    Yet when the other far doth rome,
It leanes, and hearkens after it,
    And growes erect, as it comes home.

Such wilt thou be to mee, who must
    Like th'other foot, obliquely runne;
Thy firmnes makes my circle just,
    And makes me end, where I begunne.

---

[1] The trepidation, or libration, of the ninth, the Crystalline, sphere, invented to account for the precession of the equinoxes, communicated itself to all the other spheres. Unlike earthquakes, it was harmless and not portentous.

The Extasie

Where, like a pillow on a bed,
   A Pregnant banke swel'd up, to rest
The violets reclining head,
   Sat we two, one anothers best;

Our hands were firmely cimented
   With a fast balme, which thence did spring,
Our eye-beames[1] twisted, and did thred
   Our eyes, upon one double string;

So to'entergraft our hands, as yet
   Was all our meanes to make us one,
And pictures on our eyes to get
   Was all our propagation.[2]

As 'twixt two equall Armies, Fate
   Suspends uncertaine victorie,
Our soules, (which to advance their state,
   Were gone out,) hung 'twixt her, and mee.

And whil'st our soules negotiate there,
   Wee like sepulchrall statues lay;
All day, the same our postures were,
   And wee said nothing, all the day.

If any, so by love refin'd,
   That he soules language understood,
And by good love were grown all minde,
   Within convenient distance stood,

He (though he knew not which soule spake,
   Because both meant, both spake the same)
Might thence a new concoction take,
   And part farre purer than he came.

[1] One theory of sight held that it was caused by the contact of a beam emitted from the eye with the object seen.

[2] They were 'looking babies', that is, seeing the image of each reflected in the eyes of the other.

This Extasie doth unperplex
  (We said) and tell us what we love,
Wee see by this, it was not sexe,
  Wee see, we saw not what did move:

But as all severall soules containe
  Mixture of things, they know not what,
Love, these mixt soules, doth mixe againe,
  And makes both one, each this and that.

A single violet transplant,
  The strength, the colour, and the size,
(All which before was poore, and scant,)
  Redoubles still, and multiplies.

When love, with one another so
  Interinanimates two soules,
That abler soule, which thence doth flow,
  Defects of lonelinesse controules.

Wee then, who are this new soule, know,
  Of what we are compos'd, and made,
For, th'Atomies of which we grow,
  Are soules, whom no change can invade.

But O alas, so long, so farre
  Our bodies why doe wee forbeare?
They'are ours, though they'are not wee, Wee are
  Th'intelligences, they the spheare.[1]

We owe them thankes, because they thus,
  Did us, to us, at first convay,
Yeelded their forces, sense, to us,
  Nor are drosse to us, but allay.

---

[1] *spheare*: the whole physical cosmos, made up of concentric spheres
moved by intelligences, or angels.

On man heavens influence workes not so,
　　But that it first imprints the ayre,
Soe soule into the soule may flow,
　　Though it to body first repaire.

As our blood labours to beget
　　Spirits, as like soules as it can,
Because such fingers need[1] to knit
　　That subtile knot, which makes us man:[2]

So must pure lovers soules descend
　　T'affections, and to faculties,
That sense may reach and apprehend,
　　Else a great Prince in prison lies.

To'our bodies turne wee then, that so
　　Weake men on love reveal'd may looke;
Loves mysteries in soules doe grow,
　　But yet the body is his booke.

And if some lover, such as wee,
　　Have heard this dialogue of one,
Let him still marke us, he shall see
　　Small change, when we'are to bodies gone.

Loves Deitie

I long to talke with some old lovers ghost,
　　Who dyed before the god of Love was borne:
I cannot thinke that hee, who then lov'd most,
　　Sunke so low, as to love one which did scorne.

---

[1] *need*: are necessary.

[2] In the old physiology, the spirits were rarified and subtle substances
n the blood, concocted in the liver, purified in the heart and further sub-
tilized in the brain. By them the brain's commands were communicated to
the muscles. The union of soul and body, through the working of the
spirits, 'makes us man'.

But since this god produc'd a destinie,
And that vice-nature, custome, lets it be;
   I must love her, that loves not mee.

Sure, they which made him god, meant not so much:
   Nor he, in his young godhead practis'd it.
But when an even flame two hearts did touch,
   His office was indulgently to fit
Actives to passives: Correspondencie
Only his subject was. It cannot bee
   Love, till I love her, that loves mee.

But every moderne god will now extend
   His vast prerogative, as far as Jove.
To rage, to lust, to write to, to commend,
   All is the purlewe[1] of the God of Love.
Oh were wee wak'ned by this Tyrannie
To'ungod this child againe, it could not bee
   That I should love, who loves not mee.

Rebell and Atheist too, why murmure I,
   As though I felt the worst that love could doe?
Love might make me leave loving, or might trie
   A deeper plague, to make her love mee too,
Which, since she loves before, I'am loth to see;
Falshood is worse than hate; and that must bee,
   If shee whom I love, should love mee.

The Will

Before I sigh my last gaspe, let me breath,
Great love, some Legacies; Here I bequeath
Mine eyes to *Argus*, if mine eyes can see,
If they be blinde, then Love, I give them thee;

---

[1] *purlewe*: the outskirts of a forest, which, although disafforested by charter, were still subject, in respect to hunting, to the Forest Laws. The Crown was always attempting to extend its rights over the purlieus of royal forests.

My tongue to Fame; to'Embassadours mine eares;
　　To women or the sea, my teares.
Thou, Love, hast taught mee heretofore
By making mee serve her who'had twenty more,
That I should give to none, but such, as had too much before.

My constancie I to the planets give;
My truth to them, who at the Court doe live;
Mine ingenuity and opennesse,
To Jesuites; to Buffones my pensivenesse;
My silence to'any, who abroad hath beene;
　　My mony to a Capuchin.
Thou Love taught'st me, by'appointing mee
To love there, where no love receiv'd can be,
Onely to give to such as have an incapacitie.

My faith I give to Roman Catholiques;
All my good works unto the Schismaticks
Of Amsterdam; my best civility
And Courtship, to an Universitie;
My modesty I give to souldiers bare;
　　My patience let gamesters share.
Thou Love taughtst mee, by making mee
Love her that holds my love disparity,
Onely to give to those that count my gifts indignity.

I give my reputation to those
Which were my friends; Mine industrie to foes;
To Schoolemen I bequeath my doubtfulnesse;
My sicknesse to Physitians, or excesse;
To Nature, all that I in Ryme have writ;
　　And to my company my wit.
Thou Love, by making mee adore
Her, who begot this love in mee before,
Taughtst me to make, as though I gave, when I did but restore.

To him for whom the passing bell next tolls,
I give my physick bookes; my writen rowles

Of Morall counsels, I to Bedlam give;
My brazen medals,[1] unto them which live
In want of bread; To them which passe among
    All forrainers, mine English tongue.
Thou, Love, by making mee love one
Who thinkes her friendship a fit portion
For yonger lovers, dost my gifts thus disproportion.

Therefore I'll give no more; But I'll undoe
The world by dying; because love dies too.
Then all your beauties will bee no more worth
Than gold in Mines, where none doth draw it forth;
And all your graces no more use shall have
    Than a Sun dyall in a grave.
Thou Love taughtst mee, by making mee
Love her, who doth neglect both mee and thee,
To'invent, and practise this one way, to'annihilate all three.

The Relique

When my grave is broke up againe
Some second guest to entertaine,
(For graves have learn'd that woman-head
To be to more than one a Bed)
    And he that digs it, spies
A bracelet of bright haire about the bone,
    Will he not let'us alone,
And thinke that there a loving couple lies,
Who thought that this device might be some way
To make their soules, at the last busie day,
Meet at this grave, and make a little stay?

If this fall in a time, or land,
Where mis-devotion doth command,
Then, he that digges us up, will bring
Us, to the Bishop, and the King,

[1] *medals*: Roman bronze coins, valued by collectors but useless as money.

49

To make us Reliques; then
Thou shalt be'a Mary Magdalen,[1] and I
    A something else thereby;
All women shall adore us, and some men;
And since at such times, miracles are sought,
I would that age were by this paper taught
What miracles wee harmelesse lovers wrought.

    First, we lov'd well and faithfully,
    Yet knew not what wee lov'd, nor why,
    Difference of sex no more wee knew,
    Than our Guardian Angells doe;
        Comming and going, wee
Perchance might kisse, but not between those meales;
    Our hands ne'er toucht the seales,
Which nature, injur'd by late law, sets free:
These miracles wee did; but now alas,
All measure, and all language, I should passe,
Should I tell what a miracle shee was.

The Expiration

So, so, breake off this last lamenting kisse,
    Which sucks two soules, and vapors both away,
Turne thou ghost that way, and let mee turne this,
    And let our selves benight our happiest day,
We ask'd none leave to love; nor will we owe
    Any, so cheape a death, as saying, Goe;

Goe; and if that word have not quite kil'd thee,
    Ease mee with death, by bidding mee goe too.
Oh, if it have, let my word worke on mee,
    And a just office on a murderer doe.
Except it be too late, to kill me so,
    Being double dead, going, and bidding, goe.

[1] The 'bright haire' will suggest this saint to the superstitious looking
for relics; she is always represented with golden hair in art. The 'bone'
will then be taken for the arm of one of her lovers wearing her token.

To Mr Rowland Woodward[1]

Like one who'in her third widdowhood doth professe
Her selfe a Nunne, tyed to retirednesse,
So'affects my muse now, a chast fallownesse;

Since shee to few, yet to too many'hath showne
How love-song weeds, and Satyrique thornes are growne
Where seeds of better Arts, were early sown.

Though to use, and love Poëtrie, to mee,
Betroth'd to no'one Art, be no'adulterie;
Omissions of good, ill, as ill deeds bee.

For though to us it seeme, 'and be light and thinne,
Yet in those faithfull scales, where God throwes in
Mens workes, vanity weighs as much as sinne.

If our Soules have stain'd their first white, yet wee
May clothe them with faith, and deare honestie,
Which God imputes, as native puritie.

There is no Vertue, but Religion:
Wise, valiant, sober, just, are names, which none
Want, which want not Vice-covering discretion.

Seeke wee then our selves in our selves; for as
Men force the Sunne with much more force to passe,
By gathering his beames with a christall glasse;

So wee, If wee into our selves will turne,
Blowing our sparkes of vertue, may outburne
The straw, which doth about our hearts sojourne.

[1] A common friend of Donne and Wotton. He seems to have gone with Wotton to Venice in 1604. This letter, a reply to a request to be shown some poems, is probably before that date.

You know, Physitians, when they would infuse
Into any'oyle, the Soules of Simples,[1] use
Places, where they may lie still warme, to chuse.

So workes retirednesse in us; To rome
Giddily, and be every where, but at home,
Such freedome doth a banishment become.

Wee are but farmers[2] of our selves, yet may,
If we can stocke our selves, and thrive, uplay
Much, much deare treasure for the great rent day.

Manure thy self then, to thy selfe be'approv'd,
And with vaine outward things be no more mov'd,
But to know, that I love thee'and would be lov'd.

Holy Sonnets: Divine Meditations[3]

I

As due by many titles I resigne
My selfe to thee, O God, first I was made
By thee, and for thee, and when I was decay'd
Thy blood bought that, the which before was thine,
I am thy sonne, made with thy selfe to shine,
Thy servant, whose paines thou hast still repaid,
Thy sheepe, thine Image, and till I betray'd
My selfe, a temple of thy Spirit divine;
Why doth the devill then usurpe in mee?
Why doth he steale, nay ravish that's thy right?
Except thou rise and for thine owne worke fight,
Oh I shall soone despaire, when I doe see
That thou lov'st mankind well, yet wilt'not chuse me,
And Satan hates mee, yet is loth to lose mee.

[1] *Soules of Simples*: virtues of medicinal herbs.
[2] *farmers*: cultivators of land which they do not own.
[3] This short sequence of six sonnets on death and judgement was probably written in 1609.

2

Oh my blacke Soule! now thou art summoned
By sicknesse, deaths herald, and champion;
Thou art like a pilgrim, which abroad hath done
Treason, and durst not turne to whence hee is fled,
Or like a thiefe, which till deaths doome be read,
Wisheth himselfe delivered from prison;
But damn'd and hal'd to execution,
Wisheth that still he might be imprisoned;
Yet grace, if thou repent, thou canst not lacke;
But who shall give thee that grace to beginne?
Oh make thy selfe with holy mourning blacke,
And red with blushing, as thou art with sinne;
Or wash thee in Christs blood, which hath this might
That being red, it dyes red soules to white.

3

This is my playes last scene, here heavens appoint
My pilgrimages last mile; and my race
Idly, yet quickly runne, hath this last pace,
My spans last inch, my minutes last point,
And gluttonous death, will instantly unjoynt
My body, and soule, and I shall sleepe a space,
But my'ever-waking part shall see that face,
Whose feare already shakes my every joynt:
Then, as my soule, to'heaven her first seate, takes flight,
And earth-borne body, in the earth shall dwell,
So, fall my sinnes, that all may have their right,
To where they'are bred, and would presse me, to hell.
Impute me righteous, thus purg'd of evill,
For thus I leave the world, the flesh, and devill.

4

At the round earths imagin'd corners, blow
Your trumpets, Angells, and arise, arise

From death, you numberlesse infinities
Of soules, and to your scattred bodies goe,
All whom the flood did, and fire shall o'erthrow,
All whom warre, dearth, age, agues, tyrannies,
Despaire, law, chance, hath slaine, and you whose eyes,
Shall behold God, and never tast deaths woe.
But let them sleepe, Lord, and mee mourne a space,
For, if above all these, my sinnes abound,
'Tis late to aske abundance of thy grace,
When wee are there; here on this lowly ground,
Teach mee how to repent; for that's as good
As if thou'hadst seal'd my pardon, with thy blood.

5

If poysonous mineralls, and if that tree,
Whose fruit threw death on else immortall us,
If lecherous goats, if serpents envious
Cannot be damn'd; Alas; why should I bee?
Why should intent or reason, borne in mee,
Make sinnes, else equall, in mee, more heinous?
And mercy being easie, and glorious
To God, in his sterne wrath, why threatens hee?
But who am I, that dare dispute with thee?
O God, Oh! of thine onely worthy blood,
And my teares, make a heavenly Lethean flood,
And drowne in it my sinnes blacke memorie.
That thou remember them, some claime as debt,
I thinke it mercy, if thou wilt forget.

6

Death be not proud, though some have called thee
Mighty and dreadfull, for, thou art not soe,
For, those, whom thou think'st, thou dost overthrow,
Die not, poore death, nor yet canst thou kill mee;
From rest and sleepe, which but thy pictures bee,

Much pleasure, then from thee, much more must flow,
And soonest our best men with thee doe goe,
Rest of their bones, and soules deliverie.
Thou art slave to Fate, chance, kings, and desperate men,
And dost with poyson, warre, and sicknesse dwell,
And poppie, or charmes can make us sleepe as well,
And better than thy stroake; why swell'st thou then?
One short sleepe past, wee wake eternally,
And death shall be no more, Death thou shalt die.

Holy Sonnet[1]

Batter my heart, three person'd God; for, you
As yet but knocke, breathe, shine, and seeke to mend;
That I may rise, and stand, o'erthrow mee, 'and bend
Your force, to breake, blowe, burn and make me new.
I, like an usurpt towne, to'another due,
Labour to'admit you, but Oh, to no end,
Reason your viceroy in mee, mee should defend,
But is captiv'd, and proves weake or untrue,
Yet dearely'I love you, and would be lov'd faine,
But am betroth'd unto your enemie,
Divorce mee, 'untie, or breake that knot againe,
Take mee to you, imprison mee, for I
Except you'enthrall mee, never shall be free,
Nor ever chast, except you ravish mee.

(Poems, 1633)

Holy Sonnet[2]

Since she whome I lovd, hath payd her last debt
To Nature, and to hers, and my good is dead,
And her soule early into heaven ravished,
Wholy in heavenly things my mind is sett.

[1] Written probably at the same time as the last six sonnets.
[2] Ann Donne died in 1617 at the age of thirty-three. She had borne her husband twelve children, of whom seven survived her.

Here the admyring her my mind did whett
To seeke thee God; so streames do shew the head,
But though I have found thee, and thou my thirst hast fed,
A holy thirsty dropsy melts mee yett.
But why should I begg more love, when as thou
Dost wooe my soule, for hers offring all thine:
And dost not only feare least I allow
My love to saints and Angels, things divine,
But in thy tender jealousy dost doubt
Least the World, fleshe, yea Devill putt thee out.

(New York Public Library, Westmoreland MS)

Good Friday, 1613. Riding Westward

Let mans Soule be a Spheare, and then, in this,
The intelligence that moves, devotion is,
And as the other Spheares, by being growne
Subject to forraigne motions, lose their owne,
And being by others hurried every day,
Scarce in a yeare their naturall forme obey:
Pleasure or businesse, so, our Soules admit
For their first mover, and are whirld by it.
Hence is't, that I am carryed towards the West
This day, when my Soules forme bends toward the East.[1]
There I should see a Sunne, by rising set,
And by that setting endlesse day beget;
But that Christ on this Crosse, did rise and fall,
Sinne had eternally benighted all.
Yet dare I'almost be glad, I do not see
That spectacle of too much weight for mee.

[1] The spheres had more than one motion. Their own natural motion, each being guided by an Intelligence, was from West to East; but the motion of the *Primum Mobile* hurled them against this, from East to West, every day. Other motions, such as the trepidation of the ninth sphere, prevented the separate spheres from obeying their 'naturall forme', or directing Intelligence.

Who sees Gods face, that is selfe life, must dye;
What a death were it then to see God dye?
It made his owne Lieutenant Nature shrinke,
It made his footstoole crack, and the Sunne winke.
Could I behold those hands which span the Poles,
And tune all spheares at once, peirc'd with those holes?
Could I behold that endlesse height which is
Zenith to us, and to'our Antipodes,
Humbled below us? or that blood which is
The seat of all our Soules, if not of his,
Make durt of dust, or that flesh which was worne
By God, for his apparell, rag'd, and torne?
If on these things I durst not looke, durst I
Upon his miserable mother cast mine eye,
Who was Gods partner here, and furnish'd thus
Halfe of that Sacrifice, which ransom'd us?
Though these things, as I ride, be from mine eye,
They'are present yet unto my memory,
For that looks towards them; and thou look'st towards mee,
O Saviour, as thou hang'st upon the tree;
I turne my backe to thee, but to receive
Corrections, till thy mercies bid thee leave.
O thinke mee worth thine anger, punish mee,
Burne off my rusts, and my deformity,
Restore thine Image, so much, by thy grace,
That thou may'st know mee, and I'll turne my face.

A Hymne to Christ, at the Authors last going into Germany[1]

In what torne ship soever I embarke,
That ship shall be my embleme of thy Arke;
What sea soever swallow mee, that flood
Shall be to mee an embleme of thy blood;

[1] Donne went as chaplain to Lord Doncaster on a mission of mediation to the German Princes in May 1619.

Though thou with clouds of anger do disguise
Thy face; yet through that maske I know those eyes,
  Which, though they turne away sometimes,
    They never will despise.

I sacrifice this Iland unto thee,
And all whom I lov'd there, and who lov'd mee;
When I have put our seas twixt them and mee,
Put thou thy sea betwixt my sinnes and thee.
As the trees sap doth seeke the root below
In winter, in my winter now I goe,
  Where none but thee, th'Eternall root
    Of true Love I may know.

Nor thou nor thy religion dost controule,
The amorousnesse of an harmonious Soule,
But thou would'st have that love thy selfe: As thou
Art jealous, Lord, so I am jealous now,
Thou lov'st not, till from loving more, thou free
My soule: Who ever gives, takes libertie:
  O, if thou car'st not whom I love
    Alas, thou lov'st not mee.

Seale then this bill of my Divorce to All,
On whom those fainter beames of love did fall;
Marry those loves, which in youth scattered bee
On Fame, Wit, Hopes (false mistresses) to thee.
Churches are best for Prayer, that have least light:
To see God only, I goe out of sight:
  And to scape stormy dayes, I chuse
    An Everlasting night.

(Poems, 1633)

JOHN DONNE

Hymne to God my God, in my sicknesse[1]

Since I am comming to that Holy roome,
  Where, with thy Quire of Saints for evermore,
I shall be made thy Musique; As I come
   I tune the Instrument here at the dore,
   And what I must doe then, thinke now before.

Whilst my Physitians by their love are growne
  Cosmographers, and I their Mapp, who lie
Flat on this bed, that by them may be showne
   That this is my South-west discoverie[2]
   Per fretum febris, by these streights to die,

I joy, that in these straits, I see my West;
  For, though theire currants yeeld return to none,
What shall my West hurt me? As West and East
   In all flatt Maps (and I am one) are one,[3]
   So death doth touch the Resurrection.

Is the Pacifique Sea my home? Or are
  The Easterne riches? Is *Jerusalem*?[4]
Anyan, and *Magellan*, and *Gibraltare*,
   All streights, and none but streights, are wayes to them,
   Whether where *Japhet* dwelt, or *Cham*, or *Sem*.

We thinke that *Paradise* and *Calvarie*,
  Christs Crosse, and *Adams* tree, stood in one place;
Looke Lord, and finde both *Adams* met in me;

---

[1] Written, according to Walton, eight days before Donne died. Another contemporary witness dates the poem Dec. 1623, as written in the same grave illness as gave rise to the *Devotions*.

[2] The South is the hot quarter, the West is that of the Sun's declension. He is to die by the 'raging heat' (*fretum*) of fever, or to travel by the strait (*fretum*) of fever.

[3] On a flat map, before it is pasted on a globe, the extreme points will be the same.

[4] Paradise had been located in the Southern Sea, in the farthest East, beyond Cathay, and in Mesopotamia, near Jerusalem.

As the first *Adams* sweat surrounds my face,
May the last *Adams* blood my soule embrace.

So, in his purple wrapp'd receive mee Lord,
  By these his thornes give me his other Crowne;
And as to others soules I preach'd thy word,
  Be this my Text, my Sermon to mine owne,
    Therfore that he may raise the Lord throws down.

(Poems, 1635)

A Hymne to God the Father[1]

Wilt thou forgive that sinne where I begunne,
  Which is my sin, though it were done before?
Wilt thou forgive those sinnes through which I runne,
  And doe them still: though still I doe deplore?
    When thou hast done, thou hast not done,
      For, I have more.

Wilt thou forgive that sinne by which I wonne
  Others to sinne? and, made my sinne their doore?
Wilt thou forgive that sinne which I did shunne
  A yeare, or two: but wallowed in, a score?
    When thou hast done, thou hast not done,
      For, I have more.

I have a sinne of feare, that when I have spunne
  My last thred, I shall perish on the shore;
Sweare by thy selfe, that at my death thy Sunne
  Shall shine as it shines now, and heretofore;
    And, having done that, Thou hast done,
      I have no more.[2]

(Poems, 1633)

[1] Walton relates that Donne wrote this poem in his illness of 1623 and caused it later to be set to music. The pun on his own name on which the poem turns gave him the epigram on his marriage: 'John Donne, Ann Donne—Undone'.

[2] For a defence of the adoption of manuscript readings into the text of this poem, see my edition of *The Divine Poems of John Donne*.

BEN JONSON

(1573–1637)

Epitaph on S.P. *a Child of* Queen Elizabeth's *Chappel*[1]

Weepe with me all you that read
    This little storie:
And know, for whom a teare you shed,
    Death's selfe is sorry.
'Twas a child, that so did thrive
    In grace, and feature,
As *Heaven* and *Nature* seem'd to strive
    Which own'd the creature.
Yeeres he numbred scarse thirteene
    When *Fates* turn'd cruell,
Yet three fill'd *Zodiackes* had he beene
    The stages jewell;
And did act (what now we mone)
    Old men so duely,
As, sooth, the *Parcae* thought him one,
    He plai'd so truely.
So, by error, to his fate
    They all consented;
But viewing him since (alas, too late)
    They have repented.
And have sought (to give new birth)
    In baths to steepe him;
But, being so much too good for earth,
    Heaven vowes to keepe him.

(Epigrammes, 1616)

[1] Solomon Pavy, who had performed in plays Jonson wrote for the Children of the Queen's Revels, died in July 1602.

My Picture left in Scotland[1]

I now thinke, Love is rather deafe, than blind,
  For else it could not be,
        That she,
Whom I adore so much, should so slight me,
  And cast my love behind:
I'm sure my language to her, was as sweet,
        And every close did meet
      In sentence, of as subtile feet,
          As hath the youngest Hee,
      That sits in shadow of *Apollo's* tree.

Oh, but my conscious feares,
      That flie my thoughts betweene,
      Tell me that she hath seene
    My hundred of gray haires,
    Told seven and fortie years,
Read so much waste, as she cannot imbrace
  My mountaine belly, and my rockie face,
And all these through her eyes, have stopt her eares.

A Hymne to God the Father

      Heare mee, O God!
      A broken heart,
      Is my best part:
    Use still thy rod
      That I may prove
      Therein, thy Love.

    If thou hadst not
      Beene sterne to mee,
      But left me free,
    I had forgot
      My selfe and thee.

[1] Written 1618–19, when Jonson visited Drummond in Scotland.

For, sin's so sweet,
 As minds ill bent
 Rarely repent,
Untill they meet
 Their punishment.

Who more can crave
 Than thou hast done?
 That gav'st a Sonne,
To free a slave,
 First made of nought;
 With all since bought.

Sinne, Death, and Hell,
 His glorious Name
 Quite overcame,
Yet I rebell,
 And slight the same.

But, I'le come in,
 Before my losse
 Me farther tosse,
As sure to win
 Under his Crosse.

       (*Underwoods*, 1641)

EDWARD, LORD HERBERT OF CHERBURY

(1583–1648)

To his Watch, when he could not sleep

Uncessant Minutes, whil'st you move you tell
 The time that tells our life, which though it run
 Never so fast or farr, your new begun
Short steps shall overtake; for though life well

May scape his own Account, it shall not yours,
    You are Death's Auditors, that both divide
And summ what ere that life inspir'd endures
    Past a beginning, and through you we bide

The doom of Fate, whose unrecall'd Decree
    You date, bring, execute; making what's new,
    Ill and good, old, for as we die in you,
You die in Time, Time in Eternity.

Elegy over a Tomb[1]

Must I then see, alas! eternal night
    Sitting upon those fairest eyes,
And closing all those beams, which once did rise
    So radiant and bright,
That light and heat in them to us did prove
        Knowledge and Love?

Oh, if you did delight no more to stay
    Upon this low and earthly stage,
But rather chose an endless heritage,
    Tell us at least, we pray,
Where all the beauties that those ashes ow'd
        Are now bestow'd?

Doth the Sun now his light with yours renew?
    Have Waves the curling of your hair?
Did you restore unto the Sky and Air,
    The red, and white, and blew?
Have you vouchsafed to flowrs since your death
        That sweetest breath?

Had not Heav'ns Lights else in their houses slept,
    Or to some private life retir'd?

[1] Dated 1617.

Must not the Sky and Air have else conspir'd,
  And in their Regions wept?
Must not each flower else the earth could breed
   Have been a weed?

But thus enrich'd may we not yield some cause
  Why they themselves lament no more?
That must have chang'd the course they held before,
  And broke their proper Laws,
Had not your beauties giv'n this second birth
   To Heaven and Earth?

Tell us, for Oracles must still ascend,
  For those that crave them at your tomb:
Tell us, where are those beauties now become,
  And what they now intend:
Tell us, alas, that cannot tell our grief,
   Or hope relief.

Sonnet of Black Beauty

Black beauty, which above that common light,
  Whose Power can no colours here renew
  But those which darkness can again subdue,
Dost still remain unvary'd to the sight,

And like an object equal to the view,
  Art neither chang'd with day, nor hid with night;
  When all these colours which the world call bright,
And which old Poetry doth so persue,

Are with the night so perished and gone,
  That of their being there remains no mark,
Thou still abidest so intirely one,
  That we may know thy blackness is a spark
Of light inaccessible, and alone
  Our darkness which can make us think it dark.

*An Ode upon a Question moved, Whether Love
should continue for ever?*

Having interr'd her Infant-birth,
   The watry ground that late did mourn,
   Was strew'd with flow'rs for the return
Of the wish'd Bridegroom of the earth.

The well accorded Birds did sing
   Their hymns unto the pleasant time,
   And in a sweet consorted chime
Did welcom in the chearful Spring.

To which, soft whistles of the Wind,
   And warbling murmurs of a Brook,
   And vari'd notes of leaves that shook,
An harmony of parts did bind.

While doubling joy unto each other,
   All in so rare concent was shown,
   No happiness that came alone,
Nor pleasure that was not another.

When with a love none can express,
   That mutually happy pair,
   Melander and *Celinda* fair,
The season with their loves did bless.

Walking thus towards a pleasant Grove,
   Which did, it seem'd, in new delight
   The pleasures of the time unite,
To give a triumph to their love,

They stay'd at last, and on the Grass
   Reposed so, as o'r his breast
   She bow'd her gracious head to rest,
Such a weight as no burden was.

66

While over eithers compass'd waste
   Their folded arms were so compos'd,
   As if in straitest bonds inclos'd,
They suffer'd for joys they did taste.

Long their fixt eyes to Heaven bent,
   Unchanged, they did never move,
   As if so great and pure a love
No Glass but it could represent.

When with a sweet, though troubled look,
   She first brake silence, saying, Dear friend,
   O that our love might take no end,
Or never had beginning took!

I speak not this with a false heart,
   (Wherewith his hand she gently strain'd)
   Or that would change a love maintain'd
With so much faith on either part.

Nay, I protest, though Death with his
   Worst Counsel should divide us here,
   His terrors could not make me fear,
To come where your lov'd presence is.

Only if loves fire with the breath
   Of life be kindled, I doubt
   With our last air 'twill be breath'd out,
And quenched with the cold of death.

That if affection be a line,
   Which is clos'd up in our last hour;
   Oh how 'twould grieve me, any pow'r
Could force so dear a love as mine!

She scarce had done, when his shut eyes
   An inward joy did represent,
   To hear *Celinda* thus intent
To a love he so much did prize.

Then with a look, it seem'd, deny'd
    All earthly pow'r but hers, yet so,
    As if to her breath he did ow
This borrow'd life, he thus repli'd;

O you, wherein, they say, Souls rest,
    Till they descend pure heavenly fires,
    Shall lustful and corrupt desires
With your immortal seed be blest?

And shall our Love, so far beyond
    That low and dying appetite,
    And which so chast desires unite,
Not hold in an eternal bond?

Is it, because we should decline,
    And wholly from our thoughts exclude
    Objects that may the sense delude,
And study only the Divine?

No sure, for if none can ascend
    Ev'n to the visible degree
    Of things created, how should we
The invisible comprehend?

Or rather since that Pow'r exprest
    His greatness in his works alone,
    Being here best in his Creatures known,
Why is he not lov'd in them best?

But is't not true, which you pretend,
    That since our love and knowledge here,
    Only as parts of life appear,
So they with it should take their end.

O no, Beloved, I am most sure,
    Those vertuous habits we acquire,
    As being with the Soul intire,
Must with it evermore endure.

For if where sins and vice reside,
   We find so foul a guilt remain,
   As never dying in his stain,
Still punish'd in the Soul doth bide,

Much more that true and real joy,
   Which in a vertuous love is found,
   Must be more solid in its ground,
Than Fate or Death can e'r destroy.

Else should our Souls in vain elect,
   And vainer yet were Heavens laws,
   When to an everlasting Cause
They gave a perishing Effect.

Nor here on earth then, nor above,
   Our good affection can impair,
   For where God doth admit the fair,
Think you that he excludeth Love?

These eyes again then, eyes shall see,
   And hands again these hands enfold,
   And all chast pleasures can be told
Shall with us everlasting be.

For if no use of sense remain
   When bodies once this life forsake,
   Or they could no delight partake,
Why should they ever rise again?

And if every imperfect mind
   Make love the end of knowledge here,
   How perfect will our love be, where
All imperfection is refin'd?

Let then no doubt, *Celinda*, touch,
   Much less your fairest mind invade,
   Were not our souls immortal made,
Our equal loves can make them such.

So when one wing can make no way,
 Two joyned can themselves dilate,
 So can two persons propagate,
When singly either would decay.

So when from hence we shall be gone,
 And be no more, nor you, nor I,
 As one anothers mystery,
Each shall be both, yet both be one.

This said, in her up-lifted face,
 Her eyes which did that beauty crown,
 Were like two starrs, that having faln down,
Look up again to find their place:

While such a moveless silent peace
 Did seize on their becalmed sense,
 One would have thought some Influence
Their ravish'd spirits did possess.

(Poems, 1665)

AURELIAN TOWNSHEND

(1583?–1651?)

To the Countesse of Salisbury[1]

Victorious beauty, though your eyes
 Are able to subdue an hoast,
 And therefore are unlike to boast
The taking of a little prize,
Do not a single heart dispise.

---

[1] Title found in MS. Malone 13. Catherine Howard, sister of the notorious Frances Howard, Countess of Essex, married William Cecil in 1608. He succeeded his father, the first Earl, Townshend's patron, in 1612.

It came alone, but yet so arm'd
　　With former love, I durst have sworne
　　That where a privy coat was worne,
With characters of beauty charm'd,
Thereby it might have scapt unharm'd.

But neither steele nor stony breast
　　Are proofe against those lookes of thine,
　　Nor can a Beauty lesse divine
Of any heart be long possest,
Where thou pretend'st an interest.

Thy Conquest in regard of me
　　Alasse is small, but in respect
　　Of her that did my Love protect,
Were it divulg'd, deserv'd to be
Recorded for a Victory.

And such a one, as some that view
　　Her lovely face perhaps may say,
　　Though you have stolen my heart away,
If all your servants prove not true,
May steale a heart or two from you.

　　　　　　(Playford, *Select Musical Ayres*, 1652)

Youth and Beauty

Thou art so fair, and yong withall,
　　Thou kindl'st yong desires in me,
Restoreing life to leaves that fall,
　　And sight to Eyes that hardly see
　　Halfe those fresh Beauties bloom in thee.

Those, under sev'rall Hearbs and Flow'rs
　　Disguis'd, were all *Medea* gave,
When she recall'd Times flying howrs,

71

And aged *Æson* from his grave,
For Beauty can both kill and save.

Youth it enflames, but age it cheers,
I would go back, but not return
To twenty but to twice those yeers;
Not blaze, but ever constant burn,
For fear my Cradle prove my Urn.

A Dialogue betwixt Time and a Pilgrime

PILGR.   Aged man, that mowes these fields.
TIME.   Pilgrime speak, what is thy will?
PILGR.   Whose soile is this that such sweet Pasture yields?
Or who art thou whose Foot stands never still?
Or where am I?   TIME.   In love.
  PILGR.   His Lordship lies above.
TIME.   Yes and below, and round about
Wherein all sorts of flow'rs are growing
Which as the early Spring puts out,
Time fals as fast a mowing.
PILGR.   If thou art Time, these Flow'rs have Lives,
And then I fear,
Under some Lilly she I love
May now be growing there.
TIME.   And in some Thistle or some spyre of grasse,
My syth thy stalk before hers come may passe.
PILGR.   Wilt thou provide it may.   TIME.   No.
  PILGR.   Alleage the cause.
TIME.   Because Time cannot alter but obey Fates laws.
CHO.   Then happy those whom Fate, that is the stronger,
Together twists their threads, and yet draws hers
the longer.

(H. Lawes, *Ayres and Dialogues*, 1653)

Song

Though regions farr devided
  And tedious tracts of tyme,
By my misfortune guided,
  Make absence thought a cryme;
Though wee weare set a sunder
  As far, as East from West,
Love still would worke this wonder,
  Thou shouldst be in my breast.

How slow alasse are paces,
  Compar'd to thoughts that flye
In moments back to places,
  Whole ages scarce descry.
The body must have pauses;
  The mynde requires noe rest;
Love needs no second causes
  To guide thee to my breast.

Accept in that poore dwelling,
  But welcome, nothing great,
With pride no turrets swelling,
  But lowly as the seate;
Wher, though not much delighted,
  In peace thou mayst be blest,
Unfeasted yet unfrighted
  By rivals, in my breast.

But this is not the dyet,
  That doth for glory strive;
Poor beawties seek in quiet
  To keepe one heart alive.
The price of his ambition,
  That lookes for such a guest,
Is hopelesse of fruition
  To beate an empty breast.

See then my last lamenting.
    Upon a cliffe I'le sit,
Rock Constancy presenting,
    Till I grow part of it;
My teares a quicksand feeding,
    Whereon noe foote can rest,
My sighs a tempest breeding
    About my stony breast.

Those armes, wherin wide open
    Loves fleete was wont to put,
Shall layd acrosse betoken
    That havens mouth is shut.
Myne eyes noe light shall cherish
    For ships at sea distrest,
But darkeling let them perish
    Or split against my breast.

Yet if I can discover
    When thine before it rides,
To shew I was thy lover
    I'le smooth my rugged sides,
And so much better measure
    Afford thee than the rest,
Thou shalt have noe displeasure
    By knocking at my breast.

To the Lady May[1]

Your smiles are not, as other womens bee,
Only the drawing of the mouth awrye;
For breasts and cheekes and forehead wee may see,
    Parts wanting motion, all stand smiling by.
Heaven hath noe mouth, and yet is sayd to smile
    After your stile;

[1] Probably the second wife of Sir Humphrey May who was made Lord Chamberlain of the Household in 1629. She married him in 1616.

Noe more hath Earth, yet that smyles too,
     Just as you doe.

Noe sympering lipps nor lookes can breed
Such smyles as from your face proceed.
The sunn must lend his goulden beames,
   Soft windes their breath, green trees their shade,
Sweet fields their flowers, cleare springs their streams,
   Ere such another smyle bee made.
But these concurring, wee may say,
So smiles the spring, and soe smyles lovely May.

                 (Bodleian Library, MS. Malone 13)

Upon Kinde and True Love[1]

'Tis not how witty, nor how free,
Nor yet how beautifull she be,
But how much kinde and true to me.
Freedome and Wit none can confine,
And Beauty like the Sun doth shine,
But kinde and true are onely mine.

Let others with attention sit,
To listen, and admire her wit,
That is a rock where I'le not split.
Let others dote upon her eyes,
And burn their hearts for sacrifice,
Beauty's a calm where danger lyes.

But Kinde and True have been long tried
A harbour where we may confide,
And safely there at anchor ride.
From change of winds there we are free,
And need not feare Storme's tyrannie,
Nor Pirat, though a Prince he be.

                        (*Choice Drollery*, 1656)

[1] Authorship doubtful.

SIR FRANCIS KYNASTON
(1587–1642)

To Cynthia. *On concealement of her beauty*

Do not conceale thy radiant eyes,
The starre-light of serenest skies,
Least wanting of their heavenly light,
They turne to *Chaos* endlesse night.

Do not conceale those tresses faire,
The silken snares of thy curl'd haire,
Least finding neither gold, nor Ore,
The curious Silke-worme worke no more.

Do not conceale those brests of thine,
More snowe white, than the Apenine,
Least if there be like cold or frost,
The Lilly be for ever lost.

Do not conceale that fragrant scent,
Thy breath, which to all flowers hath lent
Perfumes, least it being supprest,
No spices growe in all the East.

Do not conceale thy heavenly voice,
Which makes the hearts of Gods rejoyce,
Least Musicke hearing no such thing,
The Nightingale forget to sing.

Do not conceale, nor yet eclipse
Thy pearly teeth with Corrall lips,
Least that the Seas cease to bring forth
Gems, which from thee have all their worth.

Do not conceale no beauty, grace,
That's either in thy minde or face,
Least vertue overcome by vice,
Make men beleeve no Paradise.

To Cynthia. *On her changing*[1]

Dear *Cynthia*, though thou bear'st the name
Of the pale Queen of night,
Who changing yet is still the same,
Renewing still her light:
Who monthly doth her selfe conceal,
And her bright face doth hide,
That she may to *Endymion* steal,
And kisse him unespide:

Do not thou so, not being sure,
When this thy beautie's gone,
Thou such another canst procure,
And wear it as thine owne,
For the by-sliding silent houres,
Conspiratours with grief,
May crop thy beauties lovely flowres,
Time being a slie thief:

Which with his wings will flie away,
And will returne no more;
As having got so rich a prey,
Nature can not restore:
Reserve thou then, and do not waste
That beauty which is thine,
Cherish those glories which thou hast,
Let not grief make thee pine.

---

[1] One of two poems to Cynthia mourning for her mother's death.

Think that the Lilly we behold
Or July-flower may
Flourish, although the mother mold
That bred them be away.
There is no cause, nor yet no sence,
That dainty fruits should rot,
Though the tree die, and wither, whence
The Apricots were got.

(Leoline and Sydanis, 1642)

HENRY KING

(1592–1669)

Sonnet

Tell me no more how fair she is,
  I have no minde to hear
The story of that distant bliss
  I never shall come near:
By sad experience I have found
That her perfection is my wound.

And tell me not how fond I am
  To tempt a daring Fate,
From whence no triumph ever came,
  But to repent too late:
There is some hope ere long I may
In silence dote my self away.

I ask no pity (Love) from thee,
  Nor will thy justice blame,
So that thou wilt not envy mee
  The glory of my flame:
Which crowns my heart when ere it dyes,
In that it falls her sacrifice.

The Surrender

My once dear Love; hapless that I no more
Must call thee so: the rich affections store
That fed our hopes, lies now exhaust and spent,
Like summes of treasure unto Bankrupts lent.

We that did nothing study but the way
To love each other, with which thoughts the day
Rose with delight to us, and with them set,
Must learn the hateful Art how to forget.

We that did nothing wish that Heav'n could give
Beyond our selves, nor did desire to live
Beyond that wish, all these now cancell must
As if not writ in faith, but words and dust.

Yet witness those cleer vowes which Lovers make,
Witness the chast desires that never brake
Into unruly heats; witness that brest
Which in thy bosom anchor'd his whole rest,
'Tis no default in us, I dare acquite
Thy Maiden faith, thy purpose fair and white
As thy pure self. Cross Planets did envie
Us to each other, and Heaven did untie
Faster than vowes could binde. O that the Starres
When Lovers meet, should stand oppos'd in warres!

Since then some higher Destinies command,
Let us not strive, nor labour to withstand
What is past help. The longest date of grief
Can never yield a hope of our relief;
And though we waste our selves in moist laments,
Tears may drown us, but not our discontents.

Fold back our arms, take home our fruitless loves,
That must new fortunes trie, like Turtle Doves
Dislodged from their haunts. We must in tears
Unwind a love knit up in many years.

In this last kiss I here surrender thee
Back to thy self, so thou again art free.
Thou in another, sad as that, resend
The truest heart that Lover ere did lend.

Now turn from each. So fare our sever'd hearts
As the divorc'd soul from her body parts.

The Exequy. To his Matchlesse never to be forgotten Freind[1]

Accept thou Shrine of my dead Saint,
Insteed of Dirges this complaint;
And for sweet flowres to crown thy hearse,
Receive a strew of weeping verse
From thy griev'd friend, whom thou might'st see
Quite melted into tears for thee.

Dear loss! since thy untimely fate
My task hath been to meditate
On thee, on thee: thou art the book,
The library whereon I look
Though almost blind. For thee (lov'd clay)
I languish out, not live the day,
Using no other exercise
But what I practise with mine eyes:
By which wet glasses I find out
How lazily time creeps about
To one that mourns: this, onely this
My exercise and bus'ness is:
So I compute the weary houres
With sighs dissolved into showres.

[1] King married Anne Berkeley in 1617. She died in 1624, having borne
him six children of whom only two survived infancy. He married again
in 1630.

Nor wonder if my time go thus
Backward and most preposterous;
Thou hast benighted me, thy set
This Eve of blackness did beget,
Who was't my day, (though overcast)
Before thou had'st thy Noon-tide past)
And I remember must in tears,
Thou scarce had'st seen so many years
As Day tells houres. By thy cleer Sun
My life and fortune first did run;
But thou wilt never more appear
Folded within my Hemisphear,
Since both thy light and motion
Like a fled Star is fall'n and gon,
And twixt me and my soules dear wish
The earth now interposed is,
Which such a strange eclipse doth make
As ne're was read in Almanake.

I could allow thee for a time
To darken me and my sad Clime,
Were it a month, a year, or ten,
I would thy exile live till then;
And all that space my mirth adjourn,
So thou wouldst promise to return;
And putting off thy ashy shrowd
At length disperse this sorrows cloud.

But woe is me! the longest date
Too narrow is to calculate
These empty hopes: never shall I
Be so much blest as to descry
A glimpse of thee, till that day come
Which shall the earth to cinders doome,
And a fierce Feaver must calcine
The body of this world like thine,

(My little World!). That fit of fire
Once off, our bodies shall aspire
To our soules bliss: then we shall rise
And view our selves with cleerer eyes
In that calm Region, where no night
Can hide us from each others sight.

Mean time, thou hast her, earth: much good
May my harm do thee. Since it stood
With Heavens will I might not call
Her longer mine, I give thee all
My short-liv'd right and interest
In her, whom living I lov'd best:
With a most free and bounteous grief,
I give thee what I could not keep.
Be kind to her, and prethee look
Thou write into thy Dooms-day book
Each parcell of this Rarity
Which in thy Casket shrin'd doth ly:
See that thou make thy reck'ning streight,
And yield her back again by weight;
For thou must audit on thy trust
Each graine and atome of this dust,
As thou wilt answer *Him* that lent,
Not gave thee, my dear Monument.

So close the ground, and 'bout her shade
Black curtains draw, my *Bride* is laid.

Sleep on my *Love* in thy cold bed
Never to be disquieted!
My last good night! Thou wilt not wake
Till I thy fate shall overtake:
Till age, or grief, or sickness must
Marry my body to that dust
It so much loves; and fill the room
My heart keeps empty in thy Tomb.

Stay for me there; I will not faile
To meet thee in that hollow Vale.
And think not much of my delay;
I am already on the way,
And follow thee with all the speed
Desire can make, or sorrows breed.
Each minute is a short degree,
And ev'ry houre a step towards thee.
At night when I betake to rest,
Next morn I rise neerer my West
Of life, almost by eight houres saile,
Than when sleep breath'd his drowsie gale.

Thus from the Sun my Bottom stears,
And my dayes Compass downward bears:
Nor labour I to stemme the tide
Through which to *Thee* I swiftly glide.

'Tis true, with shame and grief I yield,
Thou like the *Vann* first took'st the field,
And gotten hast the victory
In thus adventuring to dy
Before me, whose more years might crave
A just precedence in the grave.
But heark! My pulse like a soft Drum
Beats my approch, tells *Thee* I come;
And slow howere my marches be,
I shall at last sit down by *Thee*.

The thought of this bids me go on,
And wait my dissolution
With hope and comfort. *Dear* (forgive
The crime) I am content to live
Divided, with but half a heart,
Till we shall meet and never part.

Sic Vita[1]

Like to the falling of a Starre;
Or as the flights of Eagles are;
Or like the fresh springs gawdy hew;
Or silver drops of morning dew;
Or like a wind that chafes the flood;
Or bubbles which on water stood;
Even such is man, whose borrow'd light
Is streight call'd in, and paid to night.

The Wind blowes out; the Bubble dies;
The Spring entomb'd in Autumn lies;
The Dew dries up; the Starre is shot;
The Flight is past; and Man forgot.

My Midnight Meditation

Ill busi'd man! why should'st thou take such care
To lengthen out thy lifes short Kalendar?
When ev'ry spectacle thou lookst upon
Presents and acts thy execution.
    Each drooping season and each flower doth cry,
    Fool! as I fade and wither, thou must dy.

The beating of thy pulse (when thou art well)
Is just the tolling of thy Passing Bell:
Night is thy Hearse, whose sable Canopie
Covers alike deceased day and thee.
    And all those weeping dewes which nightly fall,
    Are but the tears shed for thy funerall.

(Poems, 1657)

[1] This famous stanza provided a model for many imitations and parodies.
It is almost always ascribed to King in manuscript collections, but it was
first published in Francis Beaumont's *Poems*, 1640 and 1653.

HENRY KING

A Contemplation upon Flowers[1]

Brave flowers, that I could gallant it like you
And be as little vaine;
You come abroad, and make a harmeless shew,
And to your bedds of Earth againe;
You are not proud, you know your birth
For your Embroiderd garments are from Earth:

You doe obey your months, and times, but I
Would have it ever springe,
My fate would know noe winter, never dye
Nor thinke of such a thing;
Oh that I could my bed of Earth but view
And Smile, and looke as chearefully as you:

Oh teach me to see death, and not to feare
But rather to take truce;
How often have I seene you at a Beere,
And there looke fresh and spruce;
You fragrant flowers then teach me that my breath
Like yours may sweeten, and perfume my death.

(British Museum, Harleian MS. 6917)

FRANCIS QUARLES

(1592–1644)

On Those that Deserve it[2]

O when our Clergie, at the dreadfull *Day*,
Shal make their Audit; when the *Judge* shal say,

[1] Ascribed to King in the one manuscript in which it is found; but I do not believe it is his.
[2] Many Puritan clergy preferred deprivation or suspension to obedience to the Canons of 1604 which enjoined the wearing of surplices and copes, and the use of the sign of the cross in baptism.

Give your accompts: What, have my Lambs bin fed?
Say, doe they all stand sound? Is there none dead
By your defaults? Come shephards, bring them forth
That I may crowne your labours in their worth.
O what an answer will be given by some!
We have bin silenc'd: Canons strucke us dumbe;
The Great ones would not let us feed thy flock,
Unlesse we plai'd the fooles, and wore a Frock:
We were forbid unlesse wee'd yield to signe
And crosse their browes, They say, *a mark of thine*.
To say the truth, great Judge, they were not fed,
Lord, here they be; but Lord, they be all dead:
Ah cruel Shepheards! Could your conscience serve
Not to be fooles, and yet to let them sterve?
What if your Fiery spirits had bin bound
To Antick Habits; or your heads bin crown'd
With *Peacocks* Plumes; had yee bin forc'd to feed
Your Saviour's dear-bought Flock in a fools weed;
He that was scorn'd, revil'd, endur'd the *Curse*
Of a base death, in your behalfs; nay worse,
Swallow'd the cup of wrath charg'd up to th' *brim*,
Durst ye not stoope to play the fooles for him?

On Zacheus

Me thinks, I see, with what a busie hast,
Zacheus climb'd the Tree: But, O, how fast,
How full of speed, canst thou imagine (when
Our *Saviour* call'd) he powder'd downe agen!
He ne're made tryall, if the boughs were sound,
Or rotten; nor how far 'twas to the ground:
There was no danger fear'd; At such a Call,
Hee'l venture nothing, that dare feare a fall;
Needs must hee downe, by such a *Spirit* driven;
Nor could he fall, unlesse he fell to *Heaven*:
Downe came *Zacheus*, ravisht from the Tree;
Bird that was shot ne're dropt so quicke as he.

A Forme of Prayer

If thou wouldst learne, not knowing how, to pray,
Adde but a *Faith*, and say as *Beggers* say;
Master, I'm poore, and blinde, in great distresse;
Hungry and lame, and cold, and comfortlesse:
O, succour him, that's graveld on the Shelf
Of payne, and want, and cannot help himself;
Cast down thine eye upon a wretch, and take
Some pitty on me for sweet Jesus sake:
But hold! Take heed this Clause be not put in;
I never begg'd before, nor will agin:
Note this withall, That Beggers move their plaints
At all times *Ore tenus*, not *by Saints*.

(*Divine Fancies*, 1632)

Wherefore hidest thou thy face, and holdest me for thy enemie?
(Job xiii. 24)

Why dost thou shade thy lovely face? O why
Does that ecclipsing hand, so long, deny
The Sun-shine of thy soule-enliv'ning eye?

Without that *Light*, what light remaines in me?
Thou art my *Life*, my *Way*, my *Light*; in Thee
I live, I move, and by thy beames I see.

Thou art my *Life*; If thou but turne away,
My life's a thousand deaths: thou art my *Way*;
Without thee, Lord, I travell not, but stray.

My *Light* thou art; without thy glorious sight,
Mine eyes are darkned with perpetuall night.
My God, thou art my *Way*, my *Life*, my *Light*.

Thou art my *Way*; I wander, if thou flie:
Thou art my *Light*; if hid, how blind am I!
Thou art my *Life*; If thou withdraw, I die.

Mine eyes are blind and darke; I cannot see;
To whom, or whither should my darknesse flee,
But to the *Light*? And who's that *Light* but Thee?

My path is lost; my wandring steps do stray;
I cannot safely go, nor safely stay;
Whom should I see but Thee, my *Path*, my *Way*?

O, I am dead: to whom shall I, poore I,
Repaire? to whom shall my sad Ashes fly
But *Life*? And where is *Life* but in thine eye?

And yet thou turn'st away thy face, and fly'st me;
And yet I sue for Grace and thou deny'st me;
Speake, art thou angry, Lord, or onely try'st me?

Unskreene those heav'nly lamps, or tell me why
Thou shad'st thy face; Perhaps, thou thinkst, no eye
Can view those flames, and not drop downe and die.

If that be all, shine forth, and draw thee nigher;
Let me behold and die; for my desire
Is *Phoenix-like* to perish in that Fire.

Death-conquer'd *Laz'rus* was redeem'd by Thee;
If I am dead, Lord, set death's pris'ner free;
Am I more spent, or stink I worse than he?

If my pufft light be out, give leave to tine
My flameless snuffe at that bright *Lamp* of thine;
O what's thy *Light* the lesse for lighting mine?

If I have lost my *Path*, great Shepheard, say,
Shall I still wander in a doubtfull way?
Lord, shall a Lamb of Isr'el's sheepfold stray?

Thou art the Pilgim's *Path*: the blind man's *Eye*;
The dead man's *Life*; on thee my hopes rely;
If thou remove, I erre; I grope; I die.

Disclose thy Sun beames; close thy wings, and stay;
See, see, how I am blind, and dead, and stray,
O thou, that art my *Light*, my *Life*, my *Way*.

My beloved is mine, and I am his;
He feedeth among the Lillies

(Canticles ii. 16)

Ev'n like two little bank-dividing brookes,
    That wash the pebles with their wanton streames,
And having rang'd and search'd a thousand nookes,
    Meet both at length in silver-brested *Thames*,
        Where in a greater Current they conjoyne:
So I my Best-Beloved's am; so He is mine.

Ev'n so we met; and after long pursuit,
    Ev'n so we joyn'd; we both became entire;
No need for either to renew a Suit,
    For I was Flax, and he was Flames of fire:
        Our firm-united souls did more than twine;
So I my Best-Beloved's am; so He is mine.

If all those glitt'ring Monarchs that command
    The servile Quarters of this earthly Ball,
Should tender, in Exchange, their shares of land,
    I would not change my Fortunes for them all:
        Their wealth is but a Counter to my Coyne:
The world's but theirs; but my Beloved's mine.

Nay more; If the fair Thespian Ladies all
    Should heap together their diviner treasure:
That Treasure should be deem'd a price too small
    To buy a minutes Lease of halfe my Pleasure.

'Tis not the sacred wealth of all the Nine
Can buy my heart from Him, or His, from being mine.

Nor Time, nor Place, nor Chance, nor Death can bow
  My least desires unto the least remove;
He's firmly mine by Oath; I, His, by Vow;
  He's mine by Faith; and I am His by Love;
    He's mine by Water; I am His by Wine;
Thus I my Best-Beloved's am; thus He is mine.

He is my Altar; I, his Holy Place;
  I am his Guest; and he, my living Food;
I'm his, by Penitence; He, mine by Grace;
  I'm his, by Purchase; He is mine, by Blood;
    Hee's my supporting Elme; and I, his Vine;
Thus I my Best-Beloved's am; thus He is mine.

He gives me wealth, I give him all my Vowes:
  I give Him songs; He gives me length of dayes:
With wreathes of Grace he crownes my conqu'ring browes:
  And I, his Temples, with a Crowne of Praise,
    Which he accepts as an ev'rlasting signe,
That I my Best-Beloved's am; that He is mine.

(Emblemes, 1635)

GEORGE HERBERT
(1593–1633)

The Agonie

  Philosophers have measur'd mountains,
Fathom'd the depths of seas, of states, and kings,
Walk'd with a staffe to heav'n, and traced fountains:
  But there are two vast, spacious things,

The which to measure it doth more behove:
Yet few there are that sound them; Sinne and Love.

  Who would know Sinne, let him repair
Unto Mount Olivet; there shall he see
A man so wrung with pains, that all his hair,
  His skinne, his garments bloudie be.
Sinne is that presse and vice, which forceth pain
To hunt his cruell food through ev'ry vein.

  Who knows not Love, let him assay
And taste that juice, which on the crosse a pike
Did set again abroach; then let him say
  If ever he did taste the like.
Love is that liquour sweet and most divine,
Which my God feels as bloud; but I, as wine.

Redemption

Having been tenant long to a rich Lord,
  Not thriving, I resolved to be bold,
  And make a suit unto him, to afford
A new small-rented lease, and cancell th' old.
In heaven at his manour I him sought:
  They told me there, that he was lately gone
  About some land, which he had dearly bought
Long since on earth, to take possession.
I straight return'd, and knowing his great birth,
  Sought him accordingly in great resorts;
  In cities, theatres, gardens, parks, and courts:
At length I heard a ragged noise and mirth
  Of theeves and murderers: there I him espied,
  Who straight, *Your suit is granted*, said, & died.

Easter-wings[1]

Lord, who createdst man in wealth and store,
Though foolishly he lost the same,
Decaying more and more,
Till he became
Most poore:
With thee
O let me rise
As larks, harmoniously,
And sing this day thy victories:
Then shall the fall further the flight in me.

My tender age in sorrow did beginne:
And still with sicknesses and shame
Thou didst so punish sinne,
That I became
Most thinne.
With thee
Let me combine
And feel this day thy victorie:
For, if I imp[2] my wing on thine,
Affliction shall advance the flight in me.

Affliction

When first thou didst entice to thee my heart,
I thought the service brave:
So many joyes I writ down for my part,
Besides what I might have
Out of my stock of naturall delights,
Augmented with thy gracious benefits.

[1] The lines are printed vertically in the early editions, to represent the shape of wings on the page.
[2] *imp*: to engraft feathers in a damaged wing.

I looked on thy furniture so fine,
  And made it fine to me:
Thy glorious houshold-stuffe did me entwine,
  And 'tice me unto thee.
Such starres I counted mine: both heav'n and earth
Payd me my wages in a world of mirth.

What pleasures could I want, whose King I served,
  Where joyes my fellows were?
Thus argu'd into hopes, my thoughts reserved
  No place for grief or fear.
Therefore my sudden soul caught at the place,
And made her youth and fiercenesse seek thy face.

At first thou gav'st me milk and sweetnesses;
  I had my wish and way:
My dayes were straw'd with flow'rs and happinesse;
  There was no moneth but May.
But with my yeares sorrow did twist and grow,
And made a partie unawares for wo.

My flesh began[1] unto my soul in pain,
  Sicknesses cleave my bones
Consuming agues dwell in ev'ry vein,
  And tune my breath to grones.
Sorrow was all my soul; I scarce beleeved,
Till grief did tell me roundly, that I lived,

When I got health, thou took'st away my life,
  And more; for my friends die:
My mirth and edge was lost; a blunted knife
  Was of more use than I.
Thus thinne and lean without a fence or friend,
I was blown through with ev'ry storm and winde.

---

[1] *began*: began to say. The next three lines are the flesh's complaint to the soul.

Whereas my birth and spirit rather took
    The way that takes the town;
Thou didst betray me to a lingring book,
    And wrap me in a gown.
I was entangled in the world of strife,
Before I had the power to change my life.

Yet, for I threatened oft the siege to raise,
    Not simpring all mine age,
Thou often didst with Academick praise
    Melt and dissolve my rage.
I took thy sweetned pill, till I came where
I could not go away, nor persevere.

Yet lest perchance I should too happie be
    In my unhappinesse,
Turning my purge to food, thou throwest me
    Into more sicknesses.
Thus doth thy power crosse-bias me, not making
Thine own gift good, yet me from my wayes taking.

Now I am here, what thou wilt do with me
    None of my books will show:
I reade, and sigh, and wish I were a tree;
    For sure then I should grow
To fruit or shade: at least some bird would trust
Her household to me, and I should be just.

Yet, though thou troublest me, I must be meek;
    In weaknesse must be stout.
Well, I will change the service, and go seek
    Some other master out.
Ah my deare God! though I am clean forgot,
Let me not love thee, if I love thee not.

Prayer

Prayer the Churches banquet, Angels age,
  God breath in man returning to his birth,
  The soul in paraphrase, heart in pilgrimage,
The Christian plummet sounding heav'n and earth;
Engine against th' Almightie, sinners towre,
  Reversed thunder, Christ-side-piercing spear,
  The six-daies world transposing in an houre,
A kinde of tune, which all things heare and fear;
Softnesse, and peace, and joy, and love, and blisse,
  Exalted Manna, gladnesse of the best,
  Heaven in ordinarie, man well drest,
The milkie way, the bird of Paradise,
  Church-bels beyond the starres heard, the souls bloud,
  The land of spices; something understood.

The Temper

How should I praise thee, Lord! how should my rymes
  Gladly engrave thy love in steel,
  If what my soul doth feel sometimes,
    My soul might ever feel!

Although there were some fourtie heav'ns, or more,
  Sometimes I peere above them all;
  Sometimes I hardly reach a score,
    Sometimes to hell I fall.

O rack me not to such a vast extent;
  Those distances belong to thee:
  The world's too little for thy tent,
    A grave too big for me.

Wilt thou meet arms with man, that thou dost stretch
   A crumme of dust from heav'n to hell?
   Will great God measure with a wretch?
     Shall he thy stature spell?

O let me, when thy roof my soul hath hid,
   O let me roost and nestle there:
   Then of a sinner thou art rid,
     And I of hope and fear.

Yet take thy way; for sure thy way is best:
   Stretch or contract me, thy poore debter:
   This is but tuning of my breast,
     To make the musick better.

Whether I flie with angels, fall with dust,
   Thy hands made both, and I am there:
   Thy power and love, my love and trust
     Make one place ev'ry where.

Jordan[1] (I)

Who sayes that fictions onely and false hair
Become a verse? Is there in truth no beautie?
Is all good structure in a winding stair?
May no lines passe, except they do their dutie
   Not to a true, but painted chair?

Is it no verse, except enchanted groves
And sudden arbours shadow coarse-spunne lines?
Must purling streams refresh a lovers loves?
Must all be vail'd, while he that reades, divines,
   Catching the sense at two removes?

[1] In this and the other poem with the same title (p. 105) Herbert characterizes a 'baptized Muse'. The waters of Jordan are contrasted with the springs of Helicon.

Shepherds are honest people; let them sing:
Riddle who list, for me, and pull for Prime:
I envie no mans nightingale or spring;
Nor let them punish me with losse of rime,
  Who plainly say, *My God, My King*.

Deniall

When my devotions could not pierce
      Thy silent eares;
Then was my heart broken, as was my verse:
      My breast was full of fears
            And disorder:

My bent thoughts, like a brittle bow,
      Did flie asunder:
Each took his way; some would to pleasures go,
      Some to the warres and thunder
            Of alarms.

As good go any where, they say,
      As to benumme
Both knees and heart, in crying night and day,
      Come, come, my God, O come,
            But no hearing.

O that thou shouldst give dust a tongue
      To crie to thee,
And then not heare it crying! all day long
      My heart was in my knee,
            But no hearing.

Therefore my soul lay out of sight,
      Untun'd, unstrung:
My feeble spirit, unable to look right,
      Like a nipt blossome, hung
            Discontented.

O cheer and tune my heartlesse breast,
Deferre no time;
That so thy favours granting my request,
They and my minde may chime,
And mend my ryme.

Vanitie

The fleet Astronomer can bore,
And thred the spheres with his quick-piercing minde:
He views their stations, walks from doore to doore,
Surveys, as if he had design'd
To make a purchase there: he sees their dances,
And knoweth long before
Both their full-ey'd aspects, and secret glances.

The nimble Diver with his side
Cuts through the working waves, that he may fetch
His dearly-earned pearl, which God did hide
On purpose from the ventrous wretch;
That he might save his life, and also hers,
Who with excessive pride
Her own destruction and his danger wears.

The subtil Chymick can devest
And strip the creature naked, till he finde
The callow principles within their nest:
There he imparts to them his minde,
Admitted to their bed-chamber, before
They appeare trim and drest
To ordinarie suitours at the doore.

What hath not man sought out and found,
But his deare God? who yet his glorious law
Embosomes in us, mellowing the ground
With showres and frosts, with love & aw,

So that we need not say, Where's this command?
      Poore man, thou searchest round
To finde out *death*, but missest *life* at hand.

Vertue

Sweet day, so cool, so calm, so bright,
The bridall of the earth and skie:
The dew shall weep thy fall to night;
      For thou must die.

Sweet rose, whose hue angrie and brave
Bids the rash gazer wipe his eye:
Thy root is ever in its grave,
      And thou must die.

Sweet spring, full of sweet dayes and roses,
A box where sweets[1] compacted lie;
My musick shows ye have your closes,[2]
      And all must die.

Onely a sweet and vertuous soul,
Like season'd timber, never gives;
But though the whole world turn to coal,
      Then chiefly lives.

The Pearl. Matth. 13. 45[3]

I know the wayes of Learning; both the head
And pipes that feed the presse, and make it runne;
What reason hath from nature borrowed,
Or of it self, like a good huswife, spunne

---

[1] *sweets*: perfumes.   [2] *closes*: cadences.
[3] 'The kingdom of heaven is like unto a merchant man, seeking goodly pearls: who, when he had found one, sold all that he had and bought it.'

In laws and policie; what the starres conspire,
What willing nature speaks, what forc'd by fire;[1]
Both th' old discoveries, and the new-found seas,
The stock and surplus, cause and historie:
All these stand open, or I have the keyes:
      Yet I love thee.

I know the wayes of Honour, what maintains
The quick returns of courtesie and wit:
In vies of favours whether partie gains,
When glorie swells the heart, and moldeth it
To all expressions both of hand and eye,
Which on the world a true-love-knot may tie,
And bear the bundle, wheresoe're it goes:[2]
How many drammes of spirit there must be
To sell my life unto my friends or foes:
      Yet I love thee.

I know the wayes of Pleasure, the sweet strains,
The lullings and the relishes of it;
The propositions of hot bloud and brains;
What mirth and musick mean; what love and wit
Have done these twentie hundred yeares, and more:
I know the projects of unbridled store:
My stuffe is flesh, not brasse; my senses live,
And grumble oft, that they have more in me
Than he that curbs them, being but one to five:
      Yet I love thee.

I know all these, and have them in my hand:
Therefore not sealed,[3] but with open eyes

---

[1] 'What nature reveals of herself and what she is forced to reveal by the chemist's furnace.'

[2] 'I know which of two men wins in a competition to do favours, when ambition urges men to court and win the world and follow it like a servant wherever it goes.'

[3] A young hawk's eyes were 'seeled', or sewn-up, so that it should not be distracted on its return to the hawker by the lure of other sights.

I flie to thee, and fully understand
Both the main sale, and the commodities;[1]
And at what rate and price I have thy love;
With all the circumstances that may move:
Yet through these labyrinths, not my groveling wit,
But thy silk twist let down from heav'n to me,
Did both conduct and teach me, how by it
        To climbe to thee.

Man

     My God, I heard this day,
That none doth build a stately habitation,
     But he that means to dwell therein.
     What house more stately hath there been,
Or can be, than is Man? to[2] whose creation
     All things are in decay,

     For Man is ev'ry thing,
And more: He is a tree, yet bears more fruit;
     A beast, yet is, or should be more:
     Reason and speech we onely bring.
Parrats may thank us, if they are not mute,
     They go upon the score.[3]

     Man is all symmetrie,
Full of proportions, one limbe to another,
     And all to all the world besides:
     Each part may call the furthest, brother:
For head with foot hath private amitie,
     And both with moons and tides.

[1] *commodities*: goods offered in addition.
[2] *to*: compared to.
[3] Their speech is scored to our credit, not theirs.

Nothing hath got so farre,
But Man hath caught and kept it, as his prey.
His eyes dismount the highest starre:
He is in little all the sphere.
Herbs gladly cure our flesh; because that they
Finde their acquaintance there.

For us the windes do blow,
The earth doth rest, heav'n move, and fountains flow.
Nothing we see, but means our good,
As our *delight*, or as our *treasure*:
The whole is, either our cupboard of *food*,
Or cabinet of *pleasure*.

The starres have us to bed;
Night draws the curtain, which the sunne withdraws;
Musick and light attend our head.
All things unto our *flesh* are kinde
In their *descent* and *being*; to our *minde*
In their *ascent* and *cause*.

Each thing is full of dutie:
Waters united are our navigation;
Distinguished, our habitation;
Below, our drink; above, our meat;
Both are our cleanlinesse. Hath one such beautie?
Then how are all things neat?[1]

More servants wait on Man,
Than he'l take notice of: in ev'ry path
He treads down that which doth befriend him,
When sicknesse makes him pale and wan.
Oh mightie love! Man is one world, and hath
Another to attend him.

[1] 'The gathering together of waters at the Creation gave us the sea to
sail on, as their separation gave us the land: on earth they give drink, as
rain from above they give food. If such beauty can be seen in one element,
how exquisite is the whole.'

Since then, my God, thou hast
So brave a Palace built; O dwell in it,
That it may dwell with thee at last!
Till then, afford us so much wit;
That, as the world serves us, we may serve thee,
And both thy servants be.

Life

I made a posie, while the day ran by:
Here will I smell my remnant out, and tie
My life within this band.
But Time did becken to the flowers, and they
By noon most cunningly did steal away,
And wither'd in my hand.

My hand was next to them, and then my heart:
I took, without more thinking, in good part
Times gentle admonition:
Who did so sweetly deaths sad taste convey,
Making my minde to smell my fatall day;
Yet sugring the suspicion.

Farewell deare flowers, sweetly your time ye spent,
Fit, while ye liv'd, for smell or ornament,
And after death for cures.
I follow straight without complaints or grief,
Since if my scent be good, I care not if
It be as short as yours.

Mortification

How soon doth man decay!
When clothes are taken from a chest of sweets
To swaddle infants, whose young breath
Scarce knows the way;
Those clouts are little winding sheets,
Which do consigne and send them unto death.

When boyes go first to bed,
They step into their voluntarie graves,
Sleep bindes them fast; onely their breath
Makes them not dead:
Successive nights, like rolling waves,
Convey them quickly, who are bound for death.

When youth is frank and free,
And calls for musick, while his veins do swell,
All day exchanging mirth and breath
In companie;
That musick summons to the knell,
Which shall befriend him at the houre of death.

When man grows staid and wise,
Getting a house and home, where he may move
Within the circle of his breath,
Schooling his eyes;
That dumbe inclosure maketh love
Unto the coffin, that attends his death.

When age grows low and weak,
Marking his grave, and thawing ev'ry yeare,
Till all do melt, and drown his breath
When he would speak;
A chair or litter shows the biere,
Which shall convey him to the house of death.

Man, ere he is aware,
Hath put together a solemnitie,
And drest his herse, while he has breath
As yet to spare:
Yet Lord, instruct us so to die,
That all these dyings may be life in death.

Jordan (II)

When first my lines of heav'nly joyes made mention,
Such was their lustre, they did so excell,
That I sought out quaint words, and trim invention;
My thoughts began to burnish, sprout, and swell,
Curling with metaphors a plain intention,
Decking the sense, as if it were to sell.

Thousands of notions in my brain did runne,
Off'ring their service, if I were not sped:
I often blotted what I had begunne;
This was not quick enough, and that was dead.
Nothing could seem too rich to clothe the sunne,
Much less those joyes which trample on his head.

As flames do work and winde, when they ascend,
So did I weave my self into the sense.
But while I bustled, I might heare a friend
Whisper, *How wide is all this long pretence!*
There is in love a sweetnesse readie penn'd:
Copie out onely that, and save expense.

Dialogue

Sweetest Saviour, if my soul
  Were but worth the having,
Quickly should I then controll
  Any thought of waving.[1]
But when all my care and pains
Cannot give the name of gains
To thy wretch so full of stains,
What delight or hope remains?

[1] *waving*: 'waiving', or declining the offer seems the more likely sense than 'wavering'.

What, Child, is the ballance thine,
  Thine the poise and measure?
If I say, Thou shalt be mine;
  Finger not my treasure.
What the gains in having thee
Do amount to, onely he,
Who for man was sold, can see;
That transferr'd th' accounts to me.

But as I can see no merit,
  Leading to this favour:
So the way to fit me for it
  Is beyond my savour.[1]
As the reason then is thine;
So the way is none of mine:
I disclaim the whole designe:
Sinne disclaims and I resigne.

That is all, if that I could
  Get without repining;
And my clay, my creature, would
  Follow my resigning:
That as I did freely part
With my glorie and desert,
Left all joyes to feel all smart—
  Ah! no more: thou break'st my heart.

The Collar

I struck the board, and cry'd, No more.
      I will abroad.
What? shall I ever sigh and pine?
My lines and life are free; free as the rode,
    Loose as the winde, as large as store.
          Shall I be still in suit?
      Have I no harvest but a thorn
      To let me bloud, and not restore

[1] *savour*: understanding.

What I have lost with cordiall fruit?
Sure there was wine
Before my sighs did drie it: there was corn
Before my tears did drown it.
Is the yeare onely lost to me?
Have I no bayes to crown it?
No flowers, no garlands gay? all blasted?
All wasted?
Not so, my heart: but there is fruit,
And thou hast hands.
Recover all thy sigh-blown age
On double pleasures: leave thy cold dispute
Of what is fit, and not. Forsake thy cage,
Thy rope of sands,
Which pettie thoughts have made, and made to thee
Good cable, to enforce and draw,
And be thy law,
While thou didst wink and wouldst not see.
Away; take heed:
I will abroad.
Call in thy deaths head there: tie up thy fears.
He that forbears
To suit and serve his need,
Deserves his load.
But as I rav'd and grew more fierce and wilde
At every word,
Me thoughts I heard one calling, *Child!*
And I reply'd, *My Lord.*

The Pulley

When God at first made man,
Having a glasse of blessings standing by;
Let us (said he) poure on him all we can;
Let the worlds riches, which dispersed lie,
Contract into a span.

So strength first made a way;
Then beautie flow'd, then wisdome, honour, pleasure:
When almost all was out, God made a stay,
Perceiving that alone of all his treasure
     Rest in the bottome lay.

For if I should (said he)
Bestow this jewell also on my creature,
He would adore my gifts in stead of me,
And rest in Nature, not the God of Nature:
     So both should losers be.

Yet let him keep the rest,
But keep them with repining restlesnesse:
Let him be rich and wearie, that at least,
If goodnesse leade him not, yet wearinesse
     May tosse him to my breast.

The Flower

How fresh, O Lord, how sweet and clean
Are thy returns! ev'n as the flowers in spring;
    To which, besides their own demean,[1]
The late-past frosts tributes of pleasure bring.
        Grief melts away
        Like snow in May,
As if there were no such cold thing.

Who would have thought my shrivel'd heart
Could have recover'd greennesse? It was gone
    Quite under ground; as flowers depart
To see their mother-root, when they have blown;
        Where they together
        All the hard weather,
Dead to the world, keep house unknown.

[1] *demean*: demeanour.

These are thy wonders, Lord of power,
Killing and quickning, bringing down to hell
   And up to heaven in an houre;
Making a chiming of a passing-bell.
      We say amisse,
      This or that is:
Thy word is all, if we could spell.[1]

O that I once past changing were,
Fast in thy Paradise, where no flower can wither!
   Many a spring I shoot up fair,
Offring at[2] heav'n, growing and groning thither:
      Nor doth my flower
      Want a spring-showre,
My sinnes and I joining together.

But while I grow in a straight line,
Still upwards bent, as if heav'n were mine own,
   Thy anger comes, and I decline:
What frost to that? what pole is not the zone,
      Where all things burn,
      When thou dost turn,
And the least frown of thine is shown?

And now in age I bud again,
After so many deaths I live and write;
   I once more smell the dew and rain,
And relish versing: O my onely light,
      It cannot be
      That I am he
On whom thy tempests fell all night.

These are thy wonders, Lord of love,
To make us see we are but flowers that glide:
   Which when we once can finde and prove,

---

[1] Nothing *is* in itself, unchangeably: only God's word is always the same.
[2] *Offring at*: aiming at.

Thou hast a garden for us, where to bide.
        Who would be more,
        Swelling through store,
Forfeit their Paradise by their pride.

Aaron[1]

        Holinesse on the head,
    Light and perfections on the breast,
Harmonious bells below, raising the dead
    To leade them unto life and rest:
        Thus are true Aarons drest.

        Profanenesse in my head,
    Defects and darknesse in my breast,
A noise[2] of passions ringing me for dead
    Unto a place where is no rest:
        Poore priest thus am I drest.

        Onely another head
    I have, another heart and breast,
Another musick, making live not dead,
    Without whom I could have no rest:
        In him I am well drest.

        Christ is my onely head,
    My alone onely heart and breast,
My onely musick, striking me ev'n dead;
    That to the old man I may rest,
        And be in him new drest.

[1] The priestly garments of Aaron (Exodus xxviii) included a mitre with a gold plate engraved with the words 'Holiness to the Lord', a breastplate containing the URIM and THUMMIM (the Lights and Perfections) and a robe with a fringe of bells and pomegranates.
[2] *a noise*: a band of musicians.

So holy in my head,
Perfect and light in my deare breast,
My doctrine tun'd by Christ, (who is not dead,
But lives in me while I do rest)
Come people; Aaron's drest.

The Forerunners

The harbingers[1] are come. See, see their mark;
White is their colour, and behold my head.
But must they have my brain? must they dispark
Those sparkling notions, which therein were bred?
Must dulnesse turn me to a clod?
Yet have they left me, *Thou art still my God.*

Good men ye be, to leave me my best room,
Ev'n all my heart, and what is lodged there:
I passe not,[2] I, what of the rest become,
So *Thou art still my God*, be out of fear.
He will be pleased with that dittie;
And if I please him, I write fine and wittie.

Farewell sweet phrases, lovely metaphors.
But will ye leave me thus? when ye before
Of stews and brothels onely knew the doores,
Then did I wash you with my tears, and more,
Brought you to Church well drest and clad:
My God must have my best, ev'n all I had.

Lovely enchanting language, sugar-cane,
Hony of roses, whither wilt thou flie?
Hath some fond lover tic'd thee to thy bane?
And wilt thou leave the Church, and love a stie?
Fie, thou wilt soil thy broider'd coat,
And hurt thy self, and him that sings the note.

[1] Harbingers were sent ahead of a royal progress to requisition lodgings by chalking doors.　　　　　　　　　[2] *passe not*: care not.

Let foolish lovers, if they will love dung,
With canvas, not with arras, clothe their shame:
Let follie speak in her own native tongue.
True beautie dwells on high: ours is a flame
    But borrow'd thence to light us thither.
Beautie and beauteous words should go together.

Yet if you go, I passe not; take your way:
For, *Thou art still my God*, is all that ye
Perhaps with more embellishment can say.
Go birds of spring: let winter have his fee;
    Let a bleak palenesse chalk the doore,
So all within be livelier than before.

Discipline

Throw away thy rod,
Throw away thy wrath:
    O my God,
Take the gentle path.

For my hearts desire
Unto thine is bent:
    I aspire
To a full consent.

Not a word or look
I affect to own,
    But by book,
And thy book alone.

Though I fail, I weep:
Though I halt in pace,
    Yet I creep
To the throne of grace.

Then let wrath remove,
Love will do the deed:
    For with love
Stonie hearts will bleed.

Love is swift of foot;
Love's a man of warre,
    And can shoot,
And can hit from farre.

Who can scape his bow?
That which wrought on thee,
    Brought thee low,
Needs must work on me.

Throw away thy rod;
Though man frailties hath,
    Thou art God:
Throw away thy wrath.

Death

Death, thou wast once an uncouth hideous thing,
    Nothing but bones,
  The sad effect of sadder grones;
Thy mouth was open, but thou couldst not sing.

For we consider'd thee as at some six
    Or ten yeares hence,
  After the losse of life and sense,
Flesh being turn'd to dust, and bones to sticks.

We lookt on this side of thee, shooting short;
    Where we did finde
  The shells of fledge souls left behinde,
Dry dust, which sheds no tears, but may extort.

But since our Saviours death did put some bloud
       Into thy face;
    Thou art grown fair and full of grace,
Much in request, much sought for as a good.

For we do now behold thee gay and glad,
       As at dooms-day;
    When souls shall wear their new aray,
And all thy bones with beautie shall be clad.

Therefore we can go die as sleep, and trust
       Half that we have
    Unto an honest faithfull grave;
Making our pillows either down, or dust.

Love

Love bade me welcome: yet my soul drew back,
       Guiltie of dust and sinne.
But quick-ey'd Love, observing me grow slack
       From my first entrance in,
Drew nearer to me, sweetly questioning,
       If I lack'd any thing.

A guest, I answer'd, worthy to be here:
       Love said, You shall be he.
I the unkinde, ungratefull? Ah my deare,
       I cannot look on thee.
Love took my hand, and smiling did reply,
       Who made the eyes but I?

Truth Lord, but I have marr'd them: let my shame
       Go where it doth deserve.
And know you not, sayes Love, who bore the blame?
       My deare, then I will serve.
You must sit downe, sayes Love, and taste my meat:
       So I did sit and eat.

                  (*The Temple*, 1633)

THOMAS CAREW

(1594/5–1640)

An Elegie upon the death of the Deane of Pauls, *Dr* John Donne

Can we not force from widdowed Poetry,
Now thou art dead (Great DONNE) one Elegie
To crowne thy Hearse? Why yet dare we not trust
Though with unkneaded, dowe-bak't prose thy dust,
Such as the uncisor'd[1] Churchman from the flower
Of fading Rhetorique, short liv'd as his houre,
Dry as the sand that measures it, should lay
Upon thy Ashes, on the funerall day?
Have we no voice, no tune? Did'st thou dispense
Through all our language, both the words and sense?
'Tis a sad truth; The Pulpit may her plaine
And sober Christian precepts still retaine,
Doctrines it may, and wholesome Uses frame,
Grave Homilies, and Lectures, But the flame
Of thy brave Soule, (that shot such heat and light,
As burnt our earth, and made our darknesse bright,
Committed holy Rapes upon our Will,
Did through the eye the melting heart distill;
And the deepe knowledge of darke truths so teach,
As sense might judge, what phansie could not reach;)
Must be desir'd for ever. So the fire,
That fills with spirit and heat the Delphique quire,
Which kindled first by thy Promethean breath,
Glow'd here a while, lies quench't now in thy death;
The Muses garden with Pedantique weedes
O'rspred, was purg'd by thee; The lazie seeds

---

[1] With hair and beard uncut, as sign of mourning.

Of servile imitation throwne away;
And fresh invention planted, Thou didst pay
The debts of our penurious bankrupt age;
Licentious thefts, that make poëtique rage
A Mimique fury, when our soules must bee
Possest, or with Anacreons Extasie,
Or Pindars, not their owne; The subtle cheat
Of slie Exchanges, and the jugling feat
Of two-edg'd words, or whatsoever wrong
By ours was done the Greeke, or Latine tongue,
Thou hast redeem'd, and open'd Us a Mine
Of rich and pregnant phansie, drawne a line
Of masculine expression, which had good
Old Orpheus seene, Or all the ancient Brood
Our superstitious fooles admire, and hold
Their lead more precious, than thy burnish't Gold,
Thou hadst been their Exchequer, and no more
They in each others dust, had rak'd for Ore.
Thou shalt yield no precedence, but of time,
And the blinde fate of language, whose tun'd chime
More charmes the outward sense; Yet thou maist claime
From so great disadvantage greater fame,
Since to the awe of thy imperious wit
Our stubborne language bends, made only fit
With her tough-thick-rib'd hoopes to gird about
Thy Giant phansie, which had prov'd too stout
For their soft melting Phrases. As in time
They had the start, so did they cull the prime
Buds of invention many a hundred yeare,
And left the rifled fields, besides the feare
To touch their Harvest, yet from those bare lands
Of what is purely thine, thy only hands
(And that thy smallest worke) have gleaned more
Than all those times, and tongues could reape before.
  But thou art gone, and thy strict lawes will be
Too hard for Libertines in Poetrie.
They will repeale the goodly exil'd traine

Of gods and goddesses, which in thy just raigne
Were banish'd nobler Poems, now, with these
The silenc'd tales o'th'Metamorphoses
Shall stuffe their lines, and swell the windy Page,
Till Verse refin'd by thee, in this last Age,
Turne ballad rime, Or those old Idolls bee
Ador'd againe, with new apostasie;
  Oh, pardon mee, that breake with untun'd verse
The reverend silence that attends thy herse,
Whose awfull solemne murmures were to thee
More than these faint lines, A loud Elegie,
That did proclaime in a dumbe eloquence
The death of all the Arts, whose influence
Growne feeble, in these panting numbers lies
Gasping short winded Accents, and so dies:
So doth the swiftly turning wheele not stand
In th'instant we withdraw the moving hand,
But some small time maintaine a faint weake course
By vertue of the first impulsive force:
And so whil'st I cast on thy funerall pile
Thy crowne of Bayes, Oh, let it crack a while,
And spit disdaine, till the devouring flashes
Suck all the moysture up, then turne to ashes.
  I will not draw the envy to engrosse
All thy perfections, or weepe all our losse;
Those are too numerous for an Elegie,
And this too great, to be express'd by mee.
Though every pen should share a distinct part,
Yet thou art Theme enough to tyre all Art;
Let others carve the rest, it shall suffice
I on thy Tombe this Epitaph incise.

> *Here lies a King, that rul'd as hee thought fit*
> *The universall Monarchy of wit;*
> *Here lie two Flamens, and both those, the best,*
> *Apollo's first, at last, the true God's Priest.*

(Poems by J. D. with elegies upon the authors death, 1633)

Mediocritie in love rejected

Give me more love, or more disdaine;
　　The Torrid, or the frozen Zone,
Bring equall ease unto my paine;
　　The temperate affords me none:
Either extreame, of love, or hate,
Is sweeter than a calm estate.

Give me a storme; if it be love,
　　Like *Danae* in that golden showre
I swimme in pleasure; if it prove
　　Disdaine, that torrent will devoure
My Vulture-hopes; and he's possest
Of Heaven, that's but from Hell releast:
　　Then crowne my joyes, or cure my paine;
　　Give me more love, or more disdaine.

To my inconstant Mistris

When thou, poore excommunicate
　　From all the joyes of love, shalt see
The full reward, and glorious fate,
　　Which my strong faith shall purchase me,
　　Then curse thine owne inconstancie.

A fayrer hand than thine, shall cure
　　That heart, which thy false oathes did wound;
And to my soule, a soule more pure
　　Than thine, shall by Loves hand be bound,
　　And both with equall glory crown'd.

Then shalt thou weepe, entreat, complaine
　　To Love, as I did once to thee;
When all thy teares shall be as vaine
　　As mine were then, for thou shalt bee
　　Damn'd for thy false Apostasie.

Perswasions to enjoy

If the quick spirits in your eye
Now languish, and anon must dye;
If every sweet, and every grace,
Must fly from that forsaken face:
    Then (*Celia*) let us reape our joyes,
    E're time such goodly fruit destroyes.

Or, if that golden fleece must grow
For ever, free from aged snow;
If those bright Suns must know no shade,
Nor your fresh beauties ever fade:
Then feare not (*Celia*) to bestow,
What still being gather'd, still must grow.
    Thus, either *Time* his Sickle brings
    In vaine, or else in vaine his wings.

Boldnesse in love

Marke how the bashfull morne, in vaine
Courts the amorous Marigold,
With sighing blasts, and weeping raine;
Yet she refuses to unfold.
But when the Planet of the day,
Approacheth with his powerfull ray,
Then she spreads, then she receives
His warmer beames into her virgin leaves.
So shalt thou thrive in love, fond Boy;
If thy teares, and sighes discover
Thy griefe, thou never shalt enjoy
The just reward of a bold lover:
But when with moving accents, thou
Shalt constant faith, and service vow,
Thy *Celia* shall receive those charmes
With open eares, and with unfolded armes.

Maria Wentworth, Thomae *Comitis* Cleveland, *filia praemortua prima Virgineam animam exhalavit*

An. Dom. 1632. Æt. suae 18

And here the precious dust is layd;
Whose purely temper'd Clay was made
So fine, that it the guest betray'd.

Else the soule grew so fast within,
It broke the outward shell of sinne,
And so was hatch'd a Cherubin.

In heigth, it soar'd to God above;
In depth, it did to knowledge move,
And spread in breadth to generall love.

Before, a pious duty shind
To Parents, courtesie behind,
On either side an equall mind,

Good to the Poore, to kindred deare,
To servants kind, to friendship cleare,
To nothing but her selfe, severe.

So though a Virgin, yet a Bride
To every Grace, she justifi'd
A chaste Poligamie, and dy'd.

Learne from hence (Reader) what small trust
We owe this world, where vertue must
Fraile as our flesh, crumble to dust.

To Ben. Jonson
Upon occasion of his Ode of defiance annext to his Play of the new Inne[1]

Tis true (deare *Ben*:) thy just chastizing hand
Hath fixt upon the sotted Age a brand
To their swolne pride, and empty scribbling due,
It can nor judge, nor write, and yet 'tis true
Thy commique Muse from the exalted line
Toucht by thy *Alchymist*, doth since decline
From that her Zenith, and foretells a red
And blushing evening, when she goes to bed,
Yet such, as shall out-shine the glimmering light
With which all stars shall guild the following night.
Nor thinke it much (since all thy Eaglets may
Endure the Sunnie tryall) if we say
This hath the stronger wing, or that doth shine
Trickt up in fairer plumes, since all are thine;
Who hath his flock of cackling Geese compar'd
With thy tun'd quire of Swans? or else who dar'd
To call thy births deform'd? but if thou bind
By Citie-custome, or by *Gavell-kind*,[2]
In equall shares thy love on all thy race,
We may distinguish of their sexe, and place;
Though one hand form them, and though one brain strike
Soules into all, they are not all alike.
Why should the follies then of this dull age
Draw from thy Pen such an immodest rage
As seemes to blast thy (else-immortall) Bayes,
When thine owne tongue proclaimes thy ytch of praise?
Such thirst will argue drouth. No, let be hurld
Upon thy workes, by the detracting world,

[1] *The New Inne* was hissed on performance in 1629. Jonson published it in 1631, affixing at the end his Ode 'Come leave the loathed stage'.
[2] *Gavell-kind*: a form of land tenure by which at the tenant's decease his land was divided equally among his sons.

What malice can suggest; let the Rowte say,
The running sands, that (ere thou make a play)
Count the slow minutes, might a *Goodwin* frame
To swallow when th'hast done thy ship-wrackt name.
Let them the deare expence of oyle upbraid
Suckt by thy watchfull Lampe, that hath betray'd
To theft the blood of martyr'd Authors, spilt
Into thy inke, while thou growest pale with guilt.
Repine not at the Tapers thriftie waste,
That sleeks thy terser Poems, nor is haste
Prayse, but excuse; and if thou overcome
A knottie writer, bring the bootie home;
Nor think it theft, if the rich spoyles so torne
From conquered Authors, be as Trophies worne.
Let others glut on the extorted praise
Of vulgar breath, trust thou to after dayes:
Thy labour'd workes shall live, when Time devoures
Th'abortive off-spring of their hastie houres.
Thou art not of their ranke, the quarrell lyes
Within thine owne Virge, then let this suffice,
The wiser world doth greater Thee confesse
Than all men else, than Thy selfe onely lesse.

To a Lady that desired I would love her

Now you have freely given me leave to love,
What will you doe?
Shall I your mirth, or passion move
When I begin to wooe;
Will you torment, or scorne, or love me too?

Each pettie beautie can disdaine, and I
Spight of your hate
Without your leave can see, and dye;
Dispence a nobler Fate,
'Tis easie to destroy, you may create.

Then give me leave to love, and love me too,
Not with designe
To rayse, as Loves curst Rebells doe,
When puling Poets whine,
Fame to their beautie, from their blubbr'd eyne.

Griefe is a puddle, and reflects not cleare
Your beauties rayes,
Joyes are pure streames, your eyes appeare
Sullen in sadder layes,
In chearfull numbers they shine bright with prayse;

Which shall not mention to expresse you fayre
Wounds, flames, and darts,
Stormes in your brow, nets in your haire,
Suborning all your parts,
Or to betray, or torture captive hearts.

I'le make your eyes like morning Suns appeare,
As milde, and faire;
Your brow as Crystall smooth, and cleare,
And your dishevell'd hayre
Shall flow like a calme Region of the Ayre.

Rich Natures store, (which is the Poets Treasure)
I'le spend, to dresse
Your beauties, if your mine of Pleasure
In equall thankfulnesse
You but unlocke, so we each other blesse.

Song

Aske me no more where *Jove* bestowes,
When *June* is past, the fading rose:
For in your beauties orient deepe,
These flowers as in their causes, sleepe.

Aske me no more whither doth stray,
The golden Atomes of the day:
For in pure love heaven did prepare
These powders to inrich your haire.

Aske me no more whither doth hast,
The Nightingale when May is past:
For in your sweet dividing throat,
She winters and keepes warme her note.

Aske me no more where those starres light,
That downewards fall in dead of night:
For in your eyes they sit, and there,
Fixed become as in their sphere.

Aske me no more if East or West,
The Phoenix builds her spicy nest:
For unto you at last shee flies
And in your fragrant bosome dyes.

To my worthy friend Master George Sands, on his translation of the Psalmes[1]

I presse not to the Quire, nor dare I greet
The holy place with my unhallowed feet;
My unwasht Muse polutes not things Divine,
Nor mingles her prophaner notes with thine;
Here, humbly at the porch she listning stayes,
And with glad eares sucks in thy sacred layes.
So, devout penitents of Old were wont,
Some without dore, and some beneath the Font,
To stand and heare the Churches Liturgies,
Yet not assist the solemne exercise:

[1] First published in the second edition of Sandys's *A Paraphrase upon the Divine Poems*, 1638.

Sufficeth her, that she a lay-place gaine,
To trim thy Vestments, or but beare thy traine;
Though nor in tune, nor wing, she reach thy Larke,
Her Lyrick feet may dance before the Arke.
Who knowes, but that her wandring eyes that run,
Now hunting Glow-wormes, may adore the Sun,
A pure flame may, shot by Almighty power
Into her brest, the earthy flame devoure.
My eyes, in penitentiall dew may steepe
That brine, which they for sensuall love did weepe.
So (though 'gainst Natures course) fire may be quencht
With fire, and water be with water drencht.
Perhaps my restlesse soule, tyr'd with persuit
Of mortall beauty, seeking without fruit
Contentment there, which hath not, when enjoy'd
Quencht all her thirst, nor satisfi'd, though cloy'd;
Weary of her vaine search below, Above
In the first Faire may find th'immortall Love.
Prompted by thy example then, no more
In moulds of clay will I my God adore;
But teare those Idols from my heart, and write
What his blest Sp'rit, not fond Love shall indite;
Then, I no more shall court the verdant Bay,
But the dry leaveless Trunke on *Golgotha*;
And rather strive to gaine from thence one Thorne,
Than all the flourishing wreathes by Laureats worne.

(*Poems,* 1640)

OWEN FELLTHAM

(1602?–1668)

Song[1]

When, Dearest, I but think on thee,
Methinks all things that lovely be
  Are present, and my soul delighted:
For beauties that from worth arise,
Are like the grace of Deities,
  Still present with us, though unsighted.

Thus while I sit and sigh the day,
With all his spreading lights away,
  Till nights black wings do overtake me:
Thinking on thee, thy beauties then,
As sudden lights do sleeping men,
  So they by their bright rayes awake me.

Thus absence dyes, and dying proves
No absence can consist with Loves,
  That do partake of fair perfection:
Since in the darkest night they may
By their quick motion find a way
  To see each other by reflection.

The waving Sea can with such flood
Bathe some high Palace that hath stood
  Far from the Main up in the River:
Oh think not then but love can do
As much, for that's an Ocean too,
  That flows not every day, but ever.

(*Lusoria*, 1661)

[1] Printed as Suckling's in *Last Remains*, 1659.

WILLIAM HABINGTON

(1605–1654)

Against them who lay unchastity to the sex of Women[1]

They meet but with unwholesome Springs,
And Summers which infectious are:
They heare but when the Meremaid sings,
And only see the falling starre:
      Who ever dare,
Affirme no woman chaste and faire.

Goe cure your feavers: and you'le say
The Dog-dayes scorch not all the yeare:
In Copper Mines no longer stay,
But travell to the West, and there
      The right ones see:
And grant all gold's not Alchimie.

What mad man 'cause the glow-wormes flame
Is cold, sweares there's no warmth in fire?
'Cause some make forfeit of their name,
And slave themselves to mans desire;
      Shall the sex free
From guilt, damn'd to the bondage be?

Nor grieve, *Castara*, though 'twere fraile,
Thy Vertue then would brighter shine,
When thy example should prevaile,
And every womans faith be thine,
      And were there none;
'Tis Majesty to rule alone.

(*Castara, The Second Part*, 1635)

[1] A reply to Donne's 'Goe, and catche a falling starre' (p. 27).

Nox nocti indicat Scientiam. DAVID

When I survay the bright
    Coelestiall spheare:
So rich with jewels hung, that night
Doth like an Æthiop bride appeare,

My soule her wings doth spread
    And heaven-ward flies,
Th'Almighty's Mysteries to read
In the large volumes of the skies.

For the bright firmament
    Shootes forth no flame
So silent, but is eloquent
In speaking the Creators name.

No unregarded star
    Contracts its light
Into so small a Charactar,
Remov'd far from our humane sight:

But if we stedfast looke,
    We shall discerne
In it as in some holy booke,
How man may heavenly knowledge learne.

It tells the Conqueror,
    That farre-stretcht powre
Which his proud dangers traffique for,
Is but the triumph of an houre.

That from the farthest North;
    Some Nation may
Yet undiscovered issue forth,
And ore his new got conquest sway.

Some Nation yet shut in
With hills of ice
May be let out to scourge his sinne
'Till they shall equall him in vice.

And then they likewise shall
Their ruine have,
For as your selves your Empires fall,
And every Kingdome hath a grave.

Thus those Coelestiall fires,
Though seeming mute,
The fallacie of our desires
And all the pride of life confute.

For they have watcht since first
The World had birth:
And found sinne in it selfe accurst
And nothing permanent on earth.

(Castara: The Third Part, 1640)

Song

Fine young folly, though you were
That faire beauty I did sweare,
Yet you neere could reach my heart.
For we Courtiers learne at Schoole,
Onely with your sex to foole,
Y'are not worth the serious part.

When I sigh and kisse your hand,
Crosse my Armes and wondring stand;
Holding parley with your eye,
Then dilate on my desires,
Sweare the sunne nere shot such fires,
All is but a handsome lye.

When I eye your curle or Lace,
Gentle soule you think your face
Streight some murder doth commit,
And your virtue doth begin
To grow scrupulous of my sinne,
When I talke to shew my wit.

Therefore Madam weare no cloud
Nor to checke my love grow proud,
For in sooth I much doe doubt
'Tis the powder in your haire,
Not your breath perfumes the ayre,
And your Cloathes that set you out.

Yet though truth has this confest,
And I vow I love in Jest:
When I next begin to Court
And protest an amorous flame,
You'll sweare I in earnest am:
Bedlam! this is pretty sport.

(*The Queene of Arragon*, 1640)

THOMAS RANDOLPH
(1605–1635)

An Elegie

Love, give me leave to serve thee, and be wise,
To keepe thy torch in, but restore blind eyes.
I will a flame into my bosome take,
That Martyrs Court when they embrace the stake:
Not dull, and smoakie fires, but heat divine,

That burnes not to consume, but to refine.
I have a Mistresse for perfections rare
In every eye, but in my thoughts most faire.
Like Tapers on the Altar shine her eyes;
Her breath is the perfume of Sacrifice.
And whereso'ere my fancy would begin,
Still her perfection lets religion in.
I touch her like my Beads with devout care;
And come unto my Courtship as my Praier.
Wee sit, and talke, and kisse away the houres,
As chastly as the morning dews kisse flowers.
Goe wanton Lover spare thy sighs and teares,
Put on the Livery which thy dotage weares,
And call it Love, where heresie gets in
Zeal's but a coale to kindle greater sin.
Wee weare no flesh, but one another greet,
As blessed soules in separation meet.
Were't possible that my ambitious sin,
Durst commit rapes upon a *Cherubin*,
I might have lustfull thoughts to her, of all
Earths heav'nly Quire, the most Angelicall.
Looking into my brest, her forme I find
That like my Guardian-Angell keeps my mind
From rude attempts; and when affections stirre,
I calme all passions with one thought of her.
Thus they whose reasons love, and not their sence,
The spirits love: thus one Intelligence
Reflects upon his like, and by chast loves
In the same spheare this and that Angell moves.
Nor is this barren Love; one noble thought
Begets an other, and that still is brought
To bed of more; vertues and grace increase,
And such a numerous issue ne're can cease.
Where Children, though great blessings, only bee
Pleasures repriv'd to some posteritie.
Beasts love like men, if men in lust delight,
And call that Love which is but appetite.

131

When essence meets with essence, and soules joyne
In mutuall knots, thats the true Nuptiall twine:
Such Lady is my Love, and such is true;
All other Love is to your Sexe, not You.

Upon his Picture

When age hath made me what I am not now;
And every wrinckle tells me where the plow
Of time hath furrowed; when an Ice shall flow
Through every vein, and all my head wear snow:
When death displayes his coldness in my cheeke,
And I, my selfe in my own Picture seeke,
Not finding what I am, but what I was;
In doubt which to beleive, this, or my glasse;
Yet though I alter, this remaines the same
As it was drawne, retaines the primitive frame,
And first complexion; here will still be seen
Blood on the cheeke, and Downe upon the chin.
Here the smooth brow will stay, the lively eye,
The ruddy Lip, and haire of youthfull dye.
Behold what frailty we in man may see,
Whose Shadow is lesse given to change than hee.

(*Poems*, 1638)

On a maide of honour seene by a schollar in Sommerset Garden[1]

As once in blacke I disrespected walkt,
Where glittering courtiers in their Tissues stalkt,
I cast by chaunce my melancholy eye
Upon a woman (as I thought) past by.

[1] Ascribed to Randolph in manuscript, not printed as his.

But when I viewd her ruffe, and beaver reard
As if *Priapus*-like she would have feard
The ravenous *Harpyes* from the clustred grape,
Then I began much to mistrust her shape;
When viewing curiously, away she slipt,
And in a fount her whited hand she dipt,
The angry water as if wrong'd thereby,
Ranne murmuring thence a second touch to fly,
At which away she stalkes, and as she goes
She viewes the situation of each rose;
And having higher rays'd her gowne, she gaz'd
Upon her crimson stocking which amaz'd
Blusht at her open impudence, and sent
Reflection to her cheeke, for punishment.
As thus I stood the Gardiner chaunce to passe,
My friend (quoth I) what is this stately lasse?
A maide of honour Sir, said he, and goes
Leaving a riddle, was enough to pose
The crafty *Œdipus*, for I could see
Nor mayde, nor honour, sure noe honesty.

(British Museum, Add. MS. 11811)

SIR WILLIAM DAVENANT
(1606–1668)

To the Queene, *entertain'd at night by the Countesse of* Anglesey[1]

Faire as unshaded Light; or as the Day
In its first birth, when all the Yeare was May;
Sweet, as the Altars smoake, or as the new
Unfolded Bud, swell'd by the early Dew;

[1] Elizabeth, wife of Christopher Villiers, younger brother of George Villiers, Duke of Buckingham, created Earl of Anglesey in 1622.

Smooth, as the face of Waters first appear'd,
Ere Tides began to strive, or Winds were heard;
Kind, as the willing Saints, and calmer farre,
Than in their sleepes forgiven Hermits are:
You that are more, than our discreeter feare
Dares praise, with such full Art, what make you here?
Here, where the Sommer is so little seene,
That Leaves (her cheapest wealth) scarce reach at greene,
You come, as if the silver Planet were
Misled a while from her much injur'd Spheare,
And t'ease the travailes of her beames to night,
In this small Lanthorn would contract her light.

For the Lady, Olivia Porter.[1] A present upon a New-yeares day

Goe! hunt the whiter Ermine! and present
His wealthy skin, as this dayes Tribute sent
To my *Endimion's* Love; Though she be farre
More gently smooth, more soft than Ermines are!
Goe! climbe that Rock! and when thou there hast found
A Starre, contracted in a Diamond,
Give it *Endimion's* Love, whose glorious Eyes,
Darken the Starry Jewells of the Skies!
Goe! dive into the Southern Sea! and when
Th'ast found (to trouble the nice sight of Men)
A swelling Pearle; and such whose single worth,
Boasts all the wonders which the Seas bring forth;
Give it *Endimion's* Love! whose ev'ry Teare,
Would more enrich the skillfull Jeweller.

[1] Daughter of Lord Boteler, whose wife was Buckingham's favourite sister. Olivia Porter was a Catholic and an ardent proselytizer at the Court of Charles I. Her husband, Endimion Porter, was a protégé of Buckingham's and Groom of the Chamber. He had gone with Charles and Buckingham to Spain. He was a versifier, and patron of poets, and main agent in Charles's acquisition of works of art.

How I command? how slowly they obey?
The churlish *Tartar* will not hunt to day:
Nor will that lazy sallow *Indian* strive
To climbe the rock, nor that dull *Negro* dive.
Thus Poets like to Kings (by trust deceiv'd)
Give oftner what is heard of, than receiv'd.

(*Madagascar*, 1638)

Song

The Lark now leaves his watry Nest
  And climbing, shakes his dewy Wings;
He takes this Window for the East;
  And to implore your Light, he Sings,
Awake, awake, the Morn will never rise,
Till she can dress her Beauty at your Eies.

The Merchant bowes unto the Seamans Star,
  The Ploughman from the Sun his Season takes;
But still the Lover wonders what they are,
  Who look for day before his Mistress wakes.
Awake, awake, break through your Vailes of Lawne!
Then draw your Curtains, and begin the Dawne.

Endimion Porter *and* Olivia

OLIVIA

Before we shall again behold
In his diurnal race the Worlds great Eye,
  We may as silent be and cold,
As are the shades where buried Lovers ly.

ENDIMION

Olivia, 'tis no fault of Love
To lose our selves in death, but O, I fear,
   When Life and Knowledge is above
Restor'd to us, I shall not know thee there.

OLIVIA

Call it not Heaven (my Love) where we
Our selves shall see, and yet each other miss:
   So much of Heaven I find in thee
As, thou unknown, all else privation is.

ENDIMION

Why should we doubt, before we go
To find the Knowledge which shall ever last,
   That we may there each other know?
Can future Knowledge quite destroy the past?

OLIVIA

When at the Bowers in the Elizian shade
I first arrive, I shall examine where
   They dwel, who love the highest Vertue made;
For I am sure to find *Endimion* there.

ENDIMION

From this vext World when we shall both retire,
Where all are Lovers, and where all rejoyce;
   I need not seek thee in the Heavenly Quire;
For I shall know *Olivia* by her Voice.

The Philosopher and the Lover: to a Mistress dying

LOVER

Your Beauty, ripe, and calm, and fresh,
   As Eastern Summers are,
Must now, forsaking Time and Flesh,
   Add light to some small Star.

PHILOSOPHER

Whilst she yet lives, were Stars decay'd,
   Their light by hers, relief might find:
But Death will lead her to a shade
   Where Love is cold, and Beauty blinde.

LOVER

Lovers (whose Priests all Poets are)
   Think ev'ry Mistress, when she dies,
Is chang'd at least into a Starr:
   And who dares doubt the Poets wise?

PHILOSOPHER

But ask not Bodies doom'd to die,
   To what abode they go;
Since Knowledge is but sorrows Spy,
   It is not safe to know.

The Souldier going to the Field

Preserve thy sighs, unthrifty Girle!
   To purifie the Ayre;
Thy Teares to Thrid instead of Pearle,
   On Bracelets of thy Hair.

The Trumpet makes the Eccho hoarse
  And wakes the louder Drum;
Expence of grief gains no remorse,
  When sorrow should be dumb.

For I must go where lazy Peace,
  Will hide her drouzy head;
And, for the sport of Kings, encrease
  The number of the Dead.

But first I'le chide thy cruel theft:
  Can I in War delight,
Who being of my heart bereft,
  Can have no heart to fight?

Thou knowst the Sacred Laws of old,
  Ordain'd a Thief should pay,
To quit him of his Theft, seavenfold
  What he had stoln away.

Thy payment shall but double be;
  O then with speed resign
My own seduced Heart to me,
  Accompani'd with thine.

                    (*Works*, 1673)

EDMUND WALLER
(1606–1687)

To my young Lady, Lucy Sidney[1]

Why came I so untimely forth
Into a world which wanting thee
Could entertaine us with no worth
Or shadow of felicity?
    That time should mee so far remove
    From that which I was borne to love.

[1] Younger sister of Lady Dorothy Sidney, Waller's 'Sacharissa'. Her name was omitted in the second edition.

Yet fairest blossome do not slight
That age which you may know so soone;
The rosy morne resignes her light
And milder glory to the Noon;
    And then what wonders shall you doe,
    Whose dawning beauty warmes us so?

Hope waits upon the flowry prime;
And summer though it be lesse gay,
Yet is not look'd on as a time
Of declination or decay:
    For with a full hand that doth bring
    All that was promis'd by the spring.

The selfe-banished

It is not that I love you less,
Than when before your feet I lay,
But to prevent the sad increase
Of hopeless love, I keep away.

In vaine (alas!) for every thing
Which I have knowne belong to you,
Your forme does to my fancy bring,
And makes my old wounds bleed anew.

Who in the Spring from the new Sun
Already has a Fever got,
Too late begins those shafts to shun
Which *Phoebus* through his veines has shot.

Too late hee would the paine asswage,
And to thick shadowes does retire;
About with him hee beares the rage,
And in his tainted blood the fire.

But vow'd I have, and never must
Your banish'd servant trouble you;
For if I breake, you may mistrust
The vow I made to love you too.

Song

Goe lovely Rose,
Tell her that wasts her time and mee,
    That now shee knowes,
When I resemble her to thee,
    How sweet and fayr shee seems to bee.

Tell her that's young,
And shuns to have her graces spide,
    That hadst thou sprung
In deserts where no men abide,
    Thou must have uncommended dy'd.

Small is the worth
Of beauty from the light retir'd:
    Bid her come forth,
Suffer her selfe to bee desir'd,
    And not blush so to be admir'd.

Then dye, that shee
The common fate of all things rare
    May read in thee,
How small a part of time they share,
    That are so wondrous sweet and faire.

Of my Lady Isabella[1] playing on the Lute

Such moving sounds from such a careless touch,
So unconcern'd her selfe, and we so much!

[1] Lady Isabella Rich, daughter of the Earl of Holland, later married to
Sir James Thynne of Longleat.

What Art is this, that with so little pains
Transports us thus, and o'r our spirit raigns?
The trembling strings about her fingers croud,
And tell their joy for every kiss aloud;
Small force there needs to make them tremble so;
Touch'd by that hand, who would not tremble too?
Here Love takes stand, and while she charms the eare,
Empties his Quiver on the listning Deere:
Musick so softens and disarms the mind,
That not an Arrow does resistance find;
Thus the faire Tyrant celebrates the prize,
And acts her self the triumph of her eyes.
   So *Nero* once, with Harp in hand, survey'd
   His flaming *Rome*, and as it burn'd, he play'd.

An Apologie for having loved before

They that never had the use
Of the Grapes surprizing juyce,
To the first delicious cup
All their reason render up;
Neither doe, nor care to know
Whether it be best or no.

So they that are to Love enclin'd,
Sway'd by Chance, not choyce or art,
To the first that's faire or kind,
Make a present of their heart;
'Tis not she that first we love,
But whom dying we approve.

To Man that was i'th'Evening made,[1]
Stars gave the first delight,
Admiring in the gloomy shade
Those little drops of light.

[1] I cannot suggest why Waller asserts that man was created in the evening.

Then at *Aurora*, whose fair hand
Remov'd them from the skies,
Hee gazing towards the East did stand,
Shee entertain'd his eies.

But when the bright Sun did appeare,
All those he 'gan despise:
His wonder was determin'd[1] there,
And could no higher rise.

Hee neither might, nor wish'd to know
A more refulgent light:
For that, as mine your Beauties now,
Imploy'd his utmost sight.

(Poems, 1645)

Of the Last Verses in the Book[2]

When we for Age could neither read nor write,
The Subject made us able to indite.
The Soul with Nobler Resolutions deckt,
The Body stooping, does Herself erect:
No Mortal Parts are requisite to raise
Her, that Unbody'd can her Maker praise.

The Seas are quiet, when the Winds give o're;
So calm are we, when Passions are no more:
For then we know how vain it was to boast
Of fleeting Things, so certain to be lost.
Clouds of Affection from our younger Eyes
Conceal that emptiness, which Age descries.

[1] *determined*: ended.
[2] The reference is to the Divine Poems which Waller had added in the previous edition of his poems in 1682, when he was seventy-six years old.

142

The Soul's dark Cottage, batter'd and decay'd,
Lets in new Light thro chinks that time has made.
Stronger by weakness, wiser Men become
As they draw near to their Eternal home:
Leaving the Old, both Worlds at once they view,
That stand upon the Threshold of the New.

(Poems, 1686)

SIR RICHARD FANSHAWE
(1608–1666)

*An Ode, upon occasion of His Majesties Proclamation
in the yeare 1630.[1] Commanding the Gentry to reside
upon their Estates in the Country*

> Now warre is all the world about,
> And every where *Erynnis*[2] raignes,
> Or else the Torch so late put out,
>   The stench remaines.
>
> *Holland* for many yeares hath beene
> Of Christian tragedies the stage,
> Yet seldome hath she play'd a Scene
>   Of bloudyer rage.
>
> And *France* that was not long compos'd,
> With civill Drummes againe resounds,
> And ere the old are fully clos'd,
>   Receives new wounds.

[1] In 1630 Charles made peace with Spain. Holland saw the campaigns of Frederick Henry against the Imperial troops, and France, the 'Day of the Dupes'. Gustavus Adolphus, having made peace with Poland, landed on the Baltic coast to begin the campaign against the Imperial Generals Tilly and Wallenstein which culminated in the victory of Breitenfeld.

[2] *Erynnis*: a Fury, or goddess of vengeance.

The great *Gustavus* in the west,
Plucks the Imperiall Eagles wing,
Than whom the earth did ne're invest
    A fiercer King;

Revenging lost *Bohemia*,
And the proud wrongs which *Tilly* did,
And tempereth the *German* clay
    With *Spanish* bloud.

What should I tell of *Polish* Bands,
And the blouds boyling in the North?
'Gainst whom the furied *Russians*
    Their Troops bring forth:

Both confident: This in his purse,
And needy valour set on worke;
He in his Axe; which oft did worse
    Th'invading *Turke*.

Who now sustaines a *Persian* storme:
There hell (that made it) suffers schisme:
This warre (forsooth) was to reforme
    Mahumetisme.

Onely the Island which wee sowe,
(A world without the world) so farre
From present wounds, it cannot showe
    An ancient skarre.

White Peace (the beautiful'st of things)
Seemes here her everlasting rest
To fix, and spreads her downy wings
    Over the nest.

As when great *Jove*, usurping Reigne,
From the plagu'd world did her exile,
And ty'd her with a golden chaine
    To one blest Isle:

Which in a sea of plenty swamme
And Turtles sang on ev'ry bowgh,
A safe retreat to all that came
    As ours is now.

Yet wee, as if some foe were here,
Leave the despised Fields to clownes,
And come to save our selves as 'twere
    In walled Townes.

Hither we bring Wives, Babes, rich clothes
And Gemms; Till now my Soveraigne
The growing evill doth oppose:
    Counting in vaine

His care preserves us from annoy
Of enemyes his Realmes t'invade,
Unlesse hee force us to enjoy
    The peace hee made.

To rowle themselves in envy'd leasure
He therefore sends the Landed Heyres,
Whilst hee proclaimes not his owne pleasure
    So much as theirs.

The sapp and bloud o'th'land, which fled
Into the roote, and choakt the heart,
Are bid their quickning pow'r to spread
    Through ev'ry part.[1]

O, 'twas an act, not for my muse
To celebrate, nor the dull Age
Untill the country aire infuse
    A purer rage!

---

[1] The gentry will be better employed on their estates than in coming up to the capital to make trouble in Parliament. After the dissolution of 1629 Charles did not summon a Parliament for eleven years.

And if the Fields as thankfull prove
For benefits receiv'd, as seed,
They will, to quite so great a love,
    A *Virgill* breed.

A *Tityrus*, that shall not cease
Th'*Augustus* of our world to praise
In equall verse, author of peace
    And *Halcyon* dayes.

Nor let the Gentry grudge to goe
Into those places whence they grew,
But thinke them blest they may doe soe.
    Who would pursue

The smoaky glory of the Towne,
That may goe till his native earth,
And by the shining fire sit downe
    Of his owne hearth,

Free from the griping Scriveners bands,
And the more byting Mercers books;
Free from the bayt of oyled hands
    And painted looks?

The country too ev'n chopps for raine:
You that exhale it by your power,
Let the fat dropps fall downe againe
    In a full showre.

And you bright beautyes of the time,
That waste your selves here in a blaze,
Fixe to your Orbe and proper clime
    Your wandring rayes.

Let no darke corner of the Land
Be unimbellisht with one Gemme;
And those which here too thick doe stand
    Sprinkle on them.

Beleeve me Ladies you will finde
In that sweet life, more solid joyes,
More true contentment to the minde
      Than all Town-toyes.

Nor *Cupid* there lesse bloud doth spill,
But heads his shafts with chaster love,
Not feathered with a Sparrowes[1] quill,
      But of a Dove.

There shall you heare the Nightingale
(The harmelesse Syren of the wood)
How prettily she tells a tale
      Of rape and blood.[2]

The lyrricke Larke, with all beside
Of natures feathered quire: and all
The Common-wealth of Flowres in'ts pride
      Behold you shall.

The Lillie (Queene), the (Royall) Rose,
The Gillyflowre (Prince of the bloud),
The (Courtyer) Tulip (gay in clothes),
      The (Regal) Budd,

The Violet (purple Senatour),
How they doe mocke the pompe of State,
And all that at the surly doore
      Of great ones waite.

Plant Trees you may, and see them shoote
Up with your Children, to be serv'd
To your cleane boards, and the fair'st Fruite
      To be preserv'd:

[1] The Sparrow, the bird of Venus, was lecherous.
[2] The rape of Philomela by Tereus and the vengeance of her sister Progne (see Ovid, *Metam.* vi).

And learne to use their severall gummes;
'Tis innocence in the sweet blood
Of Cherrye, Apricocks and Plummes
    To be imbru'd.

The Fall[1]

The bloudy trunck of him who did possesse
    Above the rest a haplesse happy state,
This little Stone doth Seale, but not depresse,
    And scarce can stop the rowling of his fate.

Brasse Tombes which justice hath deny'd t'his fault,
    The common pity to his vertues payes,
Adorning an Imaginary vault,
    Which from our minds time strives in vaine to raze.

Ten yeares the world upon him falsly smil'd,
    Sheathing in fawning lookes the deadly knife
Long aymed at his head; That so beguild
    It more securely might bereave his Life.

Then threw him to a Scaffold from a Throne.
Much Doctrine lyes under this little Stone.

                    (*Il Pastor Fido*, &c., 1648)

[1] Translated from the Spanish of a sonnet by Gongora. Fanshawe may have been struck by its applicability to the fall of Strafford. It is not known where he was buried: the tomb erected at Wentworth Woodhouse after the Restoration is a cenotaph.

JOHN MILTON

(1608–1674)

On Shakespear. *1630*[1]

What needs my *Shakespear* for his honour'd Bones
The labour of an age in piled Stones,
Or that his hallow'd reliques should be hid
Under a Star-ypointing *Pyramid*?
Dear son of memory, great heir of Fame,
What need'st thou such weak witnes of thy name?
Thou in our wonder and astonishment
Hast built thy self a live-long Monument.
For whilst to th' shame of slow-endeavouring art,
Thy easie numbers flow, and that each heart
Hath from the leaves of thy unvalu'd Book,
Those Delphick lines with deep impression took,
Then thou our fancy of it self bereaving,
Dost make us Marble with too much conceaving;
And so Sepulcher'd in such pomp dost lie,
That Kings for such a Tomb would wish to die.

On the University Carrier[2] *who sickn'd in the time of his vacancy, being forbid to go to* London, *by reason of the* Plague

Here lies old *Hobson*, Death hath broke his girt,
And here alas, hath laid him in the dirt,
Or·els the ways being foul, twenty to one,
He's here stuck in a slough, and overthrown.

[1] First printed in the Second Folio of Shakespeare's Works, 1632.
[2] Hobson, the University Carrier, died 1 Jan. 1631.

'Twas such a shifter, that if truth were known,
Death was half glad when he had got him down;
For he had any time this ten yeers full,
Dodg'd with him, betwixt *Cambridge* and the Bull.
And surely, Death could never have prevail'd,
Had not his weekly course of carriage fail'd;
But lately finding him so long at home,
And thinking now his journeys end was come,
And that he had tane up his latest Inne,
In the kind office of a Chamberlin
Shew'd him his room where he must lodge that night,
Pull'd off his Boots, and took away the light:
If any ask for him, it shall be sed,
Hobson has supt, and's newly gone to bed.

On Time[1]

Fly envious *Time*, till thou run out thy race,
Call on the lazy leaden-stepping hours,
Whose speed is but the heavy Plummets pace;
And glut thy self with what thy womb devours,
Which is no more than what is false and vain,
And meerly mortal dross;
So little is our loss,
So little is thy gain.
For when as each thing bad thou hast entomb'd,
And last of all, thy greedy self consum'd,
Then long Eternity shall greet our bliss
With an individual kiss;
And Joy shall overtake us as a flood,
When every thing that is sincerely good
And perfectly divine,
With Truth, and Peace, and Love shall ever shine

[1] Its position in the Trinity College manuscript and in the *Poems* of 1645 suggests that this poem was written after Milton left Cambridge, at Horton. In the manuscript it has a cancelled title 'Set on a Clock Case'.

About the supreme Throne
Of him, t'whose happy-making sight alone,
When once our heav'nly guided soul shall clime,
Then all this Earthy grosnes quit,
Attir'd with Stars, we shall for ever sit,
    Triumphing over Death, and Chance, and thee O Time.

(Poems, 1645)

SIR JOHN SUCKLING
(1609–1642)

Song

Why so pale and wan fond Lover?
    Prithee why so pale?
Will, when looking well can't move her,
    Looking ill prevaile?
    Prithee why so pale?

Why so dull and mute young Sinner?
    Prithee why so mute?
Will, when speaking well can't win her,
    Saying nothing doo't?
    Prithee why so mute?

Quit, quit, for shame, this will not move,
    This will not take her;
If of her selfe she will not Love,
    Nothing can make her:
    The Devill take her.

(Aglaura, 1638)

Sonnet

Of thee (kind boy) I ask no red and white
　　To make up my delight,
　　No odd becoming graces,
Black eyes, or little know-not-whats, in faces;
Make me but mad enough, give me good store
Of Love, for her I court,
　　　　　　I ask no more,
'Tis love in love that makes the sport.

There's no such thing as that we beauty call,
　　It is meer cosenage all;
　　For though some long ago
Lik'd certain colours mingled so and so,
That doth not tie me now from chusing new;
If I a fancy take
　　　　　To black and blue,
That fancy doth it beauty make.

'Tis not the meat, but 'tis the appetite
　　Makes eating a delight,
　　And if I like one dish
More than another, that a Pheasant is;
What in our watches, that in us is found,
So to the height and nick
　　　　　We up be wound,
No matter by what hand or trick.

Sonnet

Oh! for some honest Lovers ghost,
　　Some kind unbodied post
　　Sent from the shades below.
　　I strangely long to know

Whether the nobler Chaplets wear,
Those that their mistresse scorn did bear,
  Or those that were us'd kindly.

For what-so-e'er they tell us here
  To make those sufferings dear,
    'Twill there I fear be found,
    That to the being crown'd,
T'have lov'd alone will not suffice,
Unlesse we also have been wise,
  And have our Loves enjoy'd.

What posture can we think him in,
  That here unlov'd agen
    Departs and's thither gone
    Where each sits by his own?
Or how can that *Elizium* be
Where I my Mistresse still must see
  Circled in others Armes?

For there the Judges all are just,
  And *Sophonisba*[1] must
    Be his whom she held dear;
    Not his who lov'd her here:
The sweet *Philoclea*[2] since she died
Lies by her *Pirocles* his side
  Not by *Amphialus*.

Some Bayes (perchance) or Myrtle bough
  For difference crowns the brow
    Of those kind souls that were
    The noble Martyrs here;
And if that be the onely odds
(As who can tell) ye kinder Gods,
  Give me the Woman here.

(Fragmenta Aurea, 1646)

[1] *Sophonisba*: daughter of Hasdrubal, betrothed to Masinissa, but married to Syphax.
[2] *Philoclea*: one of the two heroines of Sidney's *Arcadia*.

Song

Out upon it, I have lov'd,
   Three whole days together;
And am like to love three more,
   If it prove fair weather.

Time shall moult away his wings
   Ere he shall discover
In the whole wide world agen
   Such a constant Lover.

But the spite on't is, no praise
   Is due at all to me:
Love with me had made no staies,
   Had it any been but she.

Had it any been but she
   And that very Face,
There had been at least ere this
   A dozen dozen in her place.

(*Last Remains*, 1659)

SIDNEY GODOLPHIN
(1610–1643)

Constancye

Love unreturn'd, how ere the flame
Seeme great and pure, may still admit
Degrees of more, and a new name
And strength acceptance gives to it.

Till then, by honor ther's noe tie
Layd on it, that it ne're decay,
The minds last act by constancy
Ought to be seald, and not the way.

Did aught but loves perfection bind
Who should assigne at what degree
Of love, fayth ought to fix the mynd
And in what limits wee are free.

Soe hardly in a single harte
    Is any love conceived
That fancye still supplyes one part,
    Supposing it received.

When undeceiv'd such love retires
    'Tis but a modell lost,
A draught of what might be expires
    Built but at fancies cost.

Yet if the ruine one teare move,
    From pitty not Love sent,
Though not a Pallace, it will prove
    The most wisht monument.

Song

Or love me lesse, or love me more,
    And play not with my liberty,
Either take all, or all restore,
    Bind mee at least, or set mee free,
Let mee some nobler torture finde
    Than of a doubtfull wavering mynd,
Take all my peace, but you betray
    Myne honour too this cruell way.

'Tis true that I have nurst before
  That hope of which I now complaine,
And having little, sought noe more,
  Fearing to meet with your disdaine:
The sparks of favour you did give,
  I gently blew to make them live:
And yet have gaind by all this care
  Noe rest in hope, nor in despaire.

I see you weare that pittying smile
  Which you have still vouchsaft my smart,
Content thus cheapely to beguile
  And entertaine an harmelesse hart:
But I noe longer can give way
  To hope, which doth soe little pay;
And yet I dare noe freedome owe
  Whilst you are kind, though but in shew.

Then give me more or give me lesse
  Doe not disdaine a mutuall sence,
Or your unpittying beawties dresse
  In their owne free indifference.
But shew not a severer eye
  Sooner to give mee liberty
For I shall love the very scorne
  Which for my sake you doe put on.

Song

Noe more unto my thoughts appeare,
  At least appeare lesse Fayre,
For crazy tempers[1] justly Feare
  The goodnesse of the ayre;

---

[1] *crazy tempers*: delicate constitutions. Godolphin was 'of so nice and tender a composition, that a little rayne or winde would disorder him . . . when he ridd abroad with those in whose company he most delighted, if the winde chanced to be in his face, he would (after a little pleasant murmuringe) suddaynely turne his horse, and goe home' (Clarendon).

Whilst your pure Image hath a place
   In my Impurer Mynde,
Your very shaddow is the glasse
   Wher my defects I finde.

Shall I not Fly that brighter Light
   Which makes my Fyres look Pale,
And put that vertue out of sight
   Which makes Myne none at all?

No, no your picture doth impart
   Such valew, I not wish
The native worth to any heart
   That's unadorn'd with this.

Though poorer in desert I make
   My selfe, whilst I admyre,
The fuell which from hope I take
   I give to my desire.

If this flame lighted from your Eyes
   The subject doe calcine,
A Heart may bee your sacrifice
   Too weake to bee your shrine.

Hymn

Lord when the wise men came from farr,
Led to thy Cradle by a Starr,
Then did the shepheards too rejoyce,
Instructed by thy Angells voyce:
Blest were the wisemen in their skill,
And shepheards in their harmlesse will.

Wisemen in tracing Natures lawes
Ascend unto the highest cause,

Shepheards with humble fearefulnesse
Walke safely, though their light be lesse:
Though wisemen better know the way
It seemes noe honest heart can stray.

Ther is noe merrit in the wise
But love, (the shepheards sacrifice).
Wisemen all wayes of knowledge past,
To th'shepheards wonder come at last:
To know, can only wonder breede,
And not to know, is wonders seede.

A wiseman at the Altar bowes
And offers up his studied vowes
And is received; may not the teares,
Which spring too from a shepheards feares,
And sighs upon his fraylty spent,
Though not distinct, be eloquent?

'Tis true, the object sanctifies
All passions which within us rise,
But since noe creature comprehends
The cause of causes, end of ends,
Hee who himselfe vouchsafes to know
Best pleases his creator soe.

When then our sorrowes wee applye
To our owne wantes and poverty,
When wee looke up in all distresse
And our owne misery confesse,
Sending both thankes and prayers above,
Then though wee doe not know, we love.

                              (Bodleian Library, MS. Malone 13)

WILLIAM CARTWRIGHT

(1611–1643)

To Chloe *who wish'd her self young enough for me*

Chloe, why wish you that your years
  Would backwards run, till they meet mine,
That perfect Likeness, which endears
  Things unto things, might us Combine?
Our Ages so in date agree,
That Twins do differ more than we.

There are two Births, the one when Light
  First strikes the new awak'ned sense;
The Other when two Souls unite;
  And we must count our life from thence:
When you lov'd me, and I lov'd you,
Then both of us were born anew.

Love then to us did new Souls give,
  And in those Souls did plant new pow'rs;
Since when another life we live,
  The Breath we breathe is his, not ours;
Love makes those young, whom Age doth Chill,
And whom he finds young, keeps young still.

Love, like that Angell that shall call
  Our bodies from the silent Grave,
Unto one Age doth raise us all,
  None too much, none too little have;
Nay that the difference may be none,
He makes two not alike, but One.

And now since you and I are such,
  Tell me what's yours, and what is mine?
Our Eyes, our Ears, our Taste, Smell, Touch,
  Do (like our Souls) in one Combine;
So by this, I as well may be
Too old for you, as you for me.

A New-years-gift to Brian Lord Bishop of Sarum,[1] upon the Authors entring into holy Orders, 1638

Now that the Village-Reverence doth lye hid,
          As Ægypt's Wisdom did,
In Birds, and Beasts, and that the Tenants Soul,
          Goes with his New-year's fowl:
      So that the Cock, and Hen, speak more
      Now, than in Fables heretofore;
          And that the feather'd Things
          Truly make Love have Wings;
Though we no flying Present have to pay,
A Quill yet snatch'd from thence may sign the Day.

But being the Canon bars me Wit and Wine,
          Enjoyning the true Vine,
Being the Bayes must yeeld unto the Cross,
          And all be now one Loss,
      So that my Raptures are to steal
      And knit themselves in one pure Zeal,
          And that my each days breath
          Must be a dayly Death;
Without all Strain or Fury, I must then
Tell you this New-year brings you a new man.

[1] Brian Duppa (1588–1662), Dean of Christ Church (1628), Vice-Chancellor (1632), was tutor to the Prince of Wales. He was made Bishop of Chichester in 1638 and of Salisbury in 1641. (The poem gives him his title at date of publication.) He was one of the nine Bishops to survive until the Restoration and one of those who continued to ordain through the interregnum.

New, not as th'year, to run the same Course o'r
    Which it hath run before,
Lest in the Man himself there be a Round
    As in his Humor's found,
    And that return seem to make good
    Circling of Actions, as of Bloud;
      Motion as in a Mill
      Is busie standing still;
And by such wheeling we but thus prevaile,
To make the Serpent swallow his own Taile.

Nor new by solemnizing looser Toyes,
    And erring with less Noyse,
Taking the Flag and Trumpet from the Sin,
    So to offend within:
    As some Men silence loud Perfumes,
    And draw them into shorter Rooms,
      This will be understood
      More wary, not more Good.
Sins too may be severe, and so no doubt
The Vice but only sowr'd, not rooted out.

But new, by th'Using of each part aright,
    Changing both Step and Sight,
That false Direction come not from the Eye,
    Nor the foot tread awry,
    That neither that the way aver,
    Which doth tow'rd Fame, or Profit err,
      Nor this tread that Path, which
      Is not the right, but Rich;
That thus the Foot being fixt, thus lead the Eye,
I pitch my Walk low, but my Prospect high.

New too, to teach my Opinions not t'submit
    To Favour, or to Wit;
Nor yet to Walk on Edges, where they may
    Run safe in Broader way;

Nor to search out for New Paths, where
Nor Tracks nor Footsteps doth appear,
    Knowing that Deeps are waies,
    Where no Impression staies,
Nor servile thus, nor curious, may I then
Approve my Faith to Heaven, my Life to Men.

But I who thus present my self as New,
    Am thus made New by You:
Had not your Rayes dwelt on me, One long Night
    Had shut me up from Sight;
    Your Beams exhale me from among
    Things tumbling in the Common Throng,
      Who thus with your fire burns
      Now gives not, but Returns;
To Others then be this a day of Thrift
They do receive, but you Sir make the Gift.

(Poems, 1651)

On the Queens Return from the Low Countries[1]

Hallow the Threshold, Crown the Posts anew;
    The day shall have its due:
Twist all our Victories into one bright wreath,
    On which let Honour breath;
Then throw it round the Temples of our *Queene*;
'Tis Shee that must preserve those glories green.

When greater Tempests, than on Sea before,
    Receav'd Her on the shore,
When She was shot at, for the King's own good,
    By Villaines hir'd to Blood;

[1] Henrietta Maria, who had gone abroad in 1642 to raise money and arms for the King, returned in Feb. 1643. She was fired on as she landed. Her return was greeted by loyal Oxford with a volume of verses to which Cartwright contributed this and a Latin poem.

How bravely did Shee doe, how bravely Beare,
And shew'd, though they durst rage, Shee durst not feare.

Courage was cast about Her like a Dresse
   Of solemne Comelinesse;
A gather'd Mind, and an untroubled Face
   Did give Her dangers grace.
Thus arm'd with Innocence, secure they move,
Whose Highest Treason is but Highest Love.

As some Bright Starre, that runnes a Direct Course,
   Yet with Anothers force,
Mixeth its vertue in a full dispence
   Of one joynt influence,
Such was Her mind to th'Kings, in all was done;
The Agents Diverse, but the Action One.

Look on Her Enemies, on their Godly Lyes,
   Their Holy Perjuries,
Their Curs'd encrease of much ill gotten Wealth,
   By Rapine or by stealth.
Their crafty Friendships knit by equall guilt,
And the Crown-Martyrs blood[1] so lately spilt.

Look then upon Her selfe; Beauteous in Mind,
   Scarce Angells more refin'd;
Her actions Blancht, Her Conscience still Her sway,
   And that not fearing Day:
Then you'l confesse Shee casts a double Beame,
Much shining by Her selfe, but more by Them.

Receive Her then as the new springing Light
   After a tedious Night:
As Holy Hermits doe Revealed Truth;
   Or *Æson* did his youth.
Her presence is our Guard, our Strength, our Store;
The cold snatch some flames thence, the valiant more.

---

[1] The Crown-Martyr is Strafford, executed May 1641.

But something yet, our Holy Priests will say,
    Is wanting to the Day:
'Twere sinne to let so Blest a feast arise
    Without a Sacrifice.
True, if our Flocks were full. But being all
Are gone, the Many-headed Beast must fall.

(*Musarum Oxoniensium Epibateria*, 1643)

RICHARD CRASHAW
(1612–1649)

Wishes
To his (supposed) Mistresse

Who ere shee bee,
That not impossible shee
That shall command my heart and mee;

Where ere shee lye,
Lock't up from mortall Eye,
In shady leaves of Destiny:

Till that ripe Birth
Of studied fate stand forth,
And teach her faire steps to our Earth;

Till that Divine
Idaea, take a shrine
Of Chrystall flesh, through which to shine:

Meet you her my wishes,
Bespeake her to my blisses,
And be yee call'd my absent kisses.

I wish her Beauty,
That owes not all his Duty
To gaudy Tire, or glistring shoo-ty.

Something more than
Taffata or Tissew can,
Or rampant feather, or rich fan.

More than the spoyle
Of shop, or silkewormes Toyle
Or a bought blush, or a set smile.

A face thats best
By its owne beauty drest,
And can alone command the rest.

A face made up
Out of no other shop,
Than what natures white hand sets ope.

A cheeke where Youth,
And Blood, with Pen of Truth
Write, what the Reader sweetly ru'th.

A Cheeke where growes
More than a Morning Rose:
Which to no Boxe his being owes.

Lipps, where all Day
A lovers kisse may play,
Yet carry nothing thence away.

Lookes that oppresse
Their richest Tires but dresse
And cloath their simplest Nakednesse.

Eyes, that displaces
The Neighbour Diamond, and out faces
That Sunshine by their owne sweet Graces.

Tresses, that weare
Jewells, but to declare
How much themselves more pretious are.

Whose native Ray,
Can tame the wanton Day
Of Gems, that in their bright shades play.

Each Ruby there,
Or Pearle that dare appeare,
Bee its owne blush, bee its own Teare.

A well-tam'd Heart,
For whose more noble smart,
Love may bee long chusing a Dart.

Eyes, that bestow
Full quivers on loves Bow;
Yet pay lesse Arrowes than they owe.

Smiles, that can warme
The blood, yet teach a charme,
That Chastity shall take no harme.

Blushes, that bin
The burnish of no sin,
Nor flames of ought too hot within.

Joyes, that confesse,
Vertue their Mistresse,
And have no other head to dresse.

Feares, fond and flight,
As the coy Brides, when Night
First does the longing lover right.

Teares, quickly fled,
And vaine, as those are shed
For a dying Maydenhead.

Dayes, that need borrow
No part of their good Morrow
From a fore spent night of sorrow.

Dayes, that in spight
Of Darkenesse, by the Light
Of a cleere mind are Day all Night.

Nights, sweet as they,
Made short by lovers play,
Yet long by th'absence of the Day.

Life, that dares send
A challenge to his end,
And when it comes say *Welcome Friend.*

Sydnaean showers
Of sweet discourse, whose powers
Can Crowne old Winters head with flowers,

Soft silken Houres,
Open sunnes; shady Bowers,
Bove all; Nothing within that lowres.

What ere Delight
Can make Dayes forehead bright;
Or give Downe to the Wings of Night.

In her whole frame,
Have Nature all the Name,
Art and ornament the shame.

Her flattery,
Picture and Poesy,
Her counsell her owne vertue bee.

I wish, her store
Of worth, may leave her poore
Of wishes; And I wish—No more.

Now if Time knowes
That her whose radiant Browes,
Weave them a Garland of my vowes;

Her whose just Bayes,
My future hopes can raise,
A trophie to her present praise,

Her that dares bee,
What these Lines wish to see:
I seeke no further, it is shee.

'Tis shee, and heere
Lo I uncloath and cleare,
My wishes cloudy Character.

May shee enjoy it,
Whose merit dare apply it,
But Modesty dares still deny it.

Such worth as this is
Shall fixe my flying wishes,
And determine them to kisses.

Let her full Glory,
My fancies, fly before yee,
Be ye my fictions; But her story.

(*Delights of the Muses*, 1646)

RICHARD CRASHAW

On Hope,
By way of *Question and Answer*, *betweene*
A. Cowley, *and* R. Crashaw[1]

COWLEY

Hope, whose weake being ruin'd is
Alike, if it succeed, and if it misse.
Whom Ill, and Good doth equally confound,
And both the hornes of Fates dilemma wound.
 Vaine shadow! that doth vanish quite
 Both at full noone, and perfect night.
 The Fates have not a possibility
  Of blessing thee.
If things then from their ends wee happy call,
'Tis hope is the most hopelesse thing of all.

CRASHAW

 Deare Hope! Earths dowry, and Heavens debt,
The entity of things that are not yet.
Subt'lest, but surest being! Thou by whom
Our Nothing hath a definition.
 Faire cloud of fire, both shade, and light,
 Our life in death, our day in night.
 Fates cannot find out a capacity
  Of hurting thee.
From thee their thinne dilemma with blunt horne
Shrinkes, like the sick Moone at the wholsome morne.

---

[1] Cowley's poem, here italicized, appeared separately, with minor differ-
ences, in the following year (1647) in *The Mistress*. In *Carmen Deo Nostre*
(1652) Crashaw's poem, with considerable alterations, was printed following Cowley's. I give the first version to preserve the question and answer
form; but I have corrected the arrangement of the verses to make the
second and third of Crashaw's follow the second of Cowley's, to which
they are the answer. In the edition stanzas by Cowley and Crashaw are
made to alternate which leaves Crashaw with two stanzas at the end.

COWLEY

Hope, thou bold taster of delight,
Who, in stead of doing so, devour'st it quite.
Thou bring'st us an estate, yet leav'st us poore,
By clogging it with Legacies before.
  The joyes which wee intire should wed,
  Come deflour'd virgins to our bed.
  Good fortunes without gaine imported bee,
    So mighty Custome's paid to thee.
For joy, like Wine kept close doth better taste:
If it take ayre before, its spirits waste.

CRASHAW

Thou art Loves Legacie under lock
Of Faith: the steward of our growing stocke.
Our Crown-lands lye above, yet each meale brings
A seemly portion for the Sons of Kings.
  Nor will the Virgin-joyes wee wed
  Come lesse unbroken to our bed,
  Because that from the bridall cheeke of Blisse,
    Thou thus steal'st downe a distant kisse,
Hopes chaste kisse wrongs no more joyes maidenhead,
Than Spousall rites prejudge the marriage-bed.

  Faire *Hope!* our earlier Heaven! by thee
Young *Time* is taster to Eternity.
The generous wine with age growes strong, not sower;
Nor need wee kill thy fruit to smell thy flower.
  Thy golden head never hangs downe,
  Till in the lap of Loves full noone
  It falls, and dyes: oh no, it melts away
    As doth the dawne into the day:
As lumpes of Sugar lose themselves, and twine
Their subtile essence with the soule of Wine.

COWLEY

Hope, Fortunes cheating Lotterie,
Where for one prize an hundred blankes there bee.
Fond Archer Hope, who tak'st thine ayme so farre,
That still, or short, or wide thine arrowes are.
   Thine empty cloud the eye it selfe deceives
   With shapes that our owne fancie gives:
   A cloud, which gilt, and painted now appeares,
      But must drop presently in teares.
When thy false beames o're Reasons light prevaile,
By ignes fatui, *not North starres we sayle.*

CRASHAW

Fortune alas above the worlds law warres:
Hope kicks the curl'd heads of conspiring starres.
Her keele cuts not the waves, where our winds stirre,
And *Fates* whole Lottery is one blanke to her.
   Her shafts, and shee fly farre above,
   And forrage in the fields of light, and love.
   Sweet *Hope!* kind cheat! faire fallacy! by thee
      Wee are not where, or what wee bee,
But what, and where wee would bee: thus art thou
Our absent presence, and our future now.

COWLEY

Brother of Feare! more gaily clad
The merrier Foole o'th'two, yet quite as mad.
Sire of Repentance! Child of fond desire,
That blows the Chymicks, and the Lovers fire,
   Still leading them insensibly on,
   With the strange witchcraft of Anon.
   By thee the one doth changing Nature through
      Her endlesse Laborinths pursue,
And th'other chases woman, while she goes
More wayes, and turnes, than hunted Nature knowes.

CRASHAW

Faiths Sister! Nurse of faire desire!
Feares Antidote! a wise, and well-stay'd fire,
Temper'd 'twixt cold despaire, and torrid joy:
Queen Regent in young Loves minoritie.
 Though the vext Chymick vainly chases
 His fugitive gold through all her faces,
 And loves more fierce, more fruitlesse fires assay
 One face more fugitive than all they,
True *Hope's* a glorious Huntresse, and her chase
The God of Nature in the field of Grace.

And he answered them nothing

O Mighty *Nothing!* unto thee,
Nothing, wee owe all things that bee.
God spake once when hee all things made,
He sav'd all when hee *Nothing* said.
The world was made of *Nothing* then;
'Tis made by *Nothing* now againe.

To our Lord, upon the *Water made Wine*

Thou water turn'st to Wine (faire friend of Life)
 Thy foe to crosse the sweet Arts of thy Reigne
Distills from thence the Teares of wrath and strife,
 And so turnes wine to Water backe againe.

     (*Steps to the Temple*, 1646)

The Weeper

Loe where a wounded heart, with bleeding eyes conspire;
Is she a flaming fountaine, or a weeping fire?

  Haile, Sister Springs,
 Parents of Silver-footed rills!
  Ever bubling things!
 Thawing Crystall! Snowy hills!

Still spending, never spent; I meane
Thy faire eyes, sweet *Magdalen.*

Heavens thy faire eyes bee,
Heavens of ever falling starrs,
'Tis seed-time still with thee
And stars thou sow'st, whose harvest dares
Promise the earth to counter shine
What ever makes Heaven's forehead fine.

But we are deceived all,
Stars indeed they are too true,
For they but seeme to fall,
As heav'ns other spangles doe:
It is not for our Earth and us,
To shine in things so pretious.

Upwards thou dost weepe,
Heav'ns bosome drinkes the gentle streame,
Where the milky Rivers creepe
Thine floates above, and is the creame,
Waters above the Heavens, what they bee,
We'are taught best by thy Teares, and thee.

Every Morne from hence,
A brisk Cherub something sips,
Whose sacred influence
Adds sweetnes to his sweetest lips,
Then to his Musick, and his song
Tastes of his breakefast all day long.

Not in the Evening's eyes
When they red with weeping are
For the Sun that dyes,
Sits sorrow with a face so faire:
No where but here did ever meete
Sweetnesse so sadd, sadnesse so sweete.

When sorrow would be seene,
In her brightest Majestie,
   (For she is a Queene)
Then is she drest by none but thee.
Then, and onely then, she weares
Her proudest Pearls, I meane thy tears.

The dew no more will weepe,
   The Primroses pale cheeke to decke,
The dew no more will sleepe,
   Nuzzel'd in the Lyllies necke;
Much rather would it be thy teare,
And leave them both to tremble here.

There is no neede at all
   That the Balsome-sweating bough
So coylie should let fall
   His med'cinable teares; for now
Nature hath learn't t'extract a dew
More soveraigne, and sweet from you.

Yet let the poore drops weep
   (Weeping is the ease of woe)
Softly let them creepe,
   Sad that they are vanquisht so.
They though to others no reliefe,
Balsom may be for their own griefe.

Such the maiden Gemme
   By the purpling Vine put on
Peepes from her parent stemme
   And blushes at the Bridegroome Sun:
This watrie Blossom of thy Eyne,
Ripe, will make the richer Wine.

When some new bright guest
   Takes up among the Stars a Roome,
And Heav'n will make a feast
   Angells with Chrystall Vyalls come,

And draw from these full eyes of thine,
Their Master's Water; their owne wine.

Golden though he be,
Golden *Tagus* murmures though;
Were his way by thee,
Content and quiet he would goe:
So much more rich would he esteeme
Thy silver, than his golden streame.

Well does the *May* that lyes
Smiling in thy cheekes, confesse
The *Aprill* in thine eyes;
Mutuall sweetnesse they expresse:
No *Aprill* e're lent kinder showers,
Nor *May* return'd more faithfull flowers.

O cheekes! Beds of chast loves,
By your own showers seasonably dash't,
Eyes! nests of milkie Doves
In your own wells decently washt.
O wit of love that thus could place,
Fountaine and Garden in one face!

O sweet contest of woes
With loves, of tears with smiles disputing,
O fair and friendly foes
Each other kissing and confuting,
While raine and Sunshine, cheeks and eyes,
Close in kind contrarieties.

But can these fair flouds bee
Friends with the bosom fires that fill thee?
Can so great flames agree
Eternall teares should thus distill thee?
O flouds, O fires, O suns, O showers,
Mixt, and made friends by loves sweet powers.

'Twas his well pointed dart
That dig'd these wells, and drest this Vine,
And taught that wounded heart,
The way into those weeping Eyne.
Vaine loves avant! Bold hands forbeare,
The Lamb hath dipt his white foote here.

And now where e're he strayes
Among the Galilaean mountains,
Or more unwelcome wayes,
Hee's follow'd by two faithfull fountaines,
Two walking Baths, two weeping motions;
Portable and compendious Oceans.

O thou thy Lords faire store,
In thy so rich and rare expences,
Even when he show'd most poore,
He might provoke the wealth of Princes,
What Princes wanton'st pride e're could
Wash with silver, wipe with gold.

Who is that King, but he
Who calls't his crowne to be call'd thine,
That thus can boast to be
Waited on by a wandring mine,
A voluntary mint, that strowes
Warme silver showers, where e're he goes?

O pretious prodigall!
Faire spend-thrift of thy self! Thy measure
(Mercilesse love!) is all,
Even to the last Pearle in thy treasure:
All places, times, and objects be,
Thy teares sweet opportunity.

Does the day-star rise?
Still thy Stars doe fall, and fall;
Does day close his eyes?
Still the fountaine weeps for all:

Let night or day doe what they will,
Thou hast thy taske, thou weepest still.

Does thy song lull the aire?
Thy falling teares keep faithfull time.
Does thy sweet-breath'd praier
Up in clouds of incense climbe?
Still at each sigh, that is, each stop,
A bead, that is, a teare doth drop.

At these thy weeping gates
(Watching thy watrie motion)
Each winged moment waites,
Takes his teare, and gets him gon.
By thine eyes tinct enobled thus
Time layes him up: Hee's precious.

Not so long she lived
Shall thy tomb report of thee,
But so long she grieved,
Thus must we date thy memorie:
Others by moments, months, and years
Measure their ages, Thou by tears.

So doe perfumes expire,
So sigh tormented sweets, opprest
With proud unpittying fire;
Such tears the suffering Rose that's vext
With ungentle flames does shed
Sweating in a too warme bed.[1]

Say ye bright Brothers,
The fugitive sons of those fair eyes
Your fruitfull Mothers,
What make you here? what hopes can tice
You to be borne? what cause can borrow
You from those nests of noble sorrow?

[1] The whole verse refers to the distillation of perfumes from flowers by heat.

Whither away so fast?
For sure the sordid earth
  Your sweetness cannot taste,
  Nor does the dust deserve your Birth.
Sweet, whither haste you then? O say
Why you trip so fast away?

We goe not to seeke,
  The darlings of *Aurora's* bed,
  The Roses modest cheeke,
  Nor the Violets humble head:
Though the fields eyes too weepers bee,
Because they want such teares as wee.

Much lesse meane we to trace,
  The fortune of inferior gems,
  Prefer'd[1] to some proud face,
  Or pearch't upon fear'd diadems:
Crown'd heads are Toyes; We goe to meete,
A worthy object: Our Lord's Feet.

An Hymne of the Nativity, sung as by the Shepheards

CHORUS

Come we shepheards whose blest sight
  Hath met Loves noone in Natures night,
Come lift we up our loftier song,
  And wake the *Sun* that lyes too long.

To all our world of well-stoln joy,
  He slept, and dream't of no such thing;
While we found out Heav'ns fairer eye,
  And kist the cradle of our *King*,
Tell him he rises now too late,
To shew us ought worth looking at.

[1] *Prefer'd*: promoted.

Tell him we now can shew him more
   Than he e're shewd to mortall sight,
Than he himself e're saw before
   Which to be seen needs not his light;
Tell him *Tityrus* where th'hast been,
Tell him *Thyrsis* what th'hast seen.

TITYRUS

Gloomy night embrac't the place
   Where the noble Infant lay,
The *Babe* look't up and shew'd his face,
   In spite of darknesse it was day:
It was thy day, *Sweet*! and did rise,
Not from the *East*, but from thine eyes.

CHORUS

It was thy day, *Sweet*, *&c.*

THYRSIS

Winter chid aloud, and sent
   The angry North to wage his wars,
The North forgot his fierce intent,
   And left perfumes instead of scars,
By those sweet eyes perswasive powers,
Where he meant frost, he scatter'd flowers.

CHORUS

By those sweet Eyes, *&c.*

BOTH

We saw thee in thy Balmy Nest
   Bright *dawn* of our eternall *day*!
We saw thine eyes break from their *East*,
   And chace the trembling shades away,
We saw thee, and we blest the sight,
We saw thee by thine own sweet light.

TITYRUS

Poore world (said I) what wilt thou doe
  To entertaine this starrie *stranger*?
Is this the best thou canst bestow
  A cold, and not too cleanly *manger*?
Contend ye powers of heav'n and earth
To fit a bed for this huge birth.

CHORUS

Contend ye Powers, *&c.*

THYRSIS

Proud world (said I) cease your contest,
  And let the mighty *Babe* alone,
The Phoenix builds the Phoenix' nest
  Love's Architecture is his own.
The Babe whose Birth embraves this *morne,*
Made his own Bed e're he was borne.

CHORUS

The Babe, *&c.*

TITYRUS

I saw the curl'd drops, soft and slow,
  Come hovering ore the places head,
Offring their whitest sheets of snow,
  To furnish the fair *Infant's* Bed:
Forbeare (said I) be not too bold
Your fleece is white, but 'tis too cold.

CHORUS

Forbeare (sayd I) *&c.*

RICHARD CRASHAW

THYRSIS

I saw the obsequious *Seraphins*
   Their Rosie *Fleece* of *Fire* bestow,
For well they now can spare their wings
   Since Heaven it selfe lyes here below:
Well done (said I) but are you sure
Your downe so warme, will passe for pure?

CHORUS

Well done sayd I, *&c.*

TITYRUS

No, no, your *King's* not yet to seeke
   Where to repose his Royall *Head*,
See, see, how soone his new-bloom'd *cheeke*
   Twixt's mothers brests is gone to bed.
Sweet choice (said I) no way but so
Not to lye cold, yet sleep in snow.

CHORUS

Sweet choice, *&c.*

BOTH

We saw thee in thy Balmy nest
   Bright *Dawn* of our eternall *Day*,
We saw thine eyes breake from their *East*
   And chase the trembling shades away,
We saw thee, and we blest the sight,
We saw thee, by thine own sweet light.

CHORUS

We saw thee, *&c.*

FULL CHORUS

Wellcome, all *wonders* in one sight!
   Eternitie shut in a span,
Summer in winter, day in night,
   Heaven in Earth, and God in man;
Great little one! whose all embracing birth
Lifts earth to heav'n, stoops heav'n to earth.

Welcome, though not to gold nor silke,
   To more than *Caesar's* birthright is;
Two Sister-Seas of Virgin *Milke*,
   With many a rarely temper'd Kisse
That breathes at once both *Maide* and *Mother*,
Warmes in the one, cooles in the other.

She sings thy Teares a sleep, and dips
   Her Kisses in thy weeping eye,
She spreads the red leaves of thy lips,
   That in their buds yet blushing lye,
She 'gainst those Mother-Diamonds tries
The points of her young Eagles eyes.

Welcome, though not to those gay flyes
   Guilded i'th'beames of earthly Kings,
Slippery soules in smiling eyes,
   But to poor Shepheards, home-spun things,
Whose wealth's their flock; whose wit to be
Well read in their simplicitie.

Yet when young *Aprill's* husband showers
   Shall blesse the fruitfull *Maia's* bed,
Wee'l bring the first-borne of her flowers,
   To kisse thy feet, and crowne thy head.
To thee dread *Lamb!* whose love must keepe
The shepheards more than they their sheepe.

To thee, meeke *Majestie!* soft King
   Of simple *Graces* and sweet *Loves,*
Each of us his *Lamb* will bring,
   Each his paire of Silver Doves,
Till burnt at last in fire of thy faire eyes,
Our selves become our owne best sacrifice.

Hymn to Sainte Teresa[1]

Love thou art absolute sole Lord
Of life and death.—To prove the word,
Wee'l now appeale to none of all
Those thy old Souldiers, Great and tall
Ripe men of Martyrdome, that could reach downe,
With strong armes, their Triumphant crowne:
Such as could with lustie breath,
Speake loud into the face of death,
Their great Lord's glorious name; To none
Of those whose spatious bosomes spread a throne
For love at large to fill: spare Blood and sweat,
And see him take a privat seat,
Making his mansion in the mild
And milky soule of a soft child.
Scarce hath she learnt to lisp the name,
Of Martyr; yet she thinkes it shame
Life should so long play with that breath,
Which spent can buy so brave a death.
She never undertooke to know,
What death with love should have to doe;
Nor hath she e're yet understood
Why to shew love, she should shed blood,

[1] St. Teresa of Avila (1515–1582), foundress of the Order of Discalced (reformed) Carmelites. Her childish attempt to court martyrdom by preaching to the Moors is recounted in her autobiography, as is the vision in which a seraph plunged a fiery lance into her heart. She was canonized in 1622.

Yet though she can not tell you why,
She can *love*, and she can *dye*.
Scarce hath she blood enough, to make
A guilty sword blush for her sake;
Yet hath she a heart dare hope to prove,
How much lesse strong is Death than Love.
Be Love but there, let poore six yeares
Be pos'd with the maturest feares
Man trembles at, you streight shall find
Love knowes no nonage, nor the Mind.
'Tis *Love*, not years nor Limbs, that can
Make the *Martyr* or the *Man*.
Love toucht her *Heart*, and lo it beates
High, and burnes with such brave Heates,
Such *Thirsts* to dye, as dares drink up,
A thousand cold *Deaths* in one cup.
Good reason; for she breathes all *fire*,
Her weake brest heaves with strong desire,
Of what she may with fruitlesse wishes
Seeke for amongst her Mothers Kisses.

Since 'tis not to be had at home,
Shee'l travell for *A Martyrdome*.
No *Home* for hers confesses she,
But where she may a Martyr be.
Shee'l to the *Moores* and trade with them,
For this unvalued *Diadem*,
Shee'l offer them her dearest Breath,
With *Christ's* name in't, in change for death.
Shee'l bargain with them, and will give
Them God, and teach them how to live
In him; Or if they this deny,
For him, she'l teach them how to dye.
So shall she leave amongst them sown,
Her *Lord's* Blood, or at least her *own*.
Farewell then all the world! Adiew,

Teresa is no more for you:
Farewell all pleasures, sports, and joys,
(Never till now esteemed *Toyes*)
Farewell what ever deare may bee,
Mother's armes or Father's Knee.
Farewell house and farewell home,
She's for the *Moores*, and *Martyrdome*.

Sweet not so fast! Lo thy faire *Spouse*,
Whom thou seekst with so swift vowes
Calls thee back, and bidds thee come,
T'embrace a milder Martyrdome.
Blest powers forbid thy tender life,
Should bleed upon a barbarous Knife;
Or some base hand have power to race
Thy Brest's soft cabinet, and uncase
A soule kept there so sweet. O no;
Wise Heaven will never have it so.
Thou art *Loves* Victim; and must dye
A death more mysticall and *high*.
Into *Loves* armes thou shalt let fall
A still surviving funerall.
His is the *Dart* must make the *Death*
Whose stroake shall taste thy hallow'd *breath*;
A Dart thrice dipt in that rich *flame*,
Which writes thy spouses radiant *Name*,
Upon the roofe of Heav'n, where ay
It shines, and with a sovereigne Ray
Beates bright upon the burning faces
Of soules, which in that Name's sweet graces
Find everlasting smiles; so rare,
So spirituall, pure, and faire,
Must be th' immortall instrument,
Upon whose choice point shall be sent,
A life so lov'd; And that there be
Fit executioners for thee,

The fair'st and first borne sons of fire,
Blest *Seraphims*, shall leave their Quire,
And turne *Love's Souldiers*, upon thee,
To exercise their *Archerie*.
O how oft shalt thou complaine
Of a sweet and subtile *paine!*
Of intollerable *joyes!*
Of a *death*, in which who *dyes*
Loves his *death*, and dyes againe,
And would for ever so be slaine!
And lives, and dyes; and knowes not why
To live; But that he thus may never leave to dye.
How kindly will thy gentle *Heart*
Kisse the sweetly-killing *Dart!*
And close in his embraces keepe,
Those *delicious wounds* that *weepe*
Balsome to heale themselves with. Thus
When these thy *Deathes*, so numerous,
Shall all at last dye into one,
And melt thy soules sweet *mansion;*
Like a soft lump of Incense, hasted
By too hot a fire, and wasted
Into perfuming clouds, so fast
Shalt thou exhale to Heav'n at last,
In a resolving sigh, and then,
O what? . . . aske not the tongues of men.
Angells cannot tell. Suffice,
Thy self shall feele thine own full joyes,
And hold them fast for ever. There,
So soon as thou shalt first *appeare*,
The Moon of maiden stars, thy white
Mistresse, attended by such bright
Soules as thy shining-self, shall come,
And in her first rankes make thee roome.
Where 'mongst her snowy family
Immortall welcomes waite for thee.
O what delight, when reveal'd life shall stand,

And teach thy lips heav'n with his hand,
On which thou now maist to thy wishes,
Heape up thy *consecrated kisses!*
What joyes shall seize thy soule, when she
Bending her blessed eyes on thee
(Those second smiles of Heav'n) shall dart
Her mild rayes through thy melting Heart!
Angells thy old friends, there shall greet thee,
Glad at their owne home now to meet thee.
All thy good works which went before,
And waited for thee at the doore,
Shall owne thee there; and all in one
Weave a *Constellation*
Of crownes with which the King thy spouse,
Shall build up thy triumphant browes.
All thy old woes shall now smile on thee,
And thy Paines sit bright upon thee.
All thy sorrows here shall shine,
And thy suff'rings be divine;
Teares shall take comfort, and turn *Gems*,
And *wrongs* repent to *Diadems*.
Ev'n thy *Deaths* shall live; and new
Dresse the soule, that erst they slew.
Thy Wounds shall blush to such bright scars,
As keep accompt of the *Lamb's* wars.
Those *rare workes* where thou shalt leave writ,
Loves noble *Historie*, with wit
Taught thee by none but him, while here
They feed our *soules*, shall cloath thine there.
Each heav'nly word, by whose hid flame
Our hard hearts shall strike fire, the same
Shall flourish on thy browes, and be
Both *fire* to us, and *flame* to thee;
Whose light shall live bright, in thy Face
By *glorie*, in our Hearts by *grace*.
Thou shalt looke round about, and see
Thousands of crown'd soules throng to bee

Themselves thy *crowne*; sonnes of thy vowes,
The virgin-births, with which thy soveraigne spouse
Made fruitfull thy faire soul. Goe now
And with them all about thee, bow
To him, Put on (hee'l say) put on
(*My Rosie Love*) That thy rich Zone,
Sparkling with the sacred flames,
Of thousand soules, whose happy names
Heav'n keeps upon thy score (Thy bright
Life brought them first to kisse the light
That kindled them to stars) and so
Thou with the *Lamb*, thy Lord, shalt goe;
And where soe're he sets his white
Steps, walk with *Him* those waies of light,
Which who in death would live to see,
Must learne in life to dye like Thee.

> (*Steps to the Temple*, 1648: revised and
> expanded versions of poems first
> printed in 1646)

Charitas Nimia: or the Deare Bargain

Lord, what is man? why should he cost thee
  So deare? what had his ruine lost thee?
Lord what is man, that thou hast over-bought
  So much a thing of nought?

Love is too kind, I see, and can
Make but a simple Merchant man;
'Twas for such sorry merchandise
Bold Painters have put out his eyes.
Alas sweet Lord, what were't to thee
If there were no such wormes as wee?
  Heav'n ne're the lesse still Heav'n would bee,
    Should mankind dwell
    In the deep hell,

What have his woes to doe with thee?
    Let him goe weepe
    O're his own wounds;
    Seraphims will not sleepe
Nor *Spheares* let fall their faithfull rounds;
    Still would the youthfull Spirits sing,
    And still thy spacious Palace ring:
Still would those beautious ministers of light
    Burn all as bright,
    And bow their flaming heads before thee;
Still Thrones and Dominations would adore thee;
Still would those ever-wakeful sonnes of fire
    Keep warm thy praise
    Both nights and daies,
And teach thy lov'd name to their noble Lyre.
    Let froward dust then doe its kind,
And give it selfe for sport to the proud wind;
Why should a piece of peevish clay plead shares
In the Eternitie of thy old cares?
Why shouldst thou bow thy awfull brest to see
What mine own madnesses have done with mee?
    Should not the King still keep his Throne
    Because some desperate foole's undone?
    Or will the world's illustrious eyes
    Weepe for every worme that dyes?
    Will the gallant Sun
    E're the lesse glorious run?
    Will he hang down his Golden head,
Or e're the sooner seeke his western bed,
    Because some foolish flye
    Growes wanton, and will dye?
    If I was lost in miserie,
    What was it to thy heav'n and thee?
    What was it to thy pretious bloud
    If My foule heart call'd for a floud?
    What if my faithlesse soul and I
    Would needs fall in

With Guilt and sin?
What did the *Lamb*, that he should dye?
What did the *Lamb*, that he should need,
When the Woolfe sinnes, himselfe to bleed?
    If my base lust
Bargain'd with death, and well-beseeming dust;
    Why should the white
    Lamb's bosome write
    The purple name
    Of my sin's shame?
Why should his unstain'd brest make good
My blushes with his own Heart-blood?

O my *Saviour*, make me see,
How dearely thou hast paid for mee,
That *Lost* again my life may prove,
As then in *Death*, so now in *Love*.

                    (*Steps to the Temple*, 1648)

A Letter to the Countess of Denbigh[1]
Against Irresolution and Delay in matters of Religion

What Heav'n besieged Heart is this
Stands Trembling at the Gate of Blisse:
Holds fast the Door, yet dares not venture
Fairly to open and to enter?
Whose Definition is, A Doubt
'Twixt Life and Death, 'twixt In and Out.
Ah! linger not, lov'd Soul: A slow
And late Consent was a long No.

[1] Susan, Countess of Denbigh was a sister of Buckingham. She was first Lady of the Bedchamber to Henrietta Maria at Oxford and Paris, and while in Paris became a Roman Catholic. The Paris edition of Crashaw's poems was dedicated to her.

Who grants at last, a great while try'de,
And did his best to have Deny'de.

   What Magick-Bolts, what mystick Barrs
Maintain the Will in these strange Warrs?
What Fatall, yet fantastick, Bands
Keep the free Heart from his own Hands?
Say, lingring Fair, why comes the Birth
Of your brave Soul so slowly forth?
Plead your Pretences, (O you strong
In weaknesse) why you chuse so long
In Labour of your self to ly,
Not daring quite to Live nor Die.

   So when the Year takes cold we see
Poor Waters their own Prisoners be:
Fetter'd and lock'd up fast they lie
In a cold self-captivity.
Th'astonished Nymphs their Floud's strange Fate deplore,
To find themselves their own severer Shoar.

   Love, that lends haste to heaviest things
In you alone hath lost his wings.
Look round and reade the World's wide face,
The field of Nature or of Grace;
Where can you fix, to find Excuse
Or Pattern for the Pace you use?
Mark with what Faith Fruits answer Flowers,
And know the Call of Heav'n's kind showers:
Each mindfull Plant hasts to make good
The hope and promise of his Bud.
Seed-time's not all; there should be Harvest too.
Alas! and has the Year no Spring for you?

   Both Winds and Waters urge their way,
And murmure if they meet a stay.
Mark how the curl'd Waves work and wind,
All hating to be left behind.
Each bigge with businesse thrusts the other,
And seems to say, Make haste, my Brother.
The aiery nation of neat Doves,

That draw the Chariot of chast Loves,
Chide your delay: yea those dull things,
Whose wayes have least to doe with wings,
Make wings at least of their own Weight,
And by their Love controll their Fate.
So lumpish Steel, untaught to move,
Learn'd first his Lightnesse by his Love.

What e're Love's matter be, he moves
By th'even wings of his own Doves,
Lives by his own Laws, and does hold
In grossest Metalls his own Gold.

All things swear friends to Fair and Good,
Yea Suitours; Man alone is wo'ed,
Tediously wo'ed, and hardly wone;
Only not slow to be undone.
As if the Bargain had been driven
So hardly betwixt Earth and Heaven;
Our God would thrive too fast, and be
Too much a gainer by't, should we
Our purchas'd selves too soon bestow
On him, who has not lov'd us so.
When love of Us call'd Him to see
If wee'd vouchsafe his company,
He left his Father's Court, and came
Lightly as a Lambent Flame,
Leaping upon the Hills, to be
The Humble King of You and Me.
Nor can the cares of his whole Crown
(When one poor Sigh sends for him down)
Detain him, but he leaves behind
The late wings of the lazy Wind,
Spurns the tame Laws of Time and Place,
And breaks through all ten Heav'ns to our embrace.

Yield to his Siege, wise Soul, and see
Your Triumph in his Victory.
Disband dull Feares, give Faith the day:
To save your Life, kill your Delay.

'Tis Cowardise that keeps this Field;
And want of Courage not to Yield.
   Yield then, O yield, that Love may win
The Fort at last, and let Life in.
Yield quickly, lest perhaps you prove
Death's Prey, before the Prize of Love.
This Fort of your Fair Self if't be not wone,
He is repuls'd indeed, but You're undone.

> (*A Letter*, etc. 1653: revised version
> of poem first printed in *Carmen Deo
> Nostro*, Paris 1652)

JOHN CLEVELAND
(1613–1658)

To the State of Love, or the Senses Festival

I saw a Vision yesternight
Enough to tempt a *Seekers* sight:
I wisht my self a *Shaker* there,
And her quick pulse my trembling sphear.
It was a She so glittering bright:
You'd think her soul an *Adamite*;[1]
A person of so rare a frame,
Her bodie might be lin'd with 'same.
Beauties chiefest Maid of Honour:
You'd break a Lent with looking on her.
   Not the fair Abbess of the skies,
   With all her Nunnery of eyes,
   Can shew me such a glorious prize.

---

[1] *Adamite*: one who dispenses with clothes. Seekers, Shakers, and
Adamites were contemporary Sectaries.

And yet, because 'tis more renown
To make a shaddow shine, she's brown:
A brown, for which Heaven would disband
The Gallaxye, and stars be tann'd.
Brown by reflection, as her eye
Dazels the Summers livery
Old dormant windows must confesse
Her beams; their glimering spectacles
Struck with the splendour of her face,
Do th'office of a burning-glass.
   Now, where such radiant lights have shown,
   No wonder if her cheeks be grown
   Sun-burnt with lustre of her own.

My sight took pay, but (thank my charms)
I now empale her in mine arms,
(Loves Compasses) confining you,
Good Angels, to a compass too.
Is not the Universe strait-lac't,
When I can clasp it in the Waste?
My amorous foulds about thee hurl'd,
With *Drake*, I compass in the world.
I hoop the Firmament, and make
This my Embrace the Zodiack.
   How would thy Center take my Sense,
   When Admiration doth commence
   At the extream Circumference.

Now to the melting kisse that sips
The jelly'd Philtre of her lips,
So sweet, there is no tongue can phras't
Till transubstantiate with a taste,
Inspir'd like *Mahomet* from above,
By th'billing of my heav'nly Dove;
Love prints his Signets in her smacks,
Those Ruddy drops of squeezing wax;

Which, wheresoever she imparts,
They're Privie Seals to take up hearts.
    Our mouths incountering at the sport,
    My slippery soule had quit the fort,
    But that she stopt the Salley-port.

Next to those sweets her lips dispence,
As Twin-conserves of Eloquence;
The sweet perfume her breath affords;
Incorporating with her words;
No Rosary this Votress needs,
Her very syllables are beads.
No sooner 'twixt those Rubies born:
But Jewels are in Ear-rings worn.
With what delight her speech doth enter,
It is a kiss o'th'second venter.[1]
    And I dissolve at what I hear,
    As if another *Rosomond* were
    Couch'd in the Labyrinth of my Ear.

Yet, that's but a preludious bliss;
Two souls pickearing[2] in a kiss.
Embraces do but draw the Line,
'Tis storming that must take her in.
When bodies join and victory hovers
'Twixt the equall fluttering lovers
This is the game: make stakes my Dear,
Hark how the sprightly *Chanticlere*,
That Baron *Tell-clock* of the night,
Sounds Boot-esel[3] to Cupids knight.
    Then have at all, the pass is got,
    For coming off, oh name it not:
    Who would not die upon the spot.

(*Poems,* 1651)

[1] *the second venter*: the second marriage, lip to lip being the first, lip to heart, through the ear, the second.
[2] *pickearing*: marauding, or skirmishing in front of an army.
[3] *Boot-esel*: 'Boot and Saddle'.

The Antiplatonick

For shame, thou everlasting Wooer,
Still saying grace, and never falling to her!
Love that's in contemplation plac't,
Is *Venus* drawn but to the wast.
Unlesse your flame confesse its gender,
And your Parley cause surrender
Y'are Salamanders of a cold desire
That live untoucht amid the hottest fire.

What though she be a Dame of stone
The Widow of *Pigmalion*;
As hard and un-relenting she,
As the new-crusted *Niobe*;
Or what doth more of statue carry,
A Nunne of the Platonick Quarry!
Love melts the rigour which the rocks have bred,
A flint will break upon a Feather-bed.

For shame you pretty Female Elves
Cease for to candy up your selves:
No more, you sectaries of the Game,
No more of your calcining flame.
Women commence[1] by *Cupids* Dart
As a King hunting dubs a Hart,[2]
Loves votaries inthrall each others soul,
Till both of them live but upon Parole.

Vertue's no more in Woman-kind
But the green sicknesse of the mind.
Philosophy, their new delight,
A kind of Char-coal appetite.

[1] *commence*: graduate.
[2] 'The hart is ennobled by being hunted by a king.'

There's no Sophistry prevails
Where all-convincing love assails;
But the disputing petticoat will warp
As skillfull gamesters are to seeke at sharp.[1]

The souldier, that man of iron,
Whom ribs of *Horror* all inviron;
That's strung with Wire, instead of Veins,
In whose embraces you're in chains,
Let a Magnetick girl appear,
Straight he turns *Cupids* Cuirasseer,
Love storms his lips, and takes the Fortresse in,
For all the Bristled Turn-pikes of his chin.

Since Loves Artillery then checks
The brest-works of the firmest sex,
Come let us in affections riot,
Th'are sickly pleasures keep a Diet:
Give me a lover bold and free,
Not Eunucht with formality;
Like an Embassadour that beds a Queen
With the nice Caution of a sword between.

(Poems, 1653)

Epitaph on the Earl of Strafford[2]

Here lies Wise and Valiant Dust
Huddled up 'twixt Fit and Just:
STRAFFORD, who was hurried hence
'Twixt Treason and Convenience.
He spent his Time here in a Mist;
A *Papist*, yet a *Calvinist*.

[1] 'As clever fencers are not good at sword-play.'
[2] Strafford was executed 12 May 1641. Cleveland's authorship of this poem is very doubtful. It was circulating as an anonymous broadsheet in the summer of 1641.

His Princes nearest Joy, and Grief.
He had, yet wanted all Releefe.
The Prop and Ruine of the State;
The People's violent Love and Hate:
One in extreames lov'd and abhor'd.
Riddles lie here; or in a word,
Here lies Blood; and let it lie
Speechlesse still, and never crie.

(Poems, 1647)

ABRAHAM COWLEY

(1618–1667)

The Change

Love in her sunny Eyes doth basking play;
Love walks the pleasant Mazes of her Haire;
Love does on both her Lipps for ever stray;
And sowes and reapes a thousand kisses there.
In all her outward parts Love's alwayes seene;
   But, oh, Hee never went within.

Within Loves foes, his greatest foes abide,
    Malice, Inconstancy and Pride.
Soe the Earths face, Trees, Herbes, and Flowers do dresse;
    With other beauties numberlesse:
But at the Center Darknesse is, and Hell;
There wicked Spirits, and there the Damned dwell.

With Me alas, quite contrary it fares;
Darkness and Death lyes in my weeping eyes,
Despaire and Palenesse in my face appears,
And Griefe, and Fear, Loves greatest enemies;
But, like the Persian Tyrant, Love within
   Keeps his proud Court, and ne're is seen.

Oh take my Heart, and by that means you'l prove
    Within too stor'd enough of Love:
Give me but Yours, I'le by that change so thrive
    That Love in all my parts shall live.
So powerfull is this change, it render can,
My outside Woman, and your inside Man.

                   (*The Mistress*, 1647)

Ode: Of Wit

Tell me, O tell, what kinde of thing is *Wit*,
    Thou who *Master* art of it.
For the *First Matter* loves *Variety* less;
Less *Women* love't, either in *Love* or *Dress*.
    A thousand different shapes it bears,
    Comely in thousand shapes appears.
Yonder we saw it plain; and here 'tis now,
Like *Spirits* in a *Place*, we know not *How*.

London that vents of *false Ware* so much store,
    In no *Ware* deceives us more.
For men led by the *Colour*, and the *Shape*,
Like *Zeuxes Birds* fly to the painted *Grape*;
    Some things do through our Judgment pass
    As through a *Multiplying Glass*.
And sometimes, if the *Object* be too far,
We take a *Falling Meteor* for a *Star*.

Hence 'tis a *Wit* that greatest *word* of *Fame*
    Grows such a common Name.
And *Wits* by our *Creation* they become,
Just so, as *Tit'lar Bishops* made at *Rome*.
    'Tis not a *Tale*, 'tis not a *Jest*
    Admir'd with *Laughter* at a feast,
Nor florid *Talk* which can that *Title* gain;
The *Proofs* of *Wit* for ever must remain.

'Tis not to force some lifeless *Verses* meet
    With their five gowty feet.
All ev'ry where, like *Mans*, must be the *Soul*,
And *Reason* the *Inferior Powers* controul.
    Such were the *Numbers* which could call
    The *Stones* into the *Theban* wall.
Such *Miracles* are ceast; and now we see
No *Towns* or *Houses* rais'd by *Poetrie*.

Yet 'tis not to adorn, and gild each part;
    That shows more *Cost*, than *Art*.
Jewels at *Nose* and *Lips* but ill appear;
Rather than *all things Wit*, let *none* be there.
    Several *Lights* will not be seen,
    If there be nothing else between.
Men doubt, because they stand so thick i'th'skie,
If those be *Stars* which paint the *Galaxie*.

'Tis not when two like words make up one noise;
    Jests for *Dutch Men*, and *English Boys*.
In which who finds out *Wit*, the same may see
In *An'grams* and *Acrostiques Poetrie*.
    Much less can that have any place
    At which a *Virgin* hides her face,
Such *Dross* the *Fire* must purge away; 'tis just
The *Author blush*, there where the *Reader* must.

'Tis not such *Lines* as almost crack the *Stage*
    When *Bajazet* begins to rage.
Nor a tall *Metaphor* in the *Bombast way*,
Nor the dry chips of short lung'd *Seneca*.
    Nor upon all things to obtrude,
    And force some odd *Similitude*.
What is it then, which like the *Power Divine*
We onely can by *Negatives* define?

In a true piece of *Wit* all things must be,
    Yet all things there *agree*.
As in the *Ark*, joyn'd without force or strife,
All *Creatures* dwelt; all *Creatures* that had *Life*.
    Or as the *Primitive Forms* of all
    (If we compare great things with small)
Which without *Discord* or *Confusion* lie,
In that strange *Mirror* of the *Deitie*.

But *Love* that moulds *One Man* up out of *Two*,
    Makes me forget and injure you.
I took *you* for *my self* sure when I thought
That you in any thing were to be *Taught*.
    Correct my error with thy Pen;
    And if any ask me then,
What thing right *Wit*, and height of *Genius* is,
I'll only shew your *Lines*, and say, '*Tis This*.

On the Death of Mr. Crashaw

Poet and *Saint!* to thee alone are given
The two most sacred *Names* of *Earth* and *Heaven*.
The hard and rarest *Union* which can be
Next that of *Godhead* with *Humanitie*.
Long did the *Muses* banisht *Slaves* abide,
And built vain *Pyramids* to mortal pride;
Like *Moses* Thou (though Spells and Charms withstand)
Hast brought them nobly home back to their *Holy Land*.
   Ah wretched *We*, *Poets* of *Earth!* but *Thou*
Wert *Living* the same *Poet* which thou'rt *Now*.
Whilst *Angels* sing to thee their ayres divine,
And joy in an applause so great as *thine*.
Equal society with them to hold,
Thou need'st not make *new Songs*, but say the *Old*.
And they (kind Spirits!) shall all rejoyce to see
How little less than *They*, *Exalted Man* may be.

Still the old *Heathen Gods* in *Numbers* dwell,
The *Heav'nliest* thing on Earth still keeps up *Hell*.
Nor have we yet quite purg'd the *Christian Land*;
Still *Idols* here, like *Calves* at *Bethel* stand.
And though *Pans Death* long since all *Oracles* broke,
Yet still in Rhyme the *Fiend Apollo* spoke:
Nay with the worst of Heathen dotage We
(Vain men!) the *Monster Woman Deifie*;
Find *Stars*, and tye our *Fates* there in a *Face*,
And *Paradise* in them by whom we *lost* it, place.
What different faults corrupt our *Muses* thus?
Wanton as *Girls*, as *old Wives, Fabulous!*

      Thy spotless *Muse*, like *Mary*, did contain
The boundless *Godhead*; she did well disdain
That her *eternal Verse* employ'd should be
On a less subject than *Eternitie*;
And for a sacred *Mistress* scorn'd to take,
But her whom *God* himself scorn'd not his *Spouse* to make.
It (in a kind) *her* *Miracle* did do;
A fruitful *Mother* was, and *Virgin* too.
How well (blest Swan) did Fate contrive thy death;
And made thee render up thy tuneful breath
In thy great *Mistress* Arms? thou most divine
And richest *Off'ring* of *Loretto's Shrine!*
Where like some holy *Sacrifice* t'expire,
A *Fever* burns thee, and *Love* lights the *Fire*.
Angels (they say) brought the fam'd *Chapel* there,
And bore the sacred Load in Triumph through the aire.
'Tis surer much they brought thee there, and *They*,
And *Thou*, their charge, went *singing* all the way.

      Pardon, my *Mother Church*, if I consent
That *Angels* led him when from thee he went,
For even in *Error* sure no *Danger* is
When joyn'd with so much *Piety* as *His*.
Ah, mighty *God*, with shame I speak't, and grief,
Ah that our greatest *Faults* were in *Belief!*
And our weak *Reason* were ev'n weaker yet,

Rather than thus our *Wills* too strong for it.
His *Faith* perhaps in some nice Tenents might
Be wrong; his *Life*, I'm sure, was *in the right*.
And I my self a *Catholick* will be,
So far at least, great *Saint*, to *Pray* to thee.
   Hail, *Bard Triumphant!* and some care bestow
On *us*, the *Poets Militant* below!
Oppos'd by our old En'my, adverse *Chance*,
Attacqu'd by *Envy*, and by *Ignorance*,
Enchain'd by *Beauty*, tortur'd by *Desires*,
Expos'd by *Tyrant-Love* to savage *Beasts* and *Fires*.
Thou from low earth in nobler *Flames* didst rise,
And like *Elijah*, mount *Alive* the skies.
Elisha-like (but with a wish much less,
More fit thy *Greatness*, and my *Littleness*)
Lo here I beg (I whom thou once didst prove
So humble to *Esteem*, so Good to *Love*)
Not that thy *Spirit* might on me *Doubled* be,
I ask but *Half* thy mighty *Spirit* for Me.
And when my *Muse* soars with so strong a Wing,
'Twill learn of things *Divine*, and first of *Thee* to sing.

(*Miscellanies*, 1656)

Drinking

The thirsty *Earth* soaks up the *Rain*,
And drinks, and gapes for drink again.
The *Plants* suck in the *Earth*, and are
With constant drinking fresh and faire.
The *Sea* it self, which one would think
Should have but little need of *Drink*,
Drinks ten thousand *Rivers* up,
So fill'd that they oreflow the *Cup*.
The busie *Sun* (and one would guess
By's drunken fiery face no less)

Drinks up the *Sea*, and when h'as done,
The *Moon* and *Stars* drink up the *Sun*.
They drink and dance by their own light,
They drink and revel all the night.
Nothing in *Nature's Sober* found,
But an eternal *Health* goes round.·
Fill up the *Bowl*, then fill it high,
Fill all the *Glasses* there, For why
Should every creature drink but *I*,
Why, *Man* of *Morals*, tell me why?

(Anacreonticks, 1656)

Hymn to Light

First born of *Chaos*, who so fair didst come
    From the old *Negro's* darksome womb!
    Which when it saw the lovely Child,
The melancholly Mass put on kind looks and smil'd,

Thou Tide of Glory which no Rest dost know,
    But ever Ebb, and ever Flow!
    Thou Golden shower of a true *Jove!*
Who does in thee descend, and Heav'n to Earth make Love!

Hail active Natures watchful Life and Health!
    Her Joy, her Ornament, and Wealth!
    Hail to thy Husband Heat, and Thee!
Thou the worlds beauteous Bride, the lusty Bridegroom He!

Say from what Golden Quivers of the Sky,
    Do all thy winged Arrows fly?
    Swiftness and Power by Birth are thine:
From thy great Sire they came, thy Sire the word Divine.

'Tis, I believe, this Archery to show,
    That so much cost in Colours thou,
    And skill in Painting dost bestow,
Upon thy ancient Arms, the Gawdy Heav'nly Bow.

Swift as light Thoughts their empty Carriere run,
    Thy Race is finisht, when begun,
    Let a Post-Angel start with Thee,
And thou the Goal of Earth shalt reach as soon as He:

Thou in the Moons bright Chariot proud and gay,
    Dost thy bright wood of Stars survay;
    And all the year dost with thee bring
Of thousand flowry Lights thine own Nocturnal Spring.

Thou *Scythian*-like dost round thy Lands above
    The Suns gilt Tent for ever move,
    And still as thou in pomp dost go
The shining Pageants of the World attend thy show.

Nor amidst all these Triumphs dost thou scorn
    The humble Glow-worms to adorn,
    And with those living spangles gild,
(O Greatness without Pride!) the Bushes of the Field.

Night, and her ugly Subjects thou dost fright,
    And sleep, the lazy Owl of Night;
    Asham'd and fearful to appear
They skreen their horrid shapes with the black Hemisphere.

With 'em there hasts, and wildly takes the Alarm,
    Of painted Dreams, a busie swarm,
    At the first opening of thine eye,
The various Clusters break, the antick Atomes fly.

The guilty Serpents, and obscener Beasts
    Creep conscious to their secret rests:
    Nature to thee does reverence pay,
Ill Omens, and ill Sights removes out of thy way.

At thy appearance, Grief it self is said,
    To shake his Wings, and rowse his Head,
    And cloudy care has often took
A gentle beamy Smile reflected from thy Look.

At thy appearance, Fear it self grows bold;
  Thy Sun-shine melts away his Cold.
   Encourag'd at the sight of Thee,
To the cheek Colour comes, and firmness to the knee.

Even Lust the Master of a hardned Face,
  Blushes if thou beest in the place,
   To darknes' Curtains he retires,
In Sympathizing Night he rowls his smoaky Fires.

When, Goddess, thou liftst up thy wakened Head,
  Out of the Mornings purple bed,
   Thy Quire of Birds about thee play,
And all the joyful world salutes the rising day.

The Ghosts, and Monster Spirits, that did presume
  A Bodies Priv'lege to assume,
   Vanish again invisibly,
And Bodies gain agen their visibility.

All the Worlds bravery that delights our Eyes
  Is but thy sev'ral Liveries,
   Thou the Rich Day on them bestowest,
Thy nimble Pencil paints this Landskape as thou go'st.

A Crimson Garment in the Rose thou wear'st;
  A Crown of studded Gold thou bear'st,
   The Virgin Lillies in their White,
Are clad but with the Lawn of almost Naked Light.

The Violet, springs little Infant, stands
  Girt in thy purple Swadling-bands:
   On the fair Tulip thou dost dote;
Thou cloath'st it in a gay and party-colour'd Coat.

With Flame condenst thou dost the Jewels fix,
  And solid Colours in it mix:
   Flora her self envyes to see
Flowers fairer than her own, and durable as she.

Ah, Goddess! would thou could'st thy hand withhold,
    And be less Liberall to Gold;
      Didst thou less value to it give,
Of how much care (alas) might'st thou poor Man relieve!

To me the Sun is more delightful farr,
    And all fair Days much fairer are.
      But few, ah wondrous few there be,
Who do not Gold preferr, O Goddess, ev'n to Thee.

Through the soft wayes of Heaven, and Air, and Sea,
    Which open all their Pores to Thee;
      Like a clear River thou dost glide,
And with thy Living Stream through the close Channels slide.

But where firm Bodies thy free course oppose,
    Gently thy source the Land oreflowes;
      Takes there possession, and does make
Of Colours mingled, Light, a thick and standing Lake.

But the vast Ocean of unbounded Day
    In th'Empyraean Heaven does stay.
      Thy Rivers, Lakes, and Springs below
From thence first took their Rise, thither at last must Flow.

                    (*Works*, 1668)

RICHARD LOVELACE
(1618–1656/7)

To Lucasta, *Going to the Warres*

    Tell me not (Sweet) I am unkinde,
      That from the Nunnerie
    Of thy chaste breast, and quiet minde,
      To Warre and Armes I flie.

True; a new Mistresse now I chase,
  The first Foe in the Field;
And with a stronger Faith imbrace
  A Sword, a Horse, a Shield.

Yet this Inconstancy is such,
  As you too shall adore;
I could not love thee (Deare) so much,
  Lov'd I not Honour more.

To Amarantha, *That she would dishevell her haire*

Amarantha sweet and faire,
Ah brade no more that shining haire!
  As my curious hand or eye,
Hovering round thee let it flye.

  Let it flye as unconfin'd
As its calme Ravisher, the winde;
  Who hath left his darling th'East,
To wanton o're that spicie Nest.

  Ev'ry Tresse must be confest
But neatly tangled at the best;
  Like a Clue of golden thread,
Most excellently ravelled.

  Doe not then winde up that light
In Ribands, and o're-cloud in Night;
  Like the Sun in's early ray,
But shake your head and scatter day.

  See 'tis broke! Within this Grove
The Bower, and the walkes of Love,
  Weary lye we downe and rest,
And fanne each others panting breast.

Heere wee'l strippe and coole our fire
In Creame below, in milke-baths higher:
 And when all Wells are drawne dry,
I'le drink a teare out of thine eye.

Which our very Joyes shall leave
That sorrowes thus we can deceive;
 Or our very sorrowes weepe,
 That joyes so ripe, so little keepe.

Gratiana *dauncing and singing*

See! with what constant Motion
Even, and glorious, as the Sunne,
 Gratiana steeres that Noble Frame,
Soft as her breast, sweet as her voyce
That gave each winding Law and poyze,
 And swifter than the wings of Fame.

She beat the happy Pavement
By such a Starre made Firmament,
 Which now no more the Roofe envies;
But swells up high with *Atlas* ev'n,
Bearing the brighter, nobler Heav'n,
 And in her, all the Deities.

Each step trod out a Lovers thought
And the Ambitious hopes he brought,
 Chain'd to her brave feet with such arts,
Such sweet command, and gentle awe,
As when she ceas'd, we sighing saw
 The floore lay pav'd with broken hearts.

So did she move; so did she sing
Like the Harmonious spheres that bring

Unto their Rounds their musick's ayd;
Which she performed such a way,
As all th'inamour'd world will say
   The *Graces* daunced, and *Apollo* play'd.

The Scrutinie

Why should you sweare I am forsworn,
   Since thine I vow'd to be?
Lady it is already Morn,
   And 'twas last night I swore to thee
That fond impossibility.

Have I not lov'd thee much and long,
   A tedious twelve houres space?
I must all other Beauties wrong,
   And rob thee of a new imbrace;
Could I still dote upon thy Face.

Not, but all joy in thy browne haire,
   By others may be found;
But I must search the black and faire
   Like skilfull Minerallists that sound
For Treasure in un-plow'd-up ground.

Then, if when I have lov'd my round,
   Thou prov'st the pleasant she;
With spoyles of meaner Beauties crown'd,
   I laden will returne to thee,
Ev'n sated with Varietie.

RICHARD LOVELACE

The Grasse-hopper. To my Noble Friend,
Mr Charles Cotton

Oh thou that swing'st upon the waving haire
  Of some well-filled Oaten Beard,
Drunke ev'ry night with a Delicious teare
  Dropt thee from Heav'n, where now th'art reard.

The Joyes of Earth and Ayre are thine intire,
  That with thy feet and wings dost hop and flye;
And when thy Poppy workes thou dost retire
  To thy Carv'd Acorn-bed to lye.

Up with the Day, the Sun thou welcomst then,
  Sportst in the gilt-plats of his Beames,
And all these merry dayes mak'st merry men,
  Thy selfe, and Melancholy streames.

But ah the Sickle! Golden Eares are Cropt;
  Ceres and *Bacchus* bid good night;
Sharpe frosty fingers all your Flow'rs have topt,
  And what sithes spar'd, Winds shave off quite.

Poore verdant foole! and now green Ice! thy Joys
  Large and as lasting, as thy Peirch of Grasse,
Bid us lay in 'gainst Winter Raine, and poize
  Their flouds, with an o're flowing glasse.

Thou best of *Men* and *Friends!* we will create
  A Genuine Summer in each others breast;
And spite of this cold Time and frozen Fate
  Thaw us a warme seate to our rest.

Our sacred harthes shall burne eternally
  As Vestall Flames, the North-wind, he
Shall strike his frost-stretch'd Wings, dissolve and flye
  This *Ætna* in Epitome.

Dropping *December* shall come weeping in,
　Bewayle th'usurping of his Raigne;
But when in show'rs of old Greeke we beginne
　Shall crie, he hath his Crowne againe!

Night as cleare *Hesper* shall our Tapers whip
　From the light Casements where we play,
And the darke Hagge from her black mantle strip,
　And sticke there everlasting Day.

Thus richer than untempted Kings are we,
　That asking nothing, nothing need:
Though Lord of all what Seas imbrace; yet he
　That wants himselfe, is poore indeed.

To Althea, *from Prison*[1]

When Love with unconfined wings
　　Hovers within my Gates;
And my divine *Althea* brings
　　To whisper at the Grates:
When I lye tangled in her haire,
　　And fetterd to her eye;
The *Gods* that wanton in the Aire,
　　Know no such Liberty.

When flowing Cups run swiftly round
　　With no allaying *Thames*,
Our carelesse heads with Roses bound,
　　Our hearts with Loyall Flames;
When thirsty griefe in Wine we steepe,
　　When Healths and draughts go free,
Fishes that tipple in the Deepe,
　　Know no such Libertie.

[1] Written in 1642 when Lovelace was in prison in the Gatehouse after having presented the Kentish Petition.

When (like committed Linnets) I
   With shriller throat shall sing
The sweetnes, Mercy, Majesty,
   And glories of my KING;
When I shall voyce aloud, how Good
   He is, how Great should be;
Inlarged Winds that curle the Flood,
   Know no such Liberty.

Stone Walls doe not a Prison make,
   Nor Iron bars a Cage;
Minds innocent and quiet take
   That for an Hermitage;
If I have freedome in my Love,
   And in my soule am free;
Angels alone that sore above
   Injoy such Liberty.

(Lucasta, 1649)

ANDREW MARVELL
(1621–1678)

A Dialogue between
The Resolved Soul, and Created Pleasure

Courage my Soul, now learn to wield
The weight of thine immortal Shield.
Close on thy Head thy Helmet bright.
Ballance thy Sword against the Fight.
See where an Army, strong as fair,
With silken Banners spreads the air.
Now, if thou bee'st that thing Divine,
In this day's Combat let it shine:
And shew that Nature wants an Art
To conquer one resolved Heart.

ANDREW MARVELL

PLEASURE

Welcome the Creations Guest,
Lord of Earth, and Heavens Heir.
Lay aside that Warlike Crest,
And of Nature's banquet share:
Where the Souls of fruits and flow'rs
Stand prepar'd to heighten yours.

SOUL

I sup above, and cannot stay
To bait[1] so long upon the way.

PLEASURE

On these downy Pillows lye,
Whose soft Plumes will thither fly:
On these Roses strow'd so plain
Lest one Leaf thy Side should strain.

SOUL

My gentler Rest is on a Thought,
Conscious of doing what I ought.

PLEASURE

If thou bee'st with Perfumes pleas'd,
Such as oft the Gods appeas'd,
Thou in fragrant Clouds shalt show
Like another God below.

SOUL

A Soul that knowes not to presume
Is Heaven's and its own perfume.

[1] *bait*: stop for food on a journey.

ANDREW MARVELL

PLEASURE

Every thing does seem to vie
Which should first attract thine Eye:
But since none deserves that grace,
In this Crystal view *thy* face.

SOUL

When the Creator's skill is priz'd,
The rest is all but Earth disguis'd.

PLEASURE

Heark how Musick then prepares
For thy Stay these charming Aires;
Which the posting Winds recall,
And suspend the Rivers Fall.

SOUL

Had I but any time to lose,
On this I would it all dispose.
Cease Tempter. None can chain a mind
Whom this sweet Chordage cannot bind.

CHORUS

Earth cannot shew so brave a Sight
As when a single Soul does fence
The Batteries[1] of alluring Sense,
And Heaven views it with delight.
  Then persevere: for still new Charges sound:
  And if thou overcom'st thou shalt be crown'd.

PLEASURE

All this fair, and soft, and sweet,
  Which scatteringly doth shine,
Shall within one Beauty meet,
  And she be only thine.

[1] *fence the Batteries*: ward off the attacks.

ANDREW MARVELL

SOUL

If things of Sight such Heavens be,
What Heavens are those we cannot see?

PLEASURE

Where so e're thy Foot shall go
  The minted Gold shall lie;
Till thou purchase all below,
  And want new Worlds to buy.

SOUL

Wer't not a price who'ld value Gold?
And that's worth nought that can be sold.

PLEASURE

Wilt thou all the Glory have
  That War or Peace commend?
Half the World shall be thy Slave
  The other half thy Friend.

SOUL

What Friends, if to my self untrue?
What Slaves, unless I captive you?

PLEASURE

Thou shalt know each hidden Cause;
  And see the future Time:
Try what depth the Centre[1] draws;
  And then to Heaven climb.

SOUL

None thither mounts by the degree
Of Knowledge, but Humility.

[1] *Centre*: centre of the earth.

ANDREW MARVELL

CHORUS

Triumph, triumph, victorious Soul;
The World has not one Pleasure more:
The rest does lie beyond the Pole,
And is thine everlasting Store.

On a Drop of Dew

See how the Orient Dew,
Shed from the Bosom of the Morn
   Into the blowing Roses,
Yet careless of its Mansion new,
For[1] the clear Region where 'twas born,
   Round in its self incloses,
   And in its little Globes Extent,
Frames as it can its native Element.
How it the purple flow'r does slight,
   Scarce touching where it lyes,
But gazing back upon the Skies,
   Shines with a mournful Light;
     Like its own Tear,
Because so long divided from the Sphear.
  Restless it roules and unsecure,
   Trembling lest it grow impure:
Till the warm Sun pitty it's Pain,
And to the Skies exhale it back again.
   So the Soul, that Drop, that Ray
Of the clear Fountain of Eternal Day,
Could it within the humane flow'r be seen,
   Remembring still its former height,
   Shuns the sweet leaves and blossoms green;
   And, recollecting its own Light,
Does, in its pure and circling thoughts, express
The greater Heaven in an Heaven less.

       [1] *For*: because of.

In how coy a Figure wound,
Every way it turns away:
So the World excluding round,
Yet receiving in the Day.
Dark beneath, but bright above:
Here disdaining, there in Love,
How loose and easie hence to go:
How girt and ready to ascend.
Moving but on a point below,
It all about does upwards bend.
Such did the Manna's sacred Dew[1] destil;
White, and intire, though congeal'd and chill.
Congeal'd on Earth: but does, dissolving, run
Into the Glories of th' Almighty Sun.

The Coronet

When for the Thorns with which I long, too long,
    With many a piercing wound,
    My Saviours head have crown'd,
I seek with Garlands to redress that Wrong:
    Through every Garden, every Mead,
I gather flow'rs (my fruits are only flow'rs)
    Dismantling all the fragrant Towers[2]
That once adorn'd my Shepherdesses head.
And now when I have summ'd up all my store,
    Thinking (so I my self deceive)
    So rich a Chaplet thence to weave
As never yet the king of Glory wore:
    Alas I find the Serpent old
    That, twining in his speckled breast,

[1] 'And when the dew that lay was gone up, behold, upon the face of the wilderness there lay a small round thing, as small as the hoar frost on the ground. . . . And they gathered it morning by morning . . . and when the sun waxed hot it melted' (Exodus xvi).
[2] *Towers*: high head-dresses worn by women.

About the flow'rs disguis'd does fold,
  With wreaths of Fame and Interest.
Ah, foolish Man, that would'st debase with them,
And mortal Glory, Heavens Diadem!
But thou who only could'st the Serpent tame,
Either his slipp'ry knots at once untie,
And disentangle all his winding Snare:
Or shatter too with him my curious[1] frame:
And let these wither, so that he may die,
Though set with Skill and chosen out with Care.
That they, while Thou on both their Spoils dost tread,
May crown thy Feet, that could not crown thy Head.

Eyes and Tears

How wisely Nature did decree,
  With the same Eyes to weep and see!
That, having view'd the object vain,
  They might be ready to complain.

And, since the Self-deluding Sight,
  In a false Angle takes each hight;
These Tears which better measure all,
  Like wat'ry Lines and Plummets fall.

Two Tears, which Sorrow long did weigh
  Within the Scales of either Eye,
And then paid out in equal Poise,
  Are the true price of all my Joyes.

What in the World most fair appears,
  Yea even Laughter, turns to Tears:
And all the Jewels which we prize,
  Melt in these Pendants of the Eyes.

[1] *curious*: elaborately wrought.

I have through every Garden been,
Amongst the Red, the White, the Green;
And yet, from all the flow'rs I saw,
No Hony, but these Tears could draw.

So the all-seeing Sun each day
Distills the World with Chymick Ray;
But finds the Essence only Showers,
Which straight in pity back he powers.

Yet happy they whom Grief doth bless,
That weep the more, and see the less:
And, to preserve their Sight more true,
Bathe still their Eyes in their own Dew.

So *Magdalen*, in Tears more wise
Dissolv'd those captivating Eyes,
Whose liquid Chaines could flowing meet
To fetter her Redeemers feet.

Not full sailes hasting loaden home,
Nor the chast Ladies pregnant Womb,
Nor *Cynthia* Teeming[1] show's so fair,
As two Eyes swoln with weeping are.

The sparkling Glance that shoots Desire,
Drench'd in these Waves, does lose its fire.
Yea oft the Thund'rer pitty takes
And here the hissing Lightning slakes.

The Incense was to Heaven dear,
Not as a Perfume, but a Tear.
And Stars shew lovely in the Night,
But as they seem the Tears of Light.

---

[1] Cynthia *Teeming*: the full moon.

Ope then mine Eyes your double Sluice,
And practise so your noblest Use.
For others too can see, or sleep;
But only humane Eyes can weep.

Now like two Clouds dissolving, drop,
And at each Tear in distance stop:
Now like two Fountains trickle down:
Now like two floods o'return and drown.

Thus let your Streams o'reflow your Springs,
Till Eyes and Tears be the same things:
And each the other's difference bears;
These weeping Eyes, those seeing Tears.

Bermudas[1]

Where the remote *Bermudas* ride
In th' Oceans bosome unespy'd,
From a small Boat, that row'd along,
The listning Winds receiv'd this Song.
    What should we do but sing his Praise
That led us through the watry Maze,
Unto an Isle so long unknown,
And yet far kinder than our own?
Where he the huge Sea-Monsters wracks,
That lift the Deep upon their Backs.
He lands us on a grassy Stage;
Safe from the Storms, and Prelat's rage.
He gave us this eternal Spring,
Which here enamells every thing;
And sends the Fowls to us in care,
On daily Visits through the Air.

[1] Probably written *c.* 1653 when Marvell was living at Eton with John Oxenbridge. Oxenbridge left England for the Bermudas in 1635, returned in 1641, 'redeunte conscientiarum libertate', to leave again at the Restoration and settle in Massachusetts.

He hangs in shades the Orange bright,
Like golden Lamps in a green Night.
And does in the Pomgranates close,
Jewels more rich than *Ormus* shows.
He makes the Figs our mouths to meet;
And throws the Melons at our feet.
But Apples[1] plants of such a price,
No Tree could ever bear them twice.
With Cedars, chosen by his hand,
From *Lebanon*, he stores the Land.
And makes the hollow Seas, that roar,
Proclaime the Ambergris on shoar.
He cast (of which we rather boast)
The Gospels Pearl upon our Coast.
And in these Rocks for us did frame
A Temple, where to sound his Name.
Oh let our Voice his Praise exalt,
Till it arrive at Heavens Vault:
Which thence (perhaps) rebounding, may
Eccho beyond the *Mexique Bay*.
Thus sung they, in the *English* boat,
An holy and a chearful Note,
And all the way, to guide their Chime,
With falling Oars they kept the time.

A Dialogue between the Soul and Body

SOUL

O who shall, from this Dungeon, raise
A Soul inslav'd so many wayes?
With bolts of Bones, that fetter'd stands
In Feet; and manacled in Hands.
Here blinded with an Eye; and there
Deaf with the drumming of an Ear.

[1] Pineapples, propagated by planting suckers from the original plant.

A Soul hung up, as 'twere, in Chains
Of Nerves, and Arteries, and Veins.
Tortur'd, besides each other part,
In a vain Head, and double Heart.

BODY

Oh who shall me deliver whole,
From bonds of this Tyrannic Soul?
Which, stretcht upright, impales me so,
That mine own Precipice I go;
And warms and moves this needless[1] Frame:
(A Fever could but do the same.)
And, wanting where its spight to try,
Has made me live to let me dye.
A Body that could never rest,
Since this ill Spirit it possest.

SOUL

What Magick could me thus confine
Within anothers Grief to pine?
Where whatsoever it complain,
I feel, that cannot feel, the pain.
And all my Care its self employes,
That to preserve, which me destroys:
Constrain'd not only to indure
Diseases, but, whats worse, the Cure:
And ready oft the Port to gain,
Am Shipwrackt into Health again.

BODY

But Physick yet could never reach
The Maladies Thou me dost teach;
Whom first the Cramp of Hope does Tear:
And then the Palsie Shakes of Fear.

[1] *needless*: having no wants, quite content without the soul.

The Pestilence of Love does heat:
Or Hatred's hidden Ulcer eat.
Joy's chearful Madness does perplex:
Or Sorrow's other Madness vex.
Which Knowledge forces me to know;
And Memory will not foregoe.
What but a Soul could have the wit
To build me up for Sin so fit?
So Architects do square and hew,
Green Trees that in the Forest grew.

The Nymph complaining for the death of her Faun

The wanton Troopers riding by
Have shot my Faun and it will dye.
Ungentle men! They cannot thrive
To kill thee. Thou neer didst alive
Them any harm: alas nor could
Thy death yet do them any good.
I'me sure I never wisht them ill;
Nor do I for all this; nor will:
But, if my simple Pray'rs may yet
Prevail with Heaven to forget
Thy murder, I will Joyn my Tears
Rather than fail. But, O my fears!
It cannot dye so. Heavens King
Keeps register of every thing:
And nothing may we use in vain.
Ev'n Beasts must be with justice slain;
Else Men are made their *Deodands*.[1]
Though they should wash their guilty hands
In this warm life-blood, which doth part
From thine, and wound me to the Heart,
Yet could they not be clean: their Stain

[1] *Deodands*: things which have caused the death of a man and are therefore forfeited to the Crown for pious uses.

Is dy'd in such a Purple Grain.
There is not such another in
The World, to offer for their Sin.
   Unconstant *Sylvio*, when yet
I had not found him counterfeit,
One morning (I remember well)
Ty'd in this silver Chain and Bell,
Gave it to me: nay and I know
What he said then; I'me sure I do.
Said He, look how your Huntsman here
Hath taught a Faun to hunt his *Dear*.
But *Sylvio* soon had me beguil'd.
This waxed tame, while he grew wild,
And quite regardless of my Smart,
Left me his Faun, but took his Heart.
   Thenceforth I set my self to play
My solitary time away,
With this: and very well content,
Could so mine idle Life have spent.
For it was full of sport; and light
Of foot, and heart; and did invite,
Me to its game: it seem'd to bless
Its self in me. How could I less
Than love it? O I cannot be
Unkind, t' a Beast that loveth me.
   Had it liv'd long, I do not know
Whether it too might have done so
As *Sylvio* did: his Gifts might be
Perhaps as false or more than he.
But I am sure, for ought that I
Could in so short a time espie,
Thy Love was far more better than
The love of false and cruel men.
   With sweetest milk, and sugar, first
I it at mine own fingers nurst.
And as it grew, so every day
It wax'd more white and sweet than they.

It had so sweet a Breath! And oft
I blusht to see its foot more soft,
And white, (shall I say than my hand?)
NAY any Ladies of the Land.

   It is a wond'rous thing, how fleet
'Twas on those little silver feet.
With what a pretty skipping grace,
It oft would challenge me the Race:
And when 'thad left me far away,
'Twould stay, and run again, and stay.
For it was nimbler much than Hindes;
And trod, as on the four Winds.

   I have a Garden of my own,
But so with Roses over grown,
And Lillies, that you would it guess
To be a little Wilderness.
And all the Spring time of the year
It onely loved to be there.
Among the beds of Lillyes, I
Have sought it oft, where it should lye;
Yet could not, till it self would rise,
Find it, although before mine Eyes.
For, in the flaxen Lillies shade,
It like a bank of Lillies laid.
Upon the Roses it would feed,
Until its Lips ev'n seem'd to bleed:
And then to me 'twould boldly trip,
And print those Roses on my Lip.
But all its chief delight was still
On Roses thus its self to fill:
And its pure virgin Limbs to fold
In whitest sheets of Lillies cold.
Had it liv'd long, it would have been
Lillies without, Roses within.

   O help! O help! I see it faint:
And dye as calmely as a Saint.
See how it weeps. The Tears do come

Sad, slowly dropping like a Gumme,
So weeps the wounded Balsome: so
The Holy Frankincense doth flow.
The brotherless *Heliades*[1]
Melt in such Amber Tears as these.
   I in a golden Vial will
Keep these two crystal Tears; and fill
It till it do o'reflow with mine;
Then place it in *Diana's* Shrine.
   Now my Sweet Faun is vanish'd to
Whither the Swans and Turtles go:
In fair *Elizium* to endure,
With milk-white Lambs, and Ermins pure.
O do not run too fast: for I
Will but bespeak thy Grave, and dye.
   First my unhappy Statue shall
Be cut in Marble; and withal,
Let it be weeping too: but there
Th' Engraver sure his Art may spare;
For I so truly thee bemoane,
That I shall weep though I be Stone:
Until my Tears, still dropping, wear
My breast, themselves engraving there.
There at my feet shalt thou be laid,
Of purest Alabaster made:
For I would have thine Image be
White as I can, though not as Thee.

To his Coy Mistress

Had we but World enough, and Time,
This coyness Lady were no crime.

---

[1] The daughters of Helios, the Sun, who, mourning for their brother
Phaethon, were transformed into trees and wept tears which the Sun
hardened into amber (see Ovid, *Metam.* ii).

We would sit down, and think which way
To walk, and pass our long Loves Day.
Thou by the *Indian Ganges* side
Should'st Rubies find: I by the Tide
Of *Humber* would complain. I would
Love you ten years before the Flood:
And you should if you please refuse
Till the Conversion of the *Jews*.
My vegetable[1] Love should grow
Vaster than Empires, and more slow.
An hundred years should go to praise
Thine Eyes, and on thy Forehead Gaze.
Two hundred to adore each Breast:
But thirty thousand to the rest.
An Age at least to every part,
And the last Age should show your Heart.
For Lady you deserve this State;
Nor would I love at lower rate.

But at my back I alwaies hear
Times winged Charriot hurrying near:
And yonder all before us lye
Desarts of vast Eternity.
Thy Beauty shall no more be found;
Nor, in thy marble Vault, shall sound
My ecchoing Song: then Worms shall try
That long preserv'd Virginity:
And your quaint Honour turn to dust;
And into ashes all my Lust.
The Grave's a fine and private place,
But none I think do there embrace.

Now therefore, while the youthful hew
Sits on thy skin like morning dew,
And while thy willing Soul transpires
At every pore with instant Fires,
Now let us sport us while we may;
And now, like am'rous birds of prey,

[1] The 'vegetable soul' had only two powers: growth and reproduction.

228

Rather at once our Time devour,
Than languish in his slow-chapt[1] pow'r.
Let us roll all our Strength, and all
Our sweetness, up into one Ball:
And tear our Pleasures with rough strife,
Thorough the Iron gates of Life.
Thus, though we cannot make our Sun
Stand still, yet we will make him run.

The Fair Singer

To make a final conquest of all me,
Love did compose so sweet an Enemy,
In whom both Beauties to my death agree,
Joyning themselves in fatal Harmony;
That while she with her Eyes my Heart does bind,
She with her Voice might captivate my Mind.

I could have fled from One but singly fair:
My dis-intangled Soul it self might save,
Breaking the curled trammels of her hair.
But how should I avoid to be her Slave,
Whose subtile Art invisibly can wreath
My fetters of the very Air I breath?

It had been easie fighting in some plain,
Where Victory might hang in equal choice,
But all resistance against her is vain,
Who has th' advantage both of Eyes and Voice,
And all my Forces needs must be undone,
She having gained both the Wind and Sun.

[1] 'The power of his slowly moving jaws.'

ANDREW MARVELL

The Definition of Love

My Love is of a birth as rare
As 'tis for object strange and high:
It was begotten by despair
Upon Impossibility.

Magnanimous Despair alone
Could show me so divine a thing,
Where feeble Hope could ne'r have flown
But vainly flapt its Tinsel Wing.

And yet I quickly might arrive
Where my extended Soul is fixt,
But Fate does Iron wedges drive,
And alwaies crouds it self betwixt.

For Fate with jealous Eye does see
Two perfect Loves; nor lets them close:
Their union would her ruine be,
And her Tyrannick pow'r depose.

And therefore her Decrees of Steel
Us as the distant Poles have plac'd,
(Though Loves whole World on us doth wheel)
Not by themselves to be embrac'd.

Unless the giddy Heaven fall,
And Earth some new Convulsion tear;
And, us to joyn, the World should all
Be cramp'd into a *Planisphere*.[1]

As Lines so Loves *oblique* may well
Themselves in every Angle greet:
But ours so truly *Paralel*,
Though infinite can never meet.

[1] The projection of half the globe on to a plane. Here an astrolabe, a round plate on which the two sides showed the two hemispheres and the poles were consequently brought together.

Therefore the Love which us doth bind.
But Fate so enviously debarrs,
Is the Conjunction of the Mind,
And Opposition of the Stars.

The Picture of little T. C. *in a Prospect of Flowers*[1]

See with what simplicity
This Nimph begins her golden daies!
In the green Grass she loves to lie,
And there with her fair Aspect tames
The Wilder flow'rs, and gives them names:
But only with the Roses playes;
      And them does tell
What Colour best becomes them, and what Smell.

Who can foretel for what high cause
This Darling of the Gods was born!
Yet this is She whose chaster Laws
The wanton Love shall one day fear,
And, under her command severe,
See his Bow broke and Ensigns torn.
      Happy, who can
Appease this virtuous Enemy of Man!

O then let me in time compound,
And parly with those conquering Eyes;
Ere they have try'd their force to wound,
Ere, with their glancing wheels, they drive
In Triumph over Hearts that strive,
And them that yield but more despise.
      Let me be laid,
Where I may see thy Glories from some shade.

[1] Theophila Cornewall, born Sept. 1644: see Introduction, p. xxv.

Mean time, whilst every verdant thing
It self does at thy Beauty charm,
Reform the errours of the Spring;
Make that the Tulips may have share
Of sweetness, seeing they are fair;
And Roses of their thorns disarm:
        But most procure
That Violets may a longer Age endure.

But O young beauty of the Woods,
Whom Nature courts with fruits and flow'rs,
Gather the Flow'rs, but spare the Buds;
Lest *Flora* angry at thy crime,
To kill her Infants in their prime,
Do quickly make th' Example Yours;
        And, ere we see,
Nip in the blossome all our hopes and Thee.

The Mower to the Glo-Worms

Ye living Lamps, by whose dear light
The Nightingale does sit so late,
And studying all the Summer-night,
Her matchless Songs does meditate;

Ye Country Comets, that portend
No War, nor Princes funeral,
Shining unto no higher end
Than to presage the Grasses fall;

Ye Glo-worms, whose officious Flame
To wandring Mowers shows the way,
That in the Night have lost their aim,
And after foolish Fires do stray;

Your courteous Lights in vain you wast,
Since *Juliana* here is come,
For She my Mind hath so displac'd
That I shall never find my home.

The Garden

How vainly men themselves amaze
To win the Palm, the Oke, or Bayes;[1]
And their uncessant Labours see
Crown'd from some single Herb or Tree.
Whose short and narrow verged Shade
Does prudently their Toyles upbraid;
While all Flow'rs and all Trees do close
To weave the Garlands of repose.

Fair quiet, have I found thee here,
And Innocence thy Sister dear!
Mistaken long, I sought you then
In busie Companies of Men.
Your sacred Plants, if here below,
Only among the Plants will grow.
Society is all but rude,
To this delicious Solitude.

No white nor red was ever seen
So am'rous as this lovely green.
Fond Lovers, cruel as their Flame,
Cut in these Trees their Mistress name.
Little, Alas, they know, or heed,
How far these Beauties Hers exceed!
Fair Trees! where s'eer your barkes I wound,
No name shall but your own be found.

[1] The Palm is for victors, the Oak for rulers, the Laurel for poets.

When we have run our Passions heat,
Love hither makes his best retreat.
The *Gods*, that mortal Beauty chase,
Still in a Tree did end their race.
Apollo hunted *Daphne* so,
Only that She might Laurel grow.
And *Pan* did after *Syrinx* speed,
Not as a Nymph, but for a Reed.

What wond'rous Life in this I lead!
Ripe Apples drop about my head;
The Luscious Clusters of the Vine
Upon my Mouth do crush their Wine;
The Nectaren, and curious[1] Peach,
Into my hands themselves do reach;
Stumbling on Melons, as I pass,
Insnar'd with Flow'rs, I fall on Grass.

Mean while the Mind, from pleasure less,
Withdraws into its happiness:
The Mind, that Ocean where each kind
Does streight its own resemblance find;[2]
Yet it creates, transcending these,
Far other Worlds, and other Seas;
Annihilating all that's made
To a green Thought in a green Shade.

Here at the Fountains sliding foot,
Or at some Fruit-trees mossy root,
Casting the Bodies Vest aside,
My Soul into the boughs does glide:
There like a Bird it sits, and sings,
Then whets,[3] and combs its silver Wings;
And, till prepar'd for longer flight,
Waves in its Plumes the various Light.

[1] *curious*: exquisite.
[2] It was a common opinion that all species found on land had their counterparts in the sea.   [3] *whets*: preens.

ANDREW MARVELL

Such was that happy Garden-state,
While Man there walk'd without a Mate:
After a Place so pure, and sweet,
What other Help could yet be meet!
But 'twas beyond a Mortal's share
To wander solitary there:
Two Paradises 'twere in one
To live in Paradise alone.[1]

How well the skilful Gardner drew
Of flow'rs and herbes this Dial new;[2]
Where from above the milder Sun
Does through a fragrant Zodiack run;
And, as it works, th' industrious Bee
Computes its time as well as we.
How could such sweet and wholsome Hours
Be reckon'd but with herbs and flow'rs!

An Horatian *Ode upon* Cromwel's *Return from* Ireland[3]

The forward Youth that would appear
Must now forsake his *Muses* dear,
    Nor in the Shadows sing
    His Numbers languishing.
'Tis time to leave the Books in dust,
And oyl th' unused Armours rust:
    Removing from the Wall

[1] This and the two previous verses are not represented in Marvell's Latin version of this poem.
[2] The garden is embellished with a floral sundial.
[3] Cromwell returned from Ireland in May 1650 to take part in the Scottish campaign. He entered Scotland 22 July 1650. The poem must have been written between these dates. Fairfax, who was shortly to be Marvell's employer, resigned his post as commander-in-chief because he was unwilling to invade Scotland unless the Scots attacked England first. The poem was cancelled from all known copies except one of the edition of 1681.

235

The Corslet of the Hall.
So restless *Cromwel* could not cease
In the inglorious Arts of Peace,
    But through adventrous War
    Urged his active Star.
And, like the three-fork'd Lightning, first
Breaking the Clouds where it was nurst,
    Did thorough his own Side
    His fiery way divide.
For 'tis all one to Courage high
The Emulous or Enemy;
    And with such to inclose
    Is more than to oppose.
Then burning through the Air he went,
And Pallaces and Temples rent:
    And *Caesars* head at last
    Did through his Laurels blast.[1]
'Tis Madness to resist or blame
The force of angry Heavens flame:
    And, if we would speak true,
    Much to the Man is due.
Who, from his private Gardens, where
He liv'd reserved and austere,
    As if his highest plot
    To plant the Bergamot,[2]
Could by industrious Valour climbe
To ruine the great Work of Time,
    And cast the Kingdome old
    Into another Mold.
Though Justice against Fate complain,
And plead the antient Rights in vain:
    But those do hold or break
    As Men are strong or weak.
Nature that hateth emptiness,

---

[1] The Laurel was popularly supposed to be immune to lightning.
[2] *Bergamot*: a fine pear, introduced like many new varieties of fruit in the seventeenth century.

Allows of penetration[1] less:
    And therefore must make room
    Where greater Spirits come.
What Field of all the Civil Wars,
Where his were not the deepest Scars?
    And *Hampton* shows what part
    He had of wiser Art.
Where, twining subtile fears with hope,
He wove a Net of such a scope,
    That *Charles* himself might chase
    To *Caresbrooks* narrow case.[2]
That thence the *Royal Actor* born
The *Tragick Scaffold* might adorn:
    While round the armed Bands
    Did clap their bloody hands.
He nothing common did or mean
Upon that memorable Scene:
    But with his keener Eye
    The Axes edge did try:
Nor call'd the *Gods* with vulgar spight
To vindicate his helpless Right,
    But bow'd his comely Head,
    Down as upon a Bed.
This was that memorable Hour
Which first assur'd the forced Pow'r.
    So when they did design
    The *Capitols* first Line,
A bleeding Head where they begun,
Did fright the Architects to run;
    And yet in that the *State*
    Foresaw it's happy Fate.[3]

[1] *penetration*: occupation of the same space by two bodies simultaneously, a thing more abhorrent to Nature than a vacuum.

[2] Charles I fled from Hampton Court 11 Nov. 1647 to take refuge in Carisbrooke in the Isle of Wight. Contemporary writers ascribed this fatal step to Cromwell's guile, working on the King's fears.

[3] Pliny relates the discovery of the human head, which was said to give the Capitol its name, and that a famous Etruscan seer declared it to be a good omen.

And now the *Irish* are asham'd
To see themselves in one Year tam'd:
　So much one Man can do,
　That does both act and know.
They can affirm his Praises best,
And have, though overcome, confest
　How good he is, how just,
　And fit for highest Trust:
Nor yet grown stiffer with Command,
But still in the *Republick's* hand:
　How fit he is to sway
　That can so well obey.
He to the *Commons Feet* presents
A *Kingdome*, for his first years rents:
　And, what he may, forbears
　His Fame to make it theirs:
And has his Sword and Spoyls ungirt,
To lay them at the *Publick's* skirt.
　So when the Falcon high
　Falls heavy from the Sky,
She, having kill'd, no more does search,
But on the next green Bow to pearch;
　Where, when he first does lure,
　The Falckner has her sure.
What may not then our Isle presume
While Victory his Crest does plume!
　What may not others fear
　If thus he crown each Year!
A *Caesar* he ere long to *Gaul*,
To *Italy* an *Hannibal*,
　And to all States not free
　Shall *Clymacterick*[1] be.
The *Pict* no shelter now shall find
Within his party-colour'd Mind;[2]

---

[1] *Clymacterick*: critical, marking an epoch.

[2] *Pict* was falsely derived from *pingere*, to paint. The derivation was used by other writers to support the charge of falseness and treachery against the Scots.

But from this Valour sad[1]
Shrink underneath the Plad:
Happy if in the tufted brake
The *English Hunter* him mistake;
Nor lay his Hounds in near
The *Caledonian* Deer.
But thou the Wars and Fortunes Son
March indefatigably on;
And for the last effect
Still keep thy Sword erect:
Besides the force it has to fright
The Spirits of the shady Night,[2]
The same *Arts* that did *gain*
A *Pow'r* must it *maintain*.

(*Miscellaneous Poems*, 1681)

HENRY VAUGHAN
(1621/2–1695)

Regeneration

A Ward, and still in bonds, one day
I stole abroad,
It was high-spring, and all the way
Primros'd, and hung with shade;
Yet, was it frost within,
And surly winds
Blasted my infant buds, and sinne
Like Clouds ecclips'd my mind.

Storm'd thus: I straight perceiv'd my spring
Meere stage, and show,
My walke a monstrous, mountain'd thing
Rough-cast with Rocks, and snow;

[1] *sad*: steadfast.
[2] The cross-hilt of the sword would put evil spirits to flight.

And as a Pilgrims Eye
       Far from reliefe,
Measures the melancholy skye
       Then drops, and rains for griefe,

So sigh'd I upwards still, at last
         'Twixt steps, and falls
I reach'd the pinacle, where plac'd
       I found a paire of scales,
       I tooke them up and layd
         In th'one late paines,
The other smoake, and pleasures weigh'd
       But prov'd the heavier graines;

With that, some cryed, *Away*; straight I
         Obey'd, and led
Full East, a faire, fresh field could spy
       Some call'd it, *Jacobs Bed*;
       A Virgin-soile, which no
         Rude feet ere trod,
Where (since he stept there,) only go
       Prophets, and friends of God.

Here, I repos'd; but scarse well set,
       A grove descryed
Of stately height, whose branches met
       And mixt on every side;
       I entred, and once in
         (Amaz'd to see't),
Found all was chang'd, and a new spring
       Did all my senses greet;

The unthrift Sunne shot vitall gold
       A thousand peeces,
And heaven its azure did unfold
       Checqur'd with snowie fleeces,

The aire was all in spice
And every bush
A garland wore; Thus fed my Eyes
But all the Eare lay hush.

Only a little Fountain lent
Some use for Eares,
And on the dumbe shades language spent
The Musicke of her teares;
I drew her neere, and found
The Cisterne full
Of divers stones, some bright, and round
Others ill-shap'd, and dull.

The first (pray marke,) as quick as light
Danc'd through the floud,
But, th'last more heavy than the night
Nail'd to the Center stood;
I wonder'd much, but tyr'd
At last with thought,
My restless Eye that still desir'd
As strange an object brought;

It was a banke of flowers, where I descried
(Though 'twas mid-day,)
Some fast asleepe, others broad-eyed
And taking in the Ray,
Here musing long, I heard
A rushing wind
Which still increas'd, but whence it stirr'd
No where I could not find;

I turn'd me round, and to each shade
Dispatch'd an Eye,
To see, if any leafe had made
Least motion, or Reply,
But while I listning sought
My mind to ease

By knowing, where 'twas, or where not,
    It whisper'd; *Where I please.*

Lord, then said I, *On me one breath,*
    And let me dye before my death!

The Showre

'Twas so, I saw thy birth: That drowsie Lake
From her faint bosome breath'd thee, the disease
Of her sick waters, and Infectious Ease.
            But, now at Even
            Too grosse for heaven,
Thou fall'st in teares, and weep'st for thy mistake.

Ah! it is so with me; oft have I prest
Heaven with a lazie breath, but fruitles this
Peirc'd not; Love only can with quick accesse
            Unlock the way,
            When all else stray
The smoke, and Exhalations of the brest.

Yet, if as thou dost melt, and with thy traine
Of drops make soft the Earth, my eyes could weep
O're my hard heart, that's bound up, and asleep,
            Perhaps at last
            (Some such showres past,)
My God would give a Sun-shine after raine.

The Retreate

Happy those early dayes! when I
Shin'd in my Angell-infancy.
Before I understood this place
Appointed for my second race,
Or taught my soul to fancy ought
But a white, Celestiall thought,

When yet I had not walkt above
A mile, or two, from my first love,
And looking back (at that short space,)
Could see a glimpse of his bright-face;
When on some *gilded Cloud*, or *flowre*
My gazing soul would dwell an houre,
And in those weaker glories spy
Some shadows of eternity;
Before I taught my tongue to wound
My Conscience with a sinfull sound,
Or had the black art to dispence
A sev'rall sinne to ev'ry sence,
But felt through all this fleshly dresse
Bright *shootes* of everlastingnesse.
  O how I long to travell back
And tread again that ancient track!
That I might once more reach that plaine,
Where first I left my glorious traine,
From whence th' Inlightned spirit sees
That shady City of Palme trees;
But (ah!) my soul with too much stay
Is drunk, and staggers in the way.
Some men a forward motion love,
But I by backward steps would move,
And when this dust falls to the urn
In that state I came return.

§¹

Come, come, what doe I here?
    Since he is gone
Each day is grown a dozen year,
    And each houre, one;

¹ There are nine poems scattered through *Silex Scintillans* (six in the first part and three in the second) with no title and a paragraph mark set above them. They are concerned with the death of friends, particularly the death of one person, Vaughan's younger brother William, who died in 1648.

Come, come!
Cut off the sum,
By these soil'd teares!
(Which only thou
Know'st to be true,)
Dayes are my feares.

Ther's not a wind can stir,
Or beam passe by,
But strait I think (though far,)
Thy hand is nigh;
Come, come!
Strike these lips dumb:
This restless breath
That soiles thy name,
Will ne'r be tame
Untill in death.

Perhaps some think a tombe
No house of store,
But a dark, and seal'd up wombe,
Which ne'r breeds more.
Come, come!
Such thoughts benum;
But I would be
With him I weep
A bed, and sleep
To wake in thee.

The Morning-watch

O Joyes! Infinite sweetnes! with what flowres,
And shoots of glory, my soul breakes, and buds!
All the long houres
Of night, and Rest
Through the still shrouds

Of Sleep, and Clouds,
This Dew fell on my Breast;
O how it *Blouds*,
And *Spirits* all my Earth! heark! In what Rings,
And *Hymning Circulations* the quick world
Awakes, and sings;
The rising winds,
And falling springs,
Birds, beasts, all things
Adore him in their kinds.
Thus all is hurl'd
In sacred *Hymnes*, and *Order*, The great *Chime*
And *Symphony* of nature. Prayer is
The world in tune,
A spirit-voyce,
And vocall joyes
Whose *Eccho* is heav'ns blisse.
O let me climbe
When I lye down! The Pious soul by night
Is like a clouded starre, whose beames though said
To shed their light
Under some Cloud
Yet are above,
And shine, and move
Beyond that mistie shrowd.
So in my Bed
That Curtain'd grave, though sleep, like ashes, hide
My lamp, and life, both shall in thee abide.

§

Silence, and stealth of dayes! 'tis now
Since thou art gone,
Twelve hundred houres, and not a brow
But Clouds hang on.

As he that in some Caves thick damp
    Lockt from the light,
Fixeth a solitary lamp,
    To brave the night
And walking from his Sun, when past
    That glim'ring Ray
Cuts through the heavy mists in haste
    Back to his day,
So o'r fled minutes I retreat
    Unto that hour
Which shew'd thee last, but did defeat
    Thy light, and pow'r,
I search, and rack my soul to see
    Those beams again,
But nothing but the snuff to me
    Appeareth plain;
That dark, and dead sleeps in its known,
    And common urn,
But those fled to their Makers throne,
    There shine, and burn;
O could I track them! but souls must
    Track one the other,
And now the spirit, not the dust
    Must be thy brother.
Yet I have one *Pearle* by whose light
    All things I see,
And in the heart of Earth, and night
    Find Heaven, and thee.

Peace

My Soul, there is a Countrie
    Far beyond the stars,
Where stands a winged Sentrie
    All skilfull in the wars,

There above noise, and danger
  Sweet peace sits crown'd with smiles,
And one born in a Manger
  Commands the Beauteous files,
He is thy gracious friend,
  And (O my Soul awake!)
Did in pure love descend
  To die here for thy sake,
If thou canst get but thither,
  There growes the flowre of peace,
The Rose that cannot wither,
  Thy fortresse, and thy ease;
Leave then thy foolish ranges;
  For none can thee secure,
But one, who never changes,
  Thy God, thy life, thy Cure.

The Dawning

Ah! what time wilt thou come? when shall that crie
  The Bridegroome's Comming! fil the sky?
Shall it in the Evening run
When our words and works are done?
Or wil thy all-surprizing light
  Break at midnight?
When either sleep, or some dark pleasure
Possesseth mad man without measure;
Or shal these early, fragrant hours
  Unlock thy bowres?
And with their blush of light descry
Thy locks crown'd with eternitie;
Indeed, it is the only time
That with thy glory doth best chime,

All now are stirring, ev'ry field
    Ful hymns doth yield,
The whole Creation shakes off night,
And for thy shadow looks the light,
Stars now vanish without number,
Sleepie Planets set, and slumber,
The pursie Clouds disband, and scatter,
All expect some sudden matter,
Not one beam triumphs, but from far
    That morning-star;

O at what time soever thou
(Unknown to us,) the heavens wilt bow,
And, with thy Angels in the *Van*,
Descend to Judge poor careless man,
Grant, I may not like puddle lie
In a Corrupt securitie,
Where, if a traveller water crave,
He finds it dead, and in a grave;
But as this restless, vocall *Spring*
All day, and night doth run, and sing,
And though here born, yet is acquainted
Elsewhere, and flowing keeps untainted;
So let me all my busie age
In thy free services ingage,
And though (while here) of force I must
Have Commerce sometimes with poor dust,
And in my flesh, though vile, and low,
As this doth in her Channel, flow,
Yet let my Course, my aym, my Love,
And chief acquaintance be above;
So when that day, and hour shal come
In which thy self wil be the Sun,
Thou'lt find me drest and on my way,
Watching the Break of thy great day.

The World

I saw Eternity the other night
Like a great *Ring* of pure and endless light,
    All calm, as it was bright,
And round beneath it, Time in hours, days, years
    Driv'n by the spheres
Like a vast shadow mov'd, In which the world
    And all her train were hurl'd;
The doting Lover in his queintest strain
    Did there Complain,
Neer him, his Lute, his fancy, and his flights,
    Wits sour delights,
With gloves, and knots the silly snares of pleasure
    Yet his dear Treasure
All scatter'd lay, while he his eys did pour
    Upon a flowr.

The darksome States-man hung with weights and woe
Like a thick midnight-fog mov'd there so slow
    He did nor stay, nor go;
Condemning thoughts (like sad Ecclipses) scowl
    Upon his soul,
And Clouds of crying witnesses without
    Pursued him with one shout.
Yet dig'd the Mole, and lest his ways be found
    Workt under ground,
Where he did Clutch his prey, but one did see
    That policie,
Churches and altars fed him, Perjuries
    Were gnats and flies,
It rain'd about him bloud and tears, but he
    Drank them as free.

The fearfull miser on a heap of rust
Sate pining all his life there, did scarce trust

His own hands with the dust,
Yet would not place one peece above, but lives
    In feare of theeves.
Thousands there were as frantick as himself
    And hug'd each one his pelf,
The down-right Epicure plac'd heav'n in sense
    And scornd pretence
While others slipt into a wide Excesse
    Said little lesse;
The weaker sort slight, triviall wares Inslave
    Who think them brave,
And poor, despised truth sate Counting by
    Their victory.

Yet some, who all this while did weep and sing,
And sing, and weep, soar'd up into the *Ring*,
    But most would use no wing.
O fools (said I,) thus to prefer dark night
    Before true light,
To live in grots, and caves, and hate the day
    Because it shews the way,
The way which from this dead and dark abode
    Leads up to God,
A way where you might tread the Sun, and be
    More bright than he.
But as I did their madnes so discusse
    One whisper'd thus,
This Ring the Bride-groome did for none provide
    But for his bride.

Man

Weighing the stedfastness and state
Of some mean things which here below reside,
Where birds like watchful Clocks the noiseless date
    And Intercourse of times divide,

Where Bees at night get home and hive, and flowrs
   Early, as well as late,
Rise with the Sun, and set in the same bowrs;

  I would (said I) my God would give
The staidness of these things to man! for these
To his divine appointments ever cleave,
   And no new business breaks their peace;
The birds nor sow, nor reap, yet sup and dine,
   The flowres without clothes live,
Yet *Solomon* was never drest so fine.

  Man hath stil either toyes, or Care,
He hath no root, nor to one place is ty'd,
But ever restless and Irregular
   About this Earth doth run and ride,
He knows he hath a home, but scarce knows where,
   He sayes it is so far
That he hath quite forgot how to go there.

  He knocks at all doors, strays and roams,
Nay hath not so much wit as some stones have
Which in the darkest nights point to their homes,
   By some hid sense their Maker gave;
Man is the shuttle, to whose winding quest
   And passage through these looms
God order'd motion, but ordain'd no rest.

§

I walkt the other day (to spend my hour,)
   Into a field
Where I sometimes had seen the soil to yield
   A gallant flowre,
But Winter now had ruffled all the bowre
   And curious store
   I knew there heretofore.

Yet I whose search lov'd not to peep and peer
     I'th'face of things
Thought with my self, there might be other springs
     Besides this here
Which, like cold friends, sees us but once a year,
      And so the flowre
    Might have some other bowre.

Then taking up what I could neerest spie
     I digg'd about
That place where I had seen him to grow out,
     And by and by
I saw the warm Recluse alone to lie
      Where fresh and green
    He lived of us unseen.

Many a question Intricate and rare
     Did I there strow,
But all I could extort was, that he now
     Did there repair
Such losses as befel him in this air
      And would e'r long
    Come forth most fair and young.

This past, I threw the Clothes quite o'r his head,
     And stung with fear
Of my own frailty dropt down many a tear
     Upon his bed,
Then sighing whisper'd, *Happy are the dead!*
      What peace doth now
    Rock him asleep below?

And yet, how few believe such doctrine springs
     From a poor root
Which all the Winter sleeps here under foot
     And hath no wings
To raise it to the truth and light of things,
      But is stil trod
    By ev'ry wandring clod.

O thou! whose spirit did at first inflame
    And warm the dead,
And by a sacred Incubation fed
    With life this frame
Which once had neither being, forme, nor name,
    Grant I may so
    Thy steps track here below,

That in these Masques and shadows I may see
    Thy sacred way,
And by those hid ascents climb to that day
    Which breaks from thee
Who art in all things, though invisibly;
    Shew me thy peace,
    Thy mercy, love, and ease,

And from this Care, where dreams and sorrows raign
    Lead me above
Where Light, Joy, Leisure, and true Comforts move
    Without all pain,
There, hid in thee, shew me his life again
    At whose dumbe urn
    Thus all the year I mourn.

                    (Silex Scintillans, 1650)

§

They are all gone into the world of light!
    And I alone sit lingring here;
Their very memory is fair and bright,
    And my sad thoughts doth clear.

It glows and glitters in my cloudy brest
    Like stars upon some gloomy grove,
Or those faint beams in which this hill is drest,
    After the Sun's remove.

I see them walking in an Air of glory,
    Whose light doth trample on my days:
My days, which are at best but dull and hoary,
    Meer glimering and decays.

O holy hope! and high humility,
    High as the Heavens above!
These are your walks, and you have shew'd them me
    To kindle my cold love,

Dear, beauteous death! the Jewel of the Just,
    Shining no where, but in the dark;
What mysteries do lie beyond thy dust;
    Could man outlook that mark!

He that hath found some fledg'd birds nest, may know
    At first sight, if the bird be flown;
But what fair Well, or Grove he sings in now,
    That is to him unknown.

And yet, as Angels in some brighter dreams
    Call to the soul, when man doth sleep:
So some strange thoughts transcend our wonted theams,
    And into glory peep.

If a star were confin'd into a Tomb
    Her captive flames must needs burn there;
But when the hand that lockt her up, gives room,
    She'l shine through all the sphere.

O Father of eternal life, and all
    Created glories under thee!
Resume thy spirit from this world of thrall
    Into true liberty.

Either disperse these mists, which blot and fill
    My perspective[1] (still) as they pass,
Or else remove me hence unto that hill,
    Where I shall need no glass.

[1] *perspective*: spy-glass.

Cock-crowing[1]

Father of lights! what Sunnie seed,
What glance of day hast thou confin'd
Into this bird? To all the breed
This busie Ray thou hast assign'd;
    Their magnetisme works all night,
    And dreams of Paradise and light.

Their eyes watch for the morning hue,
Their little grain expelling night
So shines and sings, as if it knew
The path unto the house of light.
    It seems their candle, howe'r done,
    Was tinn'd and lighted at the sunne.

If such a tincture, such a touch,
So firm a longing can impowre
Shall thy own image think it much
To watch for thy appearing hour?
    If a meer blast so fill the sail,
    Shall not the breath of God prevail?

O thou immortall light and heat!
Whose hand so shines through all this frame,
That by the beauty of the seat,
We plainly see, who made the same.
    Seeing thy seed abides in me,
    Dwell thou in it, and I in thee.

[1] The basic ideas of this poem are Hermetic. Cf. 'The Soul . . . is guided in her operations by a spiritual, metaphysical grain, a seed or glance of light, simple and without any mixture, descending from the first Father of Lights. For though His full-eyed love shines on nothing but man, yet everything in the world is in some measure directed for his preservation by a spice or touch of the First Intellect' (Thomas Vaughan, *Anima Magica Abscondita*, 1650).

To sleep without thee, is to die;
Yea, 'tis a death partakes of hell:
For where thou dost not close the eye
It never opens, I can tell.
  In such a dark, Ægyptian border,
  The shades of death dwell and disorder.

If joyes, and hopes, and earnest throws,
And hearts, whose Pulse beats still for light
Are given to birds; who, but thee, knows
A love-sick souls exalted flight?
  Can souls be track'd by any eye
  But his, who gave them wings to flie?

Onely this Veyle which thou hast broke,
And must be broken yet in me,
This veyle, I say, is all the cloke
And cloud which shadows thee from me.
  This veyle thy full-ey'd love denies,
  And onely gleams and fractions spies.

O take it off! make no delay,
But brush me with thy light, that I
May shine unto a perfect day,
And warme me at thy glorious Eye!
  O take it off! or till it flee,
  Though with no Lilie,[1] stay with me!

The Starre[2]

What ever 'tis, whose beauty here below
Attracts thee thus & makes thee stream & flow,
  And wind and curle, and wink and smile,
  Shifting thy gate and guile:

[1] The Lily is the flower of light.
[2] Also Hermetical: cf. 'When thou seest the Coelestiall fires move in
their swift and glorious *Circles*, think also there are here *below* some *cold*

Though thy close commerce nought at all imbarrs
My present search, for Eagles eye not starrs,
    And still the lesser by the best
      And highest good is blest:

Yet, seeing all things that subsist and be,
Have their Commissions from Divinitie,
    And teach us duty, I will see
      What man may learn from thee.

First, I am sure, the Subject so respected
Is well disposed, for bodies once infected,
    Deprav'd or dead, can have with thee
      No hold, nor sympathie.

Next, there's in it a restless, pure desire
And longing for thy bright and vitall fire,
    Desire that never will be quench'd,
      Nor can be writh'd, nor wrench'd.

These are the Magnets which so strongly move
And work all night upon thy light and love,
    As beauteous shapes, we know not why,
      Command and guide the eye.

For where desire, celestiall, pure desire
Hath taken root, and grows, and doth not tire,
    There God a Commerce states, and sheds
      His Secret on their heads.

This is the Heart he craves; and who so will
But give it him, and grudge not; he shall feel
    That God is true, as herbs unseen
      Put on their youth and green.

Natures, which they *over-look*, and about which they *move* incessantly to
heat and concoct them.' Also, '*Heaven* itself was *originally* extracted from
Inferiors, yet not so *intirely*, but some *portion* of the *Heavenly Natures* remained still *below*, and are the *very same* in *Essence* and *Substance* with the
separated *starrs* and *skies*' (Thomas Vaughan, *Magia Adamica*).

The Night

(John ii. 3)

Through that pure *Virgin-shrine*,
That sacred vail drawn o'r thy glorious noon
That men might look and live as Glo-worms shine,
    And face the Moon:
  Wise *Nicodemus* saw such light
  As made him know his God by night.

    Most blest believer he!
Who in that land of darkness and blinde eyes
Thy long expected healing wings could see,
    When thou didst rise,
  And what can never more be done,
  Did at mid-night speak with the Sun!

    O who will tell me, where
He found thee at that dead and silent hour!
What hallow'd solitary ground did bear
    So rare a flower,
  Within whose sacred leafs did lie
  The fulness of the Deity.

    No mercy-seat of gold,
No dead and dusty *Cherub*, nor carv'd stone,
But his own living works did my Lord hold
    And lodge alone;
  Where *trees* and *herbs* did watch and peep
  And wonder, while the *Jews* did sleep.

    Dear night! this worlds defeat;
The stop to busie fools; cares check and curb;
The day of Spirits; my souls calm retreat
    Which none disturb!
  Christs progress, and his prayer time;
  The hours to which high Heaven doth chime

Gods silent, searching flight:
When my Lords head is fill'd with dew, and all
His locks are wet with the clear drops of night;
    His still, soft call;
  His knocking time; The souls dumb watch,
  When Spirits their fair kindred catch.

    Were all my loud, evil days
Calm and unhaunted as is thy dark Tent,
Whose peace but by some *Angels* wing or voice
    Is seldom rent;
  Then I in Heaven all the long year
  Would keep, and never wander here.

    But living where the Sun
Doth all things wake, and where all mix and tyre
Themselves and others, I consent and run
    To ev'ry myre,
  And by this worlds ill-guiding light,
  Erre more than I can do by night.

    There is in God (some say)
A deep, but dazling darkness; As men here
Say it is late and dusky, because they
    See not all clear
  O for that night! where I in him
  Might live invisible and dim.

The Water-fall

With what deep murmurs through times silent stealth
Doth thy transparent, cool and watry wealth
    Here flowing fall,
    And chide, and call,

As if his liquid, loose Retinue staid
Lingring, and were of this steep place afraid,
    The common pass
    Where, clear as glass,
    All must descend
    Not to an end:
But quickned by this deep and rocky grave,
Rise to a longer course more bright and brave.

    Dear stream! dear bank, where often I
    Have sate, and pleas'd my pensive eye,
    Why, since each drop of thy quick store
    Runs thither, whence it flow's before,
    Should poor souls fear a shade or night,
    Who came (sure) from a sea of light?
    Or since those drops are all sent back
    So sure to thee, that none doth lack,
    Why should frail flesh doubt any more
    That what God takes, hee'l not restore?
    O useful Element and clear!
    My sacred wash and cleanser here,
    My first consigner unto those
    Fountains of life, where the Lamb goes?
    What sublime truths, and wholesome themes,
    Lodge in thy mystical, deep streams!
    Such as dull man can never finde
    Unless that Spirit lead his minde,
    Which first upon thy face did move,
    And hatch'd all with his quickning love.
    As this loud brooks incessant fall
    In streaming rings restagnates all,
    Which reach by course the bank, and then
    Are no more seen, just so pass men.
    O my invisible estate,
    My glorious liberty, still late!
    Thou art the Channel my soul seeks,
    Not this with Cataracts and Creeks.

Quickness

False life! a foil and no more, when
   Wilt thou be gone?
Thou foul deception of all men
That would not have the true come on.

Thou art a Moon-like toil; a blinde
   Self-posing state;
A dark contest of waves and winde;
A meer tempestuous debate.

Life is a fix'd, discerning light,
   A knowing Joy;
No chance, or fit: but ever bright,
And calm and full, yet doth not cloy.

'Tis such a blissful thing, that still
   Doth vivifie,
And shine and smile, and hath the skil
To please without Eternity.

Thou art a toylsom Mole, or less
   A moving mist
But life is, what none can express,
A quickness, which my God hath kist.

      (*Silex Scintillans,* 1655)

THOMAS STANLEY
(1625–1678)

The Magnet

Ask the Empresse of the night
    How the hand which guides her sphear,
Constant in unconstant light,
    Taught the waves her yoke to bear,
And did thus by loving force
Curb or tame the rude seas course.

Ask the female Palme how shee
    First did woo her husbands love;
And the Magnet, ask how he
    Doth th'obsequious iron move;
Waters, plants and stones know this,
That they love, not what love is.

Be not then less kind than these,
    Or from love exempt alone,
Let us twine like amorous trees,
    And like rivers melt in one;
Or if thou more cruell prove
Learne of steel and stones to love.

                    (*Poems*, 1647)

The Repulse

Not that by this disdain
    I am releas'd,
And freed from thy tyrannick chain,
    Do I my self think blest;

Not that thy Flame shall burn
No more; for know
That I shall into ashes turn,
Before this fire doth so.

Nor yet that unconfin'd
I now may rove,
And with new beauties please my mind;
But that thou ne'r didst love:

For since thou hast no part
Felt of this flame,
I onely from thy tyrant heart
Repuls'd, not banish'd am.

To lose what once was mine
Would grieve me more
Than those inconstant sweets of thine
Had pleas'd my soul before.

Now I have lost the blisse
I ne'r possest
And spight of fate am blest in this,
That I was never blest.

La Belle Confidente

You earthly Souls that court a wanton flame,
Whose pale weak influence
Can rise no higher than the humble name
And narrow laws of Sence,
Learn by our friendship to create
An immaterial fire,
Whose brightnesse Angels may admire,
But cannot emulate.

Sicknesse may fright the roses from her cheek,
    Or make the Lilies fade,
But all the subtile wayes that death doth seek
    Cannot my love invade:
    Flames that are kindled by the eye,
      Through time and age expire;
    But ours that boast a reach far higher
      Can nor decay, nor die.

For when we must resign our vital breath,
    Our Loves by Fate benighted,
We by this friendship shall survive in death,
    Even in divorce united.
    Weak Love through fortune or distrust
      In time forgets to burn,
    But this pursues us to the Urn,
      And marries either's Dust.

                (*Poems*, 1651)

JOHN HALL

(1627–1656)

The Call

    Romira, stay,
And run not thus like a young Roe away,
      No enemie
Pursues thee (foolish girle) tis onely I,
    I'le keep off harms,
If thou'l be pleas'd to garrison mine arms;
      What dost thou fear
I'le turn a Traitour? may these Roses here
      To palenesse shred,
And Lillies stand disguised in new Red,

If that I lay
A snare, wherein thou wouldst not gladly stay;
    See see the Sunne
Does slowly to his azure Lodging run,
    Come sit but here
And presently hee'l quit our Hemisphere,
    So still among
Lovers, time is too short or else too long;
    Here will we spin
Legends for them that have Love Martyrs been,
    Here on this plain
Wee'l talk *Narcissus* to a flour again;
    Come here, and chose
On which of these proud plats thou would repose,
    Here maist thou shame
The rusty Violets, with the Crimson flame
    Of either cheek,
And Primroses white as thy fingers seek,
    Nay, thou maist prove
That mans most Noble Passion is to Love.

An Epicurean Ode[1]

Since that this thing we call the world
By chance on Atomes is begot,
Which though in dayly motions hurld,
    Yet weary not,
    How doth it prove
Thou art so fair and I in Love?

Since that the soul doth onely lie
Immers'd in matter, chaind in sense,
How can *Romira* thou and I
    With both dispence?
    And thus ascend
In higher flights than wings can lend.

[1] That is, based on the materialist philosophy of Epicurus.

Since man's but pasted up of Earth,
And ne're was cradled in the skies,
What *Terra Lemnia*[1] gave thee birth?
    What Diamond eyes?
    Or thou alone
To tell what others were, came down?

On an Houre-glasse

My Life is measur'd by this glasse, this glasse
By all those little Sands that thorough passe.
See how they presse, see how they strive, which shall
With greatest speed and greatest quicknesse fall.
See how they raise a little Mount, and then
With their owne weight doe levell it agen.
But when th'have all got thorough, they give o're
Their nimble sliding downe, and move no more.
Just such is man whose houres still forward run,
Being almost finisht ere they are begun;
So perfect nothings, such light blasts are we,
That ere w'are ought at all, we cease to be.
Do what we will, our hasty minutes fly,
And while we sleep, what do we else but die?
How transient are our Joyes, how short their day!
They creepe on towards us, but flie away.
How stinging are our sorrowes! where they gaine
But the least footing, there they will remaine.
How groundlesse are our hopes, how they deceive
Our childish thoughts, and onely sorrow leave!
How reall are our feares! they blast us still,
Still rend us, still with gnawing passions fill;
How senselesse are our wishes, yet how great!
With what toile we pursue them, with what sweat!
Yet most times for our hurts, so small we see,
Like Children crying for some Mercurie.

[1] A fine clay found in Lemnos, an antidote to poison and a sovereign remedy.

This gapes for Marriage, yet his fickle head
Knows not what cares waite on a Marriage bed.
This vowes Virginity, yet knowes not what
Lonenesse, griefe, discontent, attends that state.
Desires of wealth anothers wishes hold,
And yet how many have been choak'd with Gold?
This onely hunts for honour, yet who shall
Ascend the higher, shall more wretched fall.
This thirsts for knowledge, yet how is it bought
With many a sleeplesse night and racking thought?
This needs will travell, yet how dangers lay
Most secret Ambuscado's in the way?
These triumph in their Beauty, though it shall
Like a pluck't Rose or fading Lillie fall.
Another boasts strong armes, 'las Giants have
By silly Dwarfes been drag'd unto their grave.
These ruffle in rich silke, though ne're so gay,
A well plum'd Peacock is more gay than they.
Poore man, what art! A Tennis ball of Errour,
A Ship of Glasse, toss'd in a Sea of terrour,
Issuing in blood and sorrow from the wombe,
Crauling in teares and mourning to the tombe,
How slippery are thy pathes, how sure thy fall,
How art thou Nothing when th'art most of all!

(Poems, 1646)

THOMAS TRAHERNE
(1637/8–1674)

On News

News from a forrein Country came,
As if my Treasure and my Wealth lay there:
So much it did my Heart Enflame!
Twas wont to call my Soul into mine Ear.

Which thither went to Meet
The Approaching Sweet:
And on the Threshhold stood,
To entertain the Unknown Good.
It Hover'd there,
As if twould leave mine Ear.
And was so Eager to Embrace
The Joyfull Tidings as they came,
Twould almost leave its Dwelling Place,
To Entertain the Same.

As if the Tidings were the Things,
My very Joys themselves, my forrein Treasure,
Or els did bear them on their Wings;
With so much Joy they came, with so much Pleasure.
My Soul stood at the Gate
To recreate
Itself with Bliss: And to
Be pleased with Speed. A fuller View
It fain would take
Yet Journeys back would make
Unto my Heart: as if twould fain
Go out to meet, yet stay within
To fit a place, to Entertain,
And bring the Tidings in.

What Sacred Instinct did inspire
My Soul in Childhood with a Hope so Strong?
What Secret Force moved my Desire,
To expect my Joys beyond the Seas, so Yong?
Felicity I knew
Was out of View:
And being here alone,
I saw that Happiness was gone,
From Me! for this
I Thirsted Absent Bliss,

And thought that sure beyond the Seas,
Or els in som thing near at hand
I knew not yet, (since nought did please
    I knew.) my Bliss did stand.

But little did the Infant Dream
That all the Treasures of the World were by:
And that Himself was so the Cream
And Crown of all, which round about did lie.
    Yet thus it was. The Gem,
      The Diadem,
      The Ring Enclosing all
That Stood upon this Earthy Ball;
      The Heavenly Eye,
    Much Wider than the Skie,
Wherein they all included were,
The Glorious Soul that was the King
Made to possess them, did appear
    A small and little thing!

        (*Centuries of Meditation*, Bodleian Library,
        MS. Eng. th. e 50)

Shadows in the Water

In unexperienc'd Infancy
Many a sweet Mistake doth lye:
Mistake tho false, intending true;
A *Seeming* somewhat more than *View*;
    That doth instruct the Mind
    In Things that lye behind,
And many Secrets to us show
Which afterwards we com to know.

Thus did I by the Water's brink
Another World beneath me think;

And while the lofty spacious Skies
Reversed there abus'd mine Eyes,
    I fancy'd other Feet
    Came mine to touch or meet;
As by som Puddle I did play
Another World within it lay.

Beneath the Water People drown'd,
Yet with another Hev'n crown'd,
In spacious Regions seem'd to go
As freely moving to and fro:
    In bright and open Space
    I saw their very face;
Eyes, Hands, and Feet they had like mine;
Another Sun did with them shine.

'Twas strange that People there should walk,
And yet I could not hear them talk:
That thro a little watry Chink,
Which one dry Ox or Horse might drink,
    We other Worlds should see,
    Yet not admitted be;
And other Confines there behold
Of Light and Darkness, Heat and Cold.

I call'd them oft, but call'd in vain;
No Speeches we could entertain:
Yet did I there expect to find
Some other World, to please my Mind.
    I plainly saw by these
    A new *Antipodes*,
Whom, tho they were so plainly seen,
A Film kept off that stood between.

By walking Men's reversed Feet
I chanc'd another World to meet;
Tho it did not to View exceed
A Phantasm, 'tis a World indeed,

Where Skies beneath us shine,
And Earth by Art divine
Another face presents below,
Where People's feet against Ours go.

Within the Regions of the Air,
Compass'd about with Hev'ns fair,
Great Tracts of Land there may be found
Enricht with Fields and fertil Ground;
Where many num'rous Hosts,
In those far distant Coasts,
For other great and glorious Ends,
Inhabit, my yet unknown Friends.

O ye that stand upon the Brink,
Whom I so near me, thro the Chink,
With Wonder see: What Faces there,
Whose Feet, whose Bodies, do ye wear?
I my Companions see
In You, another Me.
They seemed Others, but are We;
Our second Selves those Shadows be.

Look how far off those lower Skies
Extend themselves! scarce with mine Eyes
I can them reach. O ye my Friends,
What *Secret* borders on those Ends?
Are lofty Hevens hurl'd
'Bout your inferior World?
Are ye the Representatives
Of other People's distant Lives?

Of all the Play-mates which I knew
That here I do the Image view
In other Selves; what can it mean?
But that below the purling Stream

Some unknown Joys there be
　　Laid up in store for me;
To which I shall, when that thin Skin
　　Is broken, be admitted in.

(*Poems of Felicity*, British Museum,
MS. Burney 392)

JOHN WILMOT, EARL OF ROCHESTER
(1648–1680)

The Mistress

An Age in her Embraces past,
　　Would seem a Winter's Day;
When Life and Light, with envious hast,
　　Are torn and snatch'd away.

But, oh how slowly Minutes rowl,
　　When absent from her Eyes,
That feed my Love, which is my Soul;
　　It languishes and dyes.

For then no more a Soul but shade,
　　It mournfully does move;
And haunts my Breast, by absence made
　　The living Tomb of Love.

You Wiser men despise me not,
　　Whose Love-sick Fancy raves,
On Shades of Souls, and Heav'n knows what;
　　Short Ages live in Graves.

When e're those wounding Eyes, so full
　　Of Sweetness, you did see;
Had you not been profoundly dull,
　　You had gone mad like me.

Nor Censure us, You who perceive
   My best belov'd and me,
Sigh and lament, Complain and grieve;
   You think we disagree.

Alas! 'tis Sacred Jealousie,
   Love rais'd to an Extream;
The only Proof 'twixt her and me,
   We love, and do not dream.

Fantastick Fancies fondly move,
   And in frail Joys believe,
Taking false Pleasure for true Love;
   But Pain can ne're deceive.

Kind Jealous Doubts, tormenting Fears
   And Anxious Cares, when past,
Prove our Hearts Treasure fixt and dear,
   And make us blest at last.

A Song

Absent from thee I languish still,
   Then ask me not, when I return?
The straying Fool 'twill plainly kill,
   To wish all Day, all Night to Mourn.

Dear! from thine Arms then let me flie,
   That my Fantastick mind may prove,
The Torments it deserves to try,
   That tears my fixt Heart from my Love.

When wearied with a world of Woe,
   To thy safe Bosom I retire,
Where Love and Peace and Truth does flow,
   May I contented there expire.

Lest once more wandring from that Heav'n
I fall on some base heart unblest;
Faithless to thee, False, unforgiven,
And lose my Everlasting rest.

A Song of a Young Lady. To her Ancient Lover

Ancient Person, for whom I,
All the flattering Youth defy;
Long be it e're thou grow Old,
Aking, shaking, Crazy Cold.
But still continue as thou art,
Ancient Person of my Heart.

On thy wither'd Lips and dry,
Which like barren Furrows lye,
Brooding Kisses I will pour,
Shall thy Youthful Heat restore.
Such kind Show'rs in Autumn fall,
And a second Spring recall:
Nor from thee will ever part,
Ancient Person of my Heart.

Thy Nobler parts, which but to name
In our Sex would be counted shame,
By Ages frozen grasp possest,
From their Ice shall be releast:
And sooth'd by my reviving hand,
In former Warmth and Vigor stand.
All a Lover's wish can reach,
For thy Joy my Love shall teach:
And for thy Pleasure shall improve,
All that Art can add to Love.
Yet still I love thee without Art,
Ancient Person of my Heart.

Love and Life

All my past Life is mine no more,
    The flying hours are gone:
Like transitory Dreams giv'n o're,
Whose Images are kept in store,
    By Memory alone.

The Time that is to come is not;
    How can it then be mine?
The present Moment's all my Lot,
And that, as fast as it is got,
    Phyllis, is only thine.

Then talk not of Inconstancy,
    False Hearts, and broken Vows;
If I, by Miracle, can be
This live-long Minute true to thee,
    'Tis all that Heav'n allows.

Upon Nothing

Nothing! thou Elder Brother ev'n to Shade,
Thou hadst a being ere the World was made,
And (well fixt) art alone, of ending not afraid.

Ere time and place were, time and place were not,
When Primitive *Nothing* something strait begot,
Then all proceeded from the great united—What.

Something the Gen'ral Attribute of all,
Sever'd from thee, its sole Original,
Into thy boundless self must undistinguish'd fall.

Yet something did thy mighty Pow'r command,
And from thy fruitful emptiness's hand,
Snatch'd Men, Beasts, Birds, Fire, Water, Air and Land.

Matter, the wicked'st off-spring of thy Race,
By Form assisted flew from thy Embrace,
And Rebel Light obscur'd thy reverend dusky Face.

With Form and Matter, time and place did joyn,
Body, thy Foe, with these did Leagues combine,
To spoil thy peaceful Realm, and ruine all thy Line.

But turn-Coat Time assists the Foe in vain,
And, brib'd by thee, destroys their short-liv'd Reign,
And to thy hungry Womb drives back thy Slaves again.

Tho' Mysteries are barr'd from Laick Eyes,
And the Divine alone, with Warrant, pryes
Into thy Bosom where the truth in private lies;

Yet this of thee the wise may freely say,
Thou from the virtuous nothing tak'st away,
And to be part with thee the Wicked wisely pray.

Great Negative, how vainly would the Wise
Enquire, define, distinguish, teach, devise,
Didst thou not stand to point their dull Philosophies?

Is, or *is not*, the two great ends of Fate,
And *true* or *false*, the subject of debate,
That perfect, or destroy, the vast designs of State;

When they have rack'd the *Politician's* Breast,
Within thy Bosom most securely rest,
And, when reduc'd to thee, are least unsafe and best.

But *Nothing*, why does *Something* still permit,
That Sacred Monarchs should at Council sit,
With Persons highly thought at best for nothing fit:

While weighty *Something* modestly abstains,
From Princes Coffers, and from States-Mens Brains,
And nothing there like stately *Nothing* reigns?

Nothing, who dwell'st with Fools in grave disguise,
For whom they Reverend Shapes, and Forms devise,
Lawn Sleeves, and Furs, and Gowns, when they like thee look
    wise:

French Truth, *Dutch* Prowess, *Brittish* Policy,
Hibernian Learning, *Scotch* Civility,
Spaniards Dispatch, *Danes* Wit, are mainly seen in thee.

The great Man's Gratitude to his best Friend,
Kings Promises, Whores Vows, tow'rds thee they bend,
Flow swiftly into thee, and in thee ever end.

                               (*Poems*, 1691)

THOMAS HEYRICK
(1649–1694)

On a Sunbeam

Thou Beauteous Off-spring of a Syre as Fair;
With thy kind Influence thou dost all things heat:
Thou gild'st the Heaven, the Sea, the Earth and Air,
And under massy Rocks dost Gold beget.
    Th'opaque dull *Earth* thou dost make fine,
    Thou dost i'th'*Moon* and *Planets* shine;
    And if *Astronomy* say true,
Our *Earth* to them doth seem a *Planet* too.

How unaccountable thy Journeys prove!
Thy swift Course thro the Universe doth fly,
From lofty heights in distant Heavens above,
To all that at the lowly Center ly.
    Thy Parent *Sun* once in a Day
    Thro Heaven doth steer his well-beat way;
    Thou of a swifter subtler breed
Dost every *Moment* his *Day's* Course exceed.

Thy Common presence makes thee little priz'd,
Which if we once had lost, wee'd dearly Buy:
How would the Blind hugg, what's by us despis'd!
How welcome wouldst thou in a *Dungeon* be!
    Thrice-wretched those, in Mines are bred,
    That from thy sight are buried,
    When all the Stores, for which they try,
Neither in Use, nor Beauty, equal Thee.

Could there be found an Art to fix thee down,
And of condensed Rays a Gem to make,
'Twould be the brightest Lustre of a Crown,
And an esteem invaluable take,
    New Wars would the tir'd World molest,
    And new *Ambition* fire Men's breast,
    More Battels fought for it, than e're
Before for Love, Empire, or Treasure were.

Thou'rt quickly born and dost as quickly die:
Pitty so fair a Birth to fate should fall!
Now here and now in abject Dust dost lie;
One Moment 'twixt thy Birth and Funeral.
    Art thou, like Angels, only shown,
    Then to our Grief for ever flown?
    Tell me, *Apollo*, tell me where
The *Sunbeams* go, when they do disappear.

On the Death of a Monkey

Here *Busy* and yet *Innocent* lyes Dead,
    Two things, that seldom meet:
No Plots nor Stratagems disturb'd his head,
    Or's his merry Soul did fret:
He shew'd like Superannuated *Peer*,
Grave was his look, and *Politick* his Air;
And he for *Nothing* too spent all his care.

But that he died of Discontent, 'tis fear'd,
    Head of the *Monkey* Rout;
To see so many Brother *Apes* preferr'd,
    And he himself left out:
On all below he did his Anger show'r,
Fit for a Court did all above adore,
H'had *Shows* of Reason, and few *Men* have more.

                    (*Miscellany Poems*, 1691)

RICHARD LEIGH
(1649–1728)

The Eccho

Where do these *Voices* stray,
Which *lose* in *Woods* their *Way*?
Erring each *Step* anew,
While they *false Paths* pursue.
Through many *Windings* led,
Some *crookedly proceed*,
Some to the Ear *turn back*,
Asking, which way to take.
Wandring without a Guide,
They *holla* from each side,
And *call*, and *answer* all
To one another's *Call*.

Whence may these *Sounds* proceed,
From Woods, or from the *Dead*?
Sure, *Souls* here once forlorn,
The *Living* make their Scorn,
And *Shepherds*, that liv'd here,
Now ceasing to appear,

Mock thus in sport the *Fair*,
That would not grant their *Pray'r*:
While *Nymphs* their *Voices* learn,
And *mock* them in Return.
Or if at least, the *Sound*,
Does from the *Woods* rebound
The *Woods*, of them complain,
Who *Shepherds* Vows disdain.
Woods, and *Rocks*, answer all
To the wrong'd *Lover's* Call.
How *deaf* soe're, and *hard*,
They their Complaints regard;
Which *Nymphs* with Scorn repay,
More *deaf*, more *hard*, than *they*.

Sleeping on her Couch

Thus lovely, *Sleep* did *first* appear,
　　E're yet it was with *Death* ally'd;
When the first *fair one*, like *her* here,
　　Lay down, and for a little *dy'd*.

E're *happy Souls* knew how to *dye*,
　　And trod the *rougher Paths* to *Bliss*,
Transported in an *Extasie*,
　　They *breath'd out* such *smooth waies*, as this.

Her *Hand* bears gently up her *Head*,
　　And like a *Pillow*, rais'd does keep;
But *softer* than her *Couch*, is spread,
　　Though that be *softer*, than her *Sleep*.

Alas! that death-like *Sleep*, or *Night*,
　　Should power have to close those *Eyes*;
Which once vy'd with the *fairest Light*,
　　Or what *gay Colours*, thence did rise.

Ah! that lost *Beams*, thus long have shin'd,
  To them, with *Darkness* over-spread,
Unseen, as *Day breaks*, to the *Blind*,
  Or the *Sun rises*, to the *Dead*.

That *Sun*, in all his *Eastern Pride*,
  Did never see a *Shape* so rare,
Nor *Night*, within its *black Arms* hide
  A *silent Beauty*, half so *fair*.

(*Poems*, 1675)

JOHN NORRIS OF BEMERTON
(1657–1711)

Hymn to Darkness

Hail thou most *sacred Venerable* thing,
  What Muse is worthy thee to sing?
Thee, from whose *pregnant universal* womb
All things, even *Light* thy *Rival*, first did Come.
What dares he not attempt that sings of thee,
  Thou *First* and greatest *Mystery*.
Who can the *Secrets* of thy essence tell?
Thou like the *light* of God art *inaccessible*.

Before *Great Love* this *Monument* did raise,
  This ample *Theater* of *Praise*.
Before the *folding Circles* of the Skie
Were *tuned* by him who is all *Harmony*.
Before the Morning Stars their *Hymn* began,
  Before the *Councel* held for *Man*.
Before the *birth* of either *Time* or *Place*,
Thou reign'st *unquestioned* Monarch in the *empty* Space.

Thy *native* lot thou didst to *light resign*,
    But still *half* of the Globe is *thine*.
Here with a *quiet*, but yet *aweful* hand,
Like the *best* Emperours thou dost command.
To thee the Stars *above* their *brightness* owe,
    And mortals their *repose below*.
To thy protection *Fear* and *Sorrow* flee,
And those that *weary* are of *light*, find *rest* in *thee*.

Tho *Light* and *Glory* be th'Almighty's *Throne*,
    Darkness is his *Pavilion*.
From that his radiant *Beauty*, but from thee
He has his *Terrour* and his *Majesty*.
Thus when he first proclaim'd his sacred Law
    And would his *Rebel* subjects *awe*,
Like Princes on some great *solemnity*
H'appear'd in's *Robes* of *State*, and Clad himself with *thee*.

The Blest above do thy sweet *umbrage* prize
    When *Cloy'd* with light, they *veil* their eyes.
The *Vision* of the Deity is made
More sweet and *Beatifick* by thy *Shade*.
But we poor *Tenants* of this Orb below
    Don't *here* thy excellencies know,
Till Death our understandings does *improve*,
And then our *Wiser ghosts* thy silent *night-walks* love.

But thee I *now* admire, thee would I chuse
    For my *Religion*, or my *Muse*.
'Tis hard to tell whether thy reverend shade
Has more good *Votaries* or *Poets* made,
From thy *dark Caves* were *Inspirations* given,
    And from thick *groves* went *vows* to Heaven.
Hail then thou *Muse's* and *Devotions* Spring,
'Tis *just* we should *adore*, 'tis *just* we should thee *sing*.

                (*Poems*, 1687)

SELECT READING LIST

H. J. C. Grierson, *Metaphysical Lyrics and Poems*, 1921, is a classic anthology with an important critical introduction.

G. Saintsbury, *Minor Poets of the Caroline Period*, 3 vols., 1905, 1906, 1921, collects many poets unpublished or difficult to obtain in modern editions and contains much lively critical comment.

Editions, biographies, and studies of individual authors are given in the biographical notes.

Criticism

Samuel Johnson, 'Life of Cowley', *Lives of the Poets*, 1779–81, ed. G. B. Hill, 1905 (also in the World's Classics).

T. S. Eliot, 'The Metaphysical Poets', *T.L.S.*, 1921, reprinted in *Selected Essays*, 1932.

Joan Bennett, *Four Metaphysical Poets*, 1934, revised edition, 1953.

F. R. Leavis, 'The Line of Wit', in *Revaluation*, 1936.

Helen C. White, *The Metaphysical Poets*, New York, 1936.

M. Praz, *Studies in Seventeenth Century Imagery*, 1939.

Douglas Bush, *English Literature in the Earlier Seventeenth Century*, 1945.

F. P. Wilson, *Elizabethan and Jacobean*, 1945.

Rosemond Tuve, *Elizabethan and Metaphysical Imagery*, Chicago, 1947.

Rosemary Freeman, *English Emblem Books*, 1948.

L. I. Martz, *The Poetry of Meditation*, New Haven, 1954.

BIOGRAPHICAL NOTES

WILLIAM ALABASTER, 1567–1640 (p. 12). As author of *Eliseis*, a Latin poem on the Queen, Alabaster is mentioned in *Colin Clouts Come Home Again*. His tragedy *Roxana* was praised by Johnson for its elegant Latinity. Educated at Westminster and Trinity College, Cambridge, where he was a Fellow, he went as chaplain to Essex on the Cadiz Expedition in 1596. On his return he declared himself a Catholic. His divine sonnets, which survive only in manuscript, were written at the period of his conversion when he was in prison and under pressure to recant. After some years abroad, having got into trouble with the Inquisition at Rome, he returned to England and declared himself once more a Protestant. He married and ended an adventurous life as a country parson. In the latter half of his life he was absorbed in recondite speculations on the Book of Revelation and published several cabbalistic works.

The Sonnets of William Alabaster, ed. G. M. Story and Helen
   Gardner, 1959.
L. I. Guiney, *Recusant Poets*, 1938.

THOMAS CAREW, 1594/5–1640 (p. 115). Carew came of a good Cornish family. His father, Sir Matthew Carew, was a Master in Chancery, knighted by James I. He was educated at Merton College, Oxford, and at the Middle Temple, where he was reported to study his law-books 'very little'. He found employment as secretary to his relative Sir Dudley Carleton, Ambassador at Venice, and was with him in Italy from 1613 to 1615 and again at The Hague in 1616; but he offended his benefactor and was dismissed in disgrace. He went on an embassy with Sir Edward Herbert to Paris in 1619. Otherwise, he kept himself at Court until he was made Gentleman of the Privy Chamber and Sewer in Ordinary to the King in 1630. His masque, *Caelum Britannicum*, with settings by Inigo Jones, was performed at Court with great splendour in 1634. He went north with the King and his army in 1639 in the first Bishops' War, but escaped the miseries of the Civil War by dying in 1640. 'A great libertine in his life and talke', according to Walton, Carew is described more kindly by Clarendon as 'a Person of a pleasant and facetious Wit', who 'made many Poems (especially in the amorous Way) which for Sharpness of the Fancy, and the Elegancy of the Language . . . were at least equal, if not superior to any of that time'.

Poems, ed. Rhodes Dunlap, 1949.

WILLIAM CARTWRIGHT, 1611–43 (p. 159). Cartwright went from the free school at Cirencester to Westminster and from there, as Student, to Christ Church. His play, *The Royal Slave*, was staged at Oxford for the King's visit in 1636, and was so much approved that the Queen commanded a second performance at Hampton Court. In 1638 he took Holy Orders, probably at the suggestion of his patron Brian Duppa, then Bishop of Chichester. Cartwright, who was, according to Wood, 'the most florid and seraphical Preacher in the University', preached the sermon of victory on the King's return to Oxford after Edgehill. He died of camp fever and was buried in Christ Church Cathedral. Aubrey says it is 'not to be forgott that king Charles 1st dropt a teare at the newes of his death'. It occasioned an outburst of elegiac verses, which occupy the first hundred pages of his collected *Works* (1651). That Jonson actually said of him 'My son *Cartwright* writes all like a Man' is possibly an invention of the publisher.

Plays and Poems, ed. G. B. Evans, 1951.

JOHN CLEVELAND, 1613–58 (p. 193). From the number of editions of his poems, Cleveland seems to have been by far the most popular poet of the mid-century. The son of a clergyman, he was educated at the country school at Hinckley, Leicestershire, where his father was Vicar, and at Christ's College, Cambridge. In 1634 he became a Fellow of St. John's and Reader in Rhetoric. He was active in opposing Cromwell's election as Member for Cambridge in 1640, and in 1643 removed to Oxford where the King was. From 1645 to 1646 he was Judge Advocate at Newark and held the town against the Scots. Cleveland never went into exile, nor did he come to terms with the King's enemies. He was imprisoned in 1655–6, and appealed to Cromwell in a dignified letter, declaring 'For the service of his *Majesty*, I am so far from excusing it, that I am ready to alledge it in my vindication.' The appeal to Cromwell's magnanimity was successful, and he was released, but only to die shortly after. Cleveland's great reputation was as the satirist of 'The Rebel Scot', and as a daring Royalist journalist, as well as an extravagantly witty poet.

G. Saintsbury, *Caroline Poets*, vol. iii.

ABRAHAM COWLEY, 1618–67 (p. 198). The posthumous child of a London stationer, Cowley was educated at Westminster and Trinity College, Cambridge, where he was elected Fellow in 1640. Like Crashaw, his friend at Cambridge, and Cleveland, he did not wait to be ejected, but joined the King at Oxford in 1643. From 1644 he was in France as secretary to Jermyn and the Queen. He returned to England in 1654 and, after a short spell in prison, took up medicine and became M.D. at Oxford in 1657. It is not certain whether Cowley's submission to the régime in England was genuine, or, as was claimed after the Restoration, was a cloak for Royalist activities. On the King's return he was restored to his Fellowship and given a grant of land by Henrietta Maria, a less reward than he expected. He lived a retired life in the country and turned to the writing of essays. Cowley's astonishing precocity showed itself in his *Poetical Blossoms* (1633), published while he was a schoolboy. His Biblical epic the *Davideis* displayed his ambition to be the 'Muses' Hannibal', and a further misconception of the nature of his talents is seen in the so-called Pindaric Odes, the ungainly parents of much of the worst verse of the subsequent hundred years.

Works, ed. A. R. Waller, 1905–6.
A. H. Nethercot, *Abraham Cowley, the Muses' Hannibal*, 1931.

RICHARD CRASHAW, 1612–49 (p. 164). Crashaw's father was a noted Puritan divine, who was preacher at the Temple when his only child was born. Crashaw was educated at the Charterhouse and Pembroke College, Cambridge, and in 1635, a year after he had taken his B.A. and published a book of Latin epigrams, he was elected to 'the little contented kingdom' of a Fellowship at Peterhouse. Under Matthew Wren and Cosin, Peterhouse had become the centre of Laudian High Churchmanship in Cambridge. It is not certain if Crashaw took Orders, but he appears to have had some sort of official charge at Little St. Mary's, and was also a frequent visitor to the community at Little Gidding. In 1643, after the visitation of the Parliamentary Commission had stripped the chapel at Peterhouse and broken down 'Superstitious Pictures' in Little St. Mary's, he left Cambridge, and is next heard of in Leyden. It seems likely he returned to England and was for a while at Oxford; but in 1646 he was in Paris and had by then entered the Roman Church. From Paris he went to Rome, where he found himself neglected, in spite of the recommendation of Henrietta Maria, until in 1649 he was appointed to a post at the Cathedral of Loreto, where he died in the same year. Both editions of *Steps to the Temple* were published after he left England, and the final edition of his poems, *Carmen Deo Nostro*, was published in Paris after his death.

Poems, ed. L. C. Martin, second edition, 1957.
A. Warren, *Richard Crashaw, A Study in Baroque Sensibility*, 1939.

SIR WILLIAM DAVENANT, 1606–68 (p. 133). The son of an Oxford tavern-keeper, Davenant was reputed to be the godson of Shakespeare. (According to Aubrey, he claimed him as a father.) He was page to the Duchess of Richmond and to Fulke Greville. By 1638 he had produced masques, plays, and poems which earned him the succession to Jonson as 'Poet Laureate'. He fought in both the Bishops' Wars, was involved in the Army Plot of 1641 and, after serving on land and at sea, went into exile at Paris in 1646. Charles II made him Governor of Maryland in 1650, but on his way there he was captured and put in prison, where he continued writing his heroic poem *Gondibert*. He was released in 1652, pardoned in 1654, and managed to carry on theatrical performances in London, making theatrical history by his production of the operatic *Siege of Rhodes* in 1656. At the Restoration he was granted one of the two theatrical patents. He was buried in Westminster Abbey. His published and unpublished poems were collected together in the *Works* of 1673.

JOHN DONNE, 1572–1631 (p. 16). Donne's father, a London iron-monger, died in 1576. His mother, daughter of John Heywood the writer of interludes, was, like him, a staunch Catholic. Her brothers, Jaspar, the translator of Seneca, and Ellis, were both Jesuits. Donne went early to Hart Hall, Oxford, and, according to Walton, pro-ceeded to Cambridge before he entered the Inns of Court in 1591. He sailed with Essex to Cadiz and to the Azores in 1596 and 1597, and on his return became secretary to Sir Thomas Egerton, the Lord Keeper. During his young manhood he had broken with his family tradition and had conformed to the Established Church. At the close of 1601 he wrecked his career by a secret marriage with the young niece of his employer's wife, Ann More, and found himself without employment and his wife without a dowry. After a period of living on the kindness of friends he was employed in controversies with Catholics and in 1610 wrote *Pseudo-Martyr*, a learned attempt to persuade them to take the Oath of Allegiance. Long years of poverty and insecurity came to an end in January 1615 when he took Holy Orders. He was made Reader at Lincoln's Inn in 1616 and from 1621 until his death was Dean of St. Paul's. His monument by Nicholas Stone, which survived the Great Fire, stands in Wren's Cathedral. With the exception of the two *Anniversaries*, funeral elegies on the young daughter of his patron Sir Robert Drury, Donne published none of his poems. He left his sermons carefully written out for his son to publish; but the poems, which appeared in 1633, were not printed from his own copies.

Poems, ed. H. J. C. Grierson, 2 vols., 1912;

Divine Poems, ed. Helen Gardner, 1952; *Elegies and Songs & Sonnets*, ed. Helen Gardner, 1965;

Sermons, ed. G. R. Potter and Evelyn M. Simpson, 10 vols., 1953–1962.

Edmund Gosse, *The Life and Letters of John Donne*, 1899, has not yet been replaced; K. Gransden, *John Donne*, 1954, is a brief life which corrects some of Gosse's errors.

J. B. Leishman, *The Monarch of Wit*, third edition, 1961.

SIR RICHARD FANSHAWE, 1608–66 (p. 143). Born at Ware Park in Hertfordshire, and educated at Jesus College, Cambridge, and the Inner Temple, Fanshawe went abroad in 1627 to study languages. In 1635 he was secretary to the Ambassador at Madrid. On the outbreak of the Civil War he joined the King at Oxford, where he married. He was made secretary of war to the Prince of Wales in 1646 and accompanied him out of England. He was back in England in 1647 and at the time of the King's death was in Ireland attempting to secure support for the royal cause. He fought at Worcester, was taken prisoner and released on bail. After the Restoration he was Ambassador, first in Portugal, and afterwards in Spain, where he died. Fanshawe was a good classical scholar as well as a linguist. His best known translations are of Guarini's *Il Pastor Fido* (1647), to the second issue of which in 1648 his original poems were appended, and of Camoens' *Lusiad* (1655). His wife, who shared in many of his adventures and distresses, commemorated him and their married happiness in her charming *Memoirs* (ed. H. C. Fanshawe, 1907).

OWEN FELLTHAM, 1602?–68 (p. 126). Not much is known of Felltham's life. He was born in Suffolk. At some time before 1627 he visited the Low Countries, and he was acquainted with the London wits, contributing to various volumes of verse in the 1620s and 30s.

By 1641 he had taken service with the Earl of Thomond at Great Billing in Northamptonshire, where he is buried. His *Resolves, Divine, Moral and Political* contained a hundred essays in the first edition (1623); another century was added in the second edition (1628). *Lusoria, or Occasional Pieces* was bound up with the eighth edition (1661). Felltham was a devout Anglican and fervent Royalist, who, in a poem to the memory of Charles I, referred to the dead King as 'Christ the Second'.

SIDNEY GODOLPHIN, 1610–43 (p. 154). In Suckling's 'Sessions of the Poets' Godolphin figures as 'little *Cid*'. Clarendon said of him that 'there was never so great a Mind and Spirit contained in so little Room; so large an Understanding, and so unrestrained a Fancy, in so very small a Body'; and Hobbes, in dedicating *Leviathan* to Francis Godolphin, spent a great part of the dedication in extolling his younger brother, Sidney, who 'hating no man, nor hated of any, was unfortunately slain in the beginning of the late Civil War, in the publick quarrel, by an undiscerned and undiscerning hand'. Godolphin was a Cornishman, who was educated at Exeter College, Oxford. He left without taking a degree and, according to Wood, went to the Inns of Court. He was a friend of Falkland and the circle around Jonson and wrote a fine elegy on Donne, praising his power as a preacher, as well as contributing to *Jonsonus Virbius*. He sat as Member for Helston in 1628, and again in both the Short and Long Parliaments of 1640. In spite of his delicacy and pacific temper, he joined the King's forces under Hopton on the outbreak of war and was killed in a skirmish at Chagford in Devonshire. His poems were first collected and printed by Saintsbury.

Poems, ed. W. Dighton, 1931.

FULKE GREVILLE, first LORD BROOKE, 1554–1628 (p. 3). The son of a great Warwickshire landowner of the same name, Fulke Greville was born at Beauchamp Court in that county and is buried in St. Mary's Warwick, where his epitaph records, as culminating phrase, that he was 'the Friend of Sir Philip Sidney'. They knew each other from their schooldays at Shrewsbury. When Giordano Bruno came to England in 1583–4 Greville entertained him in London. After Sidney's death Greville was active politically, without reaching any great eminence, and was also a patron of younger writers. He was knighted in 1603 and given a peerage in 1621, and, having been given by James the abandoned and half-ruined castle at Warwick, he rebuilt it. He died at the hands of a servant whose expectations under his will he had disappointed. Apart from the unauthorised edition of *Mustapha* in 1609, his works were published after his death.

Poems and Dramas, ed. G. Bullough, 1939.
The Remains, ed. G. A. Wilkes, 1965.

WILLIAM HABINGTON, 1605–54 (p. 127). In spite of his upbringing there is nothing particularly Catholic about the poetry of Habington. His father, Thomas Habington of Hindlip Hall near Worcester, a house with no less than eleven priest-holes, was involved in both the Babington and Gunpowder Plots. After his release from prison in 1606 he was confined to Worcestershire and made himself its first antiquary and historian. Compared with his father's, William's life was uneventful; he even managed to take no part in the Civil War. He was educated abroad and by 1629 was at Court. In the years between 1629 and 1640, when no Parliaments met, the laws against Catholics were relaxed and Habington moved in a close circle of Catholics favoured at the Court. He married Lucy Herbert, daughter of Lord Powys, in 1633. Their courtship and marriage is celebrated in *Castara* (1634). In the preface the author congratulated himself on having erected 'the selfe-same Altar, both to chastity and love', and attacked 'loose copies of lust happily exprest'. A second part was added in the edition of 1635, and a third part, containing devotional poems, in the edition of 1640.

Poems, ed. Kenneth Allott, 1948.

JOHN HALL, 1627–56 (p. 264). Hall was educated at the Grammar School of his native town of Durham and went up to St. John's College, Cambridge, in 1646. In the same year he published a book of essays, *Horae Vacivae*, and in the following year his *Poems* appeared, accompanied by a chorus of encomiastic verses, and dedicated to Thomas Stanley. Hall was a fervent partisan of Cromwell and is said to have been a pensioner of his. He found time, before his early death at the age of twenty-nine, to combine with polemical journalism the writing of an address to Parliament, *Concerning the Advancement of Learning and Reformation of the Universities* (1649), and the translating of Longinus under the title *The Height of Eloquence* (1652).

G. Saintsbury, *Caroline Poets*, vol. ii.

EDWARD, LORD HERBERT OF CHERBURY, 1583–1648 (p. 63).
The Herberts were a family of Norman origin which for two centuries had dominated the Welsh Border. Edward was the eldest son
of Richard and Magdalen Herbert and was educated at University
College, Oxford. While there he married a cousin several years his
senior. He was knighted by James I, in 1608 travelled to France,
accompanied by Aurelian Townshend, and fought at the siege of
Juliers in 1610. He went as ambassador to France, with Carew in his
train, in 1619 and while there wrote his *De Veritate*, which he published in 1624 on having, as he relates in his *Autobiography*, received
a sign of divine approval. The principles of natural religion outlined
there and expatiated on in later works have earned for him the title
of 'father of deism'. He was created Baron Herbert of Cherbury by
Charles I in 1629, but on the outbreak of the Civil War he attempted
to maintain neutrality. In 1644, hoping to save his library, he surren-
dered Montgomery Castle to Parliament and eighteen months later
he petitioned for and received a Parliamentary pension. Herbert was
a friend of both Donne and Jonson, and of other poets and wits.
Jonson said Donne wrote his elegy on Prince Henry 'to match Sir
Ed: Herbert in obscurenesse'.

Poems, ed. G. C. Moore Smith, 1923.
Autobiography, ed. Sidney Lee, 1906.

GEORGE HERBERT, 1593–1633 (p. 90). George Herbert was the
fifth son of Richard and Magdalen Herbert and was only three years
old when his father died. He was brought up wholly by his mother,
who did not marry her second husband, Sir John Danvers, until
1609. Herbert was educated at Westminster and Trinity College,
Cambridge, where he was elected Fellow before taking his M.A. in
1616. He was made Reader in Rhetoric in 1618 and was Public
Orator from 1620 to 1627. Like Donne, Herbert looked towards the
Court and it was only with the death of his 'Court hopes' that he
decided to 'lose himself *in an humble way*' and take Orders, an unusual
step for a man of family at this period. He was ordained deacon some
time in 1626 and spent the next years in retirement. In April 1630
he was presented with the living of Bemerton, near Salisbury, and
was ordained priest in September. Less than three years after he
died. Herbert wrote no secular verse; in his first year at Cambridge
he sent two sonnets to his mother, promising to consecrate his 'poor
Abilities in *Poetry*' to God's glory. *The Temple* was published a few

months after his death and was constantly reprinted through the century. Walton's *Life of Herbert* (1670) was not based on personal acquaintance but on good hearsay.

Works, ed. F. E. Hutchinson, 1941.
J. H. Summers, *George Herbert, his Religion and Art*, 1954.

THOMAS HEYRICK, 1649–94 (p. 277). Thomas Heyrick was a great-nephew of Robert Herrick. His father was a tradesman of Market Harborough, Leicestershire. He was educated at the school there and at Peterhouse, Cambridge, and ended his life as Curate of his native town. His *Miscellany Poems* (1691) contain some charming fancies on birds and beasts and a long Pindaric poem 'The Submarine Voyage'.

BEN JONSON, 1573–1637 (p. 61). The posthumous son of 'a grave minister of the Gospel', Jonson was educated, at a friend's expense, under Camden at Westminster. Here he laid the foundations of an erudition which makes him the most learned of our poets before Milton. Both Oxford and Cambridge gave him honorary degrees. He ran away from his step-father's trade of brick-laying to fight in the Low Countries, and is first heard of as player and playwright in 1597. In the following year, having killed a fellow actor, he escaped execution by claiming Benefit of Clergy. While in prison he became a Roman Catholic, but reverted twelve years later to the Church of England. Unlike Shakespeare, Jonson published his plays, in the folio *Works* of 1616, and the Masques which he composed in collaboration with Inigo Jones were also printed with extensive and learned annotations. From 1616 he received a court pension of £100 and was virtually 'Poet Laureate'. By his intense devotion to good literature and the strength and purity of his art, Jonson became the idol of younger men, the father of those who sealed themselves of 'the tribe of Ben'.

Ben Jonson, ed. C. H. Herford and Percy and Evelyn Simpson, 11 vols., 1925–52. The text of the *Poems* is in vol. viii and the commentary on them in vol. xi. Jonson's *Conversations with Drummond of Hawthornden* (1619) can be found, following an account of his life, in vol. i.

HENRY KING, 1592–1669 (p. 78). The eldest son of Dr. John King, Bishop of London, Henry King and his younger brother John were, like their father, educated at Westminster and Christ Church.

They went up to Oxford together as Students of Christ Church, took the degrees of B.A., M.A., B.D. and D.D. together and were both made Canons of Christ Church in 1624. It is possible that some poems ascribed to Henry were in fact written by John, who died in 1639, the year in which Henry was made Dean of Rochester. In 1642 King was made Bishop of Chichester, but was ejected from his see in the next year. He remained in England, living on the kindness of friends, until the Restoration restored him to Chichester where he died and where he is buried in the Cathedral. King was a friend of many literary men. His father, who had been chaplain to Egerton, Donne's first employer, ordained Donne, and he himself was an executor of Donne's will. His poems were published in 1657, anonymously and without their author's consent. They were re-published, still anonymously, in 1664, and, with a title-page ascribing them to Ben Jonson, in 1700.

Poems, ed. Margaret Crum, 1965.

SIR FRANCIS KYNASTON, 1587–1642 (p. 76). Not content with a B.A. from Oriel College, Oxford, Kynaston proceeded to Trinity Hall, Cambridge, for an M.A. He was knighted in 1618 and elected to the House of Commons in 1621. He founded in 1635, at his own house in Covent Garden, a private academy or *Museum Minervae*, where he and his friends as Professors taught scientific as well as literary subjects. The academy did not survive its founder. Kynaston translated the first two books of Chaucer's *Troilus and Criseyde* into Latin rhyme royal, and wrote an 'Heroick Romance' in the same measure in English, *Leoline and Sydanis*. Its plot has been praised as 'relatively lucid'. It was published in 1642, the year of Kynaston's death, with the *Cynthiades or Amorous Sonnets* appended.

G. Saintsbury, *Caroline Poets*, vol. ii.

RICHARD LEIGH, 1649–1728 (p. 279). Richard Leigh is best known for his *Censure of the Rota*, an entertaining attack on the extravagance of Dryden's *Conquest of Granada*, and for his intervention in the dispute between Marvell and Parker. He was born near Walsall of a scholarly family and was at Queen's College, Oxford. He was a doctor, but it is not known where he studied medicine or what degree he held.

Poems, ed. Hugh Macdonald, 1947.

RICHARD LOVELACE, 1618–56/7 (p. 207). The son of a Kentish landowner, Lovelace was at Charterhouse and Gloucester Hall, Oxford, where he was created M.A. on the occasion of the royal visit of 1636. Wood says of him at Oxford that he was 'the most amiable and beautiful Person that ever Eye beheld, a Person also of innate modesty, virtue and courtly deportment, which made him then, but especially after, when he retired to the great City, much admired and adored by the Female Sex'. His pleasant life as courtier and country gentleman was interrupted by the Bishops' Wars in which, like Suckling, he served. In 1642 he presented to the Commons the Kentish petition for restoring the King to his rights and was imprisoned, as a result, in the Gatehouse. He was abroad from 1643 to 1646, and on returning to England endured another spell of imprisonment, during which he prepared *Lucasta* for the press. He was released after the King's execution and spent the rest of his life in obscurity and poverty, although probably not in the extreme misery which Aubrey's account suggests.

Poems, ed. C. H. Wilkinson, 1930.

ANDREW MARVELL, 1618–78 (p. 213). The son of a clergyman of Calvinist views, preacher and master of the Almshouse at Hull, Marvell was educated at Hull Grammar School and Trinity College, Cambridge. His father was drowned while crossing the Humber in 1641, having survived long enough to rescue his son from a brief period of Catholicism. Marvell left Cambridge in this year and the next ten years of his life are obscure. From 1642 to 1646 he was abroad, tutoring part of the time in France. In 1651 he became tutor to the daughter of Lord Fairfax at Nun Appleton House in Yorkshire. Fairfax, the victor of Naseby, had retired to his Yorkshire estates, owing to his disagreement with Cromwell's policy. The career and friendships of Marvell up to this time, which it is thought most of his lyric poetry dates from, suggest that his sympathies were with moderate men, even with Royalists. But he came to an acceptance of Cromwell's 'forced power', and finally to whole-hearted admiration for him. In 1653 he became tutor to one of Cromwell's wards at Eton. In this year Milton recommended him to be his assistant in the Latin Secretaryship, although he was not appointed until 1657. Milton's nephew reports that Marvell protected Milton at the Restoration. As Member for Hull from 1659 until his death, Marvell was a staunch defender of constitutional liberties. His patriotism also found expression in political satires. The *Miscellaneous Poems* (1681) were published ostensibly by his widow, Mary Marvell. This was some kind of legal fiction, as Marvell never married.

Poems and Letters, ed. H. M. Margoliouth, second edition, 1952.
Pierre Legouis, *André Marvell, poète, puritain, patriote*, Paris, 1928; translated, abridged, and revised as *Andrew Marvell*, 1965.

JOHN MILTON, 1608–74 (p. 149). A handful of early poems allow Milton to be included in this volume. I differ from Grierson in not including the 'Nativity Ode', a poem too epic in conception and style to be called 'metaphysical'. Milton's education at St. Paul's and Christ's College, Cambridge, where he was contemporary with Cleveland, brought him into contact with some of the 'late fantasticks' whom he speaks of with scorn in the Vacation Exercise of 1628. The two poems printed here in which he condescends to the fashionable style both date from his Cambridge days. 'On Time', if originally written for a clockcase, has outgrown the epigrammatic and conceited mode suitable for such inscriptions. Like most of the writers in this volume, Milton was not a professional writer looking to his pen for a living. But unlike them he was a poet by vocation, dedicated from youth to the achievement of something of 'highest hope and hardest attempting'. It seems unsuitable, therefore, to outline the life of the author of *Paradise Lost* in this volume.

JOHN NORRIS OF BEMERTON, 1657–1711 (p. 281). The son of a Wiltshire Rector, John Norris was educated at Winchester and Exeter College, Oxford, and in 1680 was appointed by Sancroft to a vacant Fellowship at All Souls. He was ordained in 1684, married in 1689, and appointed to a living in Somerset. Three years later he became Rector of Bemerton, George Herbert's parish, where he remained until his death. Norris was a strong Churchman who attacked Whigs and Nonconformists; but his main fame is as the opponent of Locke and Toland. As a belated Christian Platonist he has a place in the history of religious thought.

FRANCIS QUARLES, 1592–1644 (p. 85). Son of a surveyor-general of victualling for the Navy, Francis Quarles was born in Essex and educated at a country school, Christ's College, Cambridge, and Lincoln's Inn. His first poem, *A Feast for Worms*, a gloomy Biblical paraphrase, appeared in 1620. From 1626 to 1630 he was in Ireland as secretary to Archbishop Ussher. In 1633 he retired to his native county of Essex; but he was appointed chronologer to the City of London in 1640, combining his duties with the composition of manuals of piety in prose. Quarles married in 1618 and had eighteen children. He was prolific as a poet also. His most famous book the *Emblems*, first published in 1635, was far the most popular book of verse of the century. A devoted member of the Church of England and a staunch Royalist, Quarles took many of the plates for his *Emblems* from Jesuit Emblem Books, and yet was rightly called by Wood an 'old puritanical poet'.

Poems, ed. A. B. Grosart, 3 vols., 1880–1.

SIR WALTER RALEGH, 1552?–1618 (p. 1). The career of Ralegh, who was the son of a Devonshire gentleman, began in the Irish Wars. On coming to Court in 1582 he rose rapidly in the Queen's favour, but by his arrogance aroused bitter enmity. He was strongly anti-Spanish in his politics. He explored Guiana in 1595, distinguished himself, in company with his rival Essex, in the attack on Cadiz in 1596, and shared with him in the unsuccess of the Islands Voyage in 1597. With the Queen's death his enemies found their opportunity. He was charged with treason, tried and sentenced to death in the first months of James's reign. Reprieved, he spent twelve years in the Tower, where he wrote his *History of the World*. He was released in 1616 to make the fatal last voyage to Guiana. Returning to England, having found no treasure, and having involved himself in fighting with the Spaniards, in which his son was killed, he was brought to trial again and executed on 29 October 1618, a sacrifice to James's pro-Spanish policy.

Poems, ed. Agnes Latham, revised edition, 1951 (Muses' Library). Philip Edwards, *Sir Walter Ralegh*, 1953.

THOMAS RANDOLPH, 1605–35 (p. 130). In the course of his short life Randolph won an extraordinary reputation as a poet, and was regarded as likely to inherit the mantle of Jonson. He came of an undistinguished family and was educated at Westminster and Trinity College, Cambridge, where he was elected to a minor Fellowship in 1629 and a major in 1632. During 1630 the University was closed because of plague and it was probably at this time that Randolph went to London and made himself known to Jonson. There are stories of doubtful veracity of his being adopted as Jonson's

'Son'. He died and is buried at Blatherwyke, Northamptonshire, where he was tutoring the children of William Stafford, nephew of the Anthony Stafford to whom he addressed his best-known poem. The cause of his death is not known. Wood ascribes it to 'indulging himself too much with the liberal conversation of his admirers'. His Poems, including the pastoral drama *Amyntas*, were published by his brother in 1638, with commendatory verses prefixed expressing 'such a sense of the loss to letters as had never before attended the death of any other English poet'.

Poems, ed. G. Thorn-Drury, 1929.

WILLIAM SHAKESPEARE, 1564–1616 (p. 9). If we are right in thinking of Shakespeare as beginning his career as a dramatist a little before 1590 and as retiring in 1612, *The Phoenix and the Turtle* was written at about the middle point of his working life, about the same time as *Hamlet*. The poem appeared in 1601 in a collection of pieces by various authors (*Vatum Chorus*) following a long and dreary allegory by Robert Chester which celebrated, under the symbols of a male Turtle-Dove and a female Phoenix, the wedded love of Chester's patron, Sir John Salusbury, and his wife Ursula, and its culmination in their daughter. Shakespeare's poem which celebrates a love which has no progeny seems to have no connexion with Chester's enterprise. It has been said that nobody would ascribe this poem to Shakespeare if it had not been printed as his. It should be added that there is no other poet of the age to whom it could be attributed.

Robert Chester, *Loves Martyr*, ed. A. B. Grosart, 1878.
Discussions of the poem will be found in editions of Shakespeare's *Sonnets and Poems* by C. K. Pooler (Arden Shakespeare), 1918; M. R. Ridley (New Temple Shakespeare), 1934; and H. E. Rollins (New Variorum), 1944.

ROBERT SOUTHWELL, 1561–95 (p. 5). From his childhood Southwell's life was directed towards the death he was to die. He was born in Norfolk and sent abroad in 1576 to study at Douai. Inspired by Jesuit teachers there and in Paris, he determined to enter the Order and became a novice at Rome in 1578. He was ordained priest in 1584 and was nominated to the dangerous English Mission at his own fervent wish. He set out with Fr. Henry Garnet in May 1586. Only one Jesuit was working in England when they landed. Southwell was closely watched from the moment of his arrival; but for some time he evaded arrest, or was left at liberty, and engaged in literary as well as more directly pastoral activity. In June 1592 he was arrested, and from then to his death was imprisoned and constantly racked and tortured. He suffered the martyrdom which he sought at Tyburn on 21 February 1595. His poems were published almost immediately.

Poems, ed. A. B. Grosart, 1872.
Pierre Janelle, *Robert Southwell the Writer*, 1935.

THOMAS STANLEY, 1625–78 (p. 262). Stanley's fame was as a scholar and translator. He was the author of a *History of Philosophy* (1655–62) and edited Aeschylus in 1663. His best known translations are those of Anacreon and of Johannes Secundus. He was descended (with a bend sinister) from the great family of Stanleys, and came of a branch which had settled in Hertfordshire and Essex. He went up to Pembroke College, Cambridge, at the age of thirteen, and he is said to have studied at Oxford also. He married very young and had a large family. His life was uneventful and, although a Royalist, he seems to have been undisturbed by the Civil War. He was a man of some means and was generous to fellow men of letters.

Poems and Translations, ed. G. M. Crump, 1962.

SIR JOHN SUCKLING, 1609–42 (p. 151). Millamant's praise of 'natural easy Suckling' and Aubrey's description of him as 'the greatest gallant of his time, and the greatest gamester, both for bowling and cards, so that no shopkeeper would trust him for 6d' fix the portrait of Suckling as Gentleman Poet. His father, also Sir John, became Master of Requests, and his mother was sister to Lionel Cranfield, Lord Middlesex, who was Lord Treasurer and a friend of Donne. Suckling was educated at Westminster (according to Aubrey), Trinity College, Cambridge, and Gray's Inn. From 1628 to 1630 he travelled, was knighted on his return, and in 1631–2 was abroad again fighting under Gustavus Adolphus. From 1632 he was at Court. His play, *Aglaura*, was produced in 1637 with gorgeous costumes, and published in the following year in folio with enormous margins. Suckling led an extravagantly clad troop to Scotland in the first Bishops' War, was involved in the Army Plot of

1641, and fled abroad to France where he died. Aubrey says he committed suicide.

Works, ed. A. H. Thompson, 1910.

AURELIAN TOWNSHEND, 1583?–1651? (p. 70). The Townshends were a Norfolk family which rose under the Tudors by the stepping-stone of the law. Aurelian was the son of John Townshend of Dereham. He came to the notice of Sir Robert Cecil, who trained him for the service of his son William, and sent him to France and Italy to improve his languages from 1600 to 1603. He went to France again (in company with Sir Edward Herbert) in 1608. Little more is known of him, except that in 1631–2 he wrote two court-masques, and that with the outbreak of the Civil War he fell on bad times. He was described in 1642 as 'a poor and pocky Poet, but a marryed man and a housekeeper in Barbican', who 'would be glad to sell an 100 verses at sixpence a piece'. The last record of him is in 1643 when he petitioned the Lords against arrest for debt; but a poem by him on the death of Charles I, preserved at Knole, shows that he managed to survive the Civil War and suggests that he found a patron in the Earl of Dorset. His daughter Mary was a famous beauty who began a career of gallantry as mistress of the Elector Palatine in 1635. She was married in 1646 at Oxford to George Kirke, Groom of the King's Chamber, the King giving her away. Townshend's poems were not collected until this century.

Poems and Masques, ed. E. K. Chambers, 1912.

THOMAS TRAHERNE, 1637/8–74 (p. 267). The only work of Traherne published in his lifetime was the polemical *Roman Forgeries* (1673). *Christian Ethics*, a rambling and repetitive work, was published posthumously (1675). Traherne's fame dates from Bertram Dobell's discovery in 1896 and 1897 of manuscripts containing poems and a prose treatise, *Centuries of Meditation*, and his identification of the author of both with the forgotten Restoration divine, Thomas Traherne. The son of a Hereford shoemaker, who was sent at the expense of a relative to Brasenose College, Oxford, Traherne was presented in 1657, the year after he took his B.A., to the living of Credenhill, Herefordshire, which he held until his death. He was ordained in October 1660. He seems to have spent most of his time at Oxford, proceeding to M.A. and B.D., with only occasional visits to his parish, until he went to London in 1667 as chaplain to Sir Orlando Bridgeman, the Lord Keeper. On Bridgeman's retirement in 1672 he went with him to Teddington, Middlesex, where he died and is buried.

Centuries, Poems and Thanksgivings, ed. H. M. Margoliouth, 1958.
G. I. Wade, *Thomas Traherne*, 1944.

HENRY VAUGHAN, 1621/2–95 (p. 239). The appellation 'the Silurist' asserts Vaughan's descent from a family in Brecknockshire, a county once inhabited by the Silures. He and his twin-brother Thomas were educated at the local school and at Jesus College, Oxford. Thomas remained at Oxford to become a well-known Hermetical Philosopher. Henry left without a degree to study law in London. Vaughan was an ardent Royalist and devoted son of the Church of England and fought in the Civil War. It is not known where he studied medicine, but he practised as a doctor at Brecknock and after at Newton by Usk. He was twice married. Vaughan's secular verse is unremarkable. The title of his two volumes of religious poetry, *Silex Scintillans* (1650 and 1655), points to the nature of the conversion which turned the tepid wooer of Amoret into a poet who brings us 'authentic tidings of invisible things'. 'Certaine Divine Raies', he wrote, 'breake out of the Soul in adversity, like sparks of fire out of the afflicted flint.' Grief at the death of friends, particularly of a brother, the defeat of his cause, and the virtual destruction of his Church are the circumstances, if not the explanation, of his conversion.

Works, ed. L. C. Martin, 1914 (second edition, 1957).
F. E. Hutchinson, *Henry Vaughan*, 1947.

EDMUND WALLER, 1606–87 (p. 138). Waller was born near Beaconsfield, where he is buried, of a family of standing and wealth, and educated at Eton and King's College, Cambridge. He was a member of Parliament at a very early age, possibly at sixteen. His first wife, an heiress, whom he married in 1631, died in 1634. From 1636 until her marriage to Lord Spencer in 1639, Waller courted Lady Dorothy Sidney, his 'Sacharissa'. He was involved as a principal in 1643 in a plot to seize London for the King. His conduct when the plot was exposed was far from heroic, though possibly not as base as Clarendon makes it appear. He was banished and heavily fined and spent seven years in exile in Paris. In 1651 he was pardoned and returned to England. After the Restoration he sat again in Parliament and distinguished himself by speeches in favour of toleration. He was a member of the Royal Society from 1661. The lucidity and ease of his writing, which caused him to be linked with Denham as a 'founder of our poesy', made the writer of his epitaph praise him as 'inter poetas sui temporis facile princeps', and add 'huic debet lingua paterna quod credas, si Graece Latineque intermitterent Musae, loqui amarent Anglice'.

Poems, ed. G. Thorn-Drury, 1905.

JOHN WILMOT, second EARL OF ROCHESTER, 1647–80 (p. 272). Henry Wilmot, the first Earl of Rochester, was Charles II's companion at Worcester and in his wanderings after the battle. He died in 1658 leaving his son little but his title and the King's favour. Rochester was educated at Burford school and at Wadham College, Oxford. He was created M.A. in 1661, after a year's residence. The most scandalous of Restoration courtiers, whose exploits included the kidnapping of the wealthy heiress whom he subsequently married, Rochester died at Woodstock at the age of thirty-three. His penitent death-bed, as described by Burnet who ministered to him, served to make his brief life even more sensational in public memory. Rochester's bibliography is a thorny subject. As a nobleman he naturally made no attempt to collect and publish his own verse, and owing to his reputation a great many indecent poems of the period were fathered upon him in the first editions of his poems. Tonson's edition of 1691 was the first to attempt to sift genuine poems from the others.

Poems, ed. V. de S. Pinto, 1953.

SIR HENRY WOTTON, 1568–1639 (p. 13). Henry Wotton came of a family which had been active in public life for two generations. He was educated at Winchester and New College, Oxford, and on leaving Oxford spent seven years abroad, during which he supplied foreign intelligence to Essex. On his return to England in 1595 he became one of Essex's secretaries, but he prudently went abroad again at the time of the Earl's arrest and settled in Italy. In 1604 he was knighted by James I and sent as ambassador to Venice where he served, with two intervals, for twenty years. In 1624 he was made Provost of Eton and three years later took deacon's orders. He was a close friend of Donne from the time they were together at Oxford and was the recipient of some of his verse-letters. He was to have written Donne's life as preface to his collected sermons, but he died leaving the task to Izaak Walton whom he had employed to collect materials. Walton went on to perform the same office for Wotton himself as preface to the *Reliquae Wottonianae* (1651). Wotton was a lover of poetry who praised the 'Dorique delicacy' of the songs in *Comus*, and a wit who endangered his own career by the jest that an Ambassador was 'an honest man sent to lie abroad for the good of his country'.

L. P. Smith, *The Life and Letters of Sir Henry Wotton*, 1907.

INDEX OF FIRST LINES

INDEX OF FIRST LINES

INDEX OF FIRST LINES

INDEX OF AUTHORS

PRINTED IN GREAT BRITAIN
AT THE UNIVERSITY PRESS, OXFORD
BY VIVIAN RIDLER
PRINTER TO THE UNIVERSITY